NG CLUB

ersey" JOE

LCOTT

CHALLENGER

LD — **15 ROUNDS**

AY EVENING

BER **5, 1947**

TURY SPORTING CLUB, Inc.

Michael S Jacobs
PROMOTER

MADISON
SQUARE
GARDEN

FRIDAY EVENING
DECEMBER
1947

5

WORKING PRESS

Row 1   40

ENTER AT EIGHTH AVE.

STADIUM
RIVER AVENUE

PORTING CLUB PRESENTS

EAVYWEIGHT
ONSHIP

IS VS

ELING

Champion

JUNE 22, 1938

TWENTIETH CENTURY SPORTING CLUB, Inc.

Michael S Jacobs
PROMOTER

IF Postponed this ticket will be
honored on postponed date only.

RAIN CHECK

Mezza Stand $3.50

ADMISSION

YANKEE STADIUM

Wednesday
JUNE 22
1938

427

JOE LOUIS: MY LIFE

JOE LOUIS: MY LIFE

BY
JOE LOUIS
WITH
EDNA AND ART RUST, Jr.

Harcourt Brace Jovanovich
New York and London

Requests for permission to make copies of any part of the
work should be mailed to: Permissions, Harcourt Brace Jovanovich, Inc., 757 Third Avenue, New York, New York 10017

Printed in the United States of America

Library of Congress Cataloging in Publication Data
Louis, Joe, 1914–
Joe Louis, my life.
1. Louis, Joe, 1914–   2. Boxers (Sports)—
United States—Biography.   3. Boxing.   I. Rust,
Edna, joint author.   II. Rust, Art, 1927–
joint author.   III. Title.
GV1132.L6A29   796.8'3'0924 [B]   77–91341
ISBN 0–15–146375–1

B   C   D   E

Art Direction: Harris Lewine
Design: Robert Aulicino

CONTENTS

By Art Rust Jr.

Get That Nigger Off the Field

ACKNOWLEDGMENTS

Alabama Archives
Michigan Historical Society
Ring Magazine
Schomburg Center for Research in Black Culture

Beverly Abrahams
Lucille Armistead
Jacqueline Barrow
Joseph Louis Barrow, Jr.
Martha Louis Barrow
Leon Bogues
St. Clair Bourne
Teddy Brenner
Lester Bromberg
Pat Brooks, Jr.
Freddie Brown
Madeline Carter
Harold Conrad
Russell Cowans
Cus D'Amato
Emmarell Barrow Davis
Angelo Dundee
Murray Gennis
Freddie Guinyard
Gaines Hutchinson
Jimmy Jacobs
Ernest Kaiser
Mr. and Mrs. George Langley
Nat Loubet
Harry Markson
Marshall Miles
Charley Morey
Bruce Nickerson
John Ort
Billy Rowe
Irving Rudd
Rose Morgan Saunders

ACKNOWLEDGMENTS

Mannie Seamon
Marva Louis Spaulding
Ivy Madden Speed
Duke Stefano
Bert Sugar
Sam Taub
Freddie Wilson

JOE LOUIS: MY LIFE

|1914|
ALABAMA

RED CLAY. YOU WOULD HAVE THOUGHT THE WHOLE world was red clay. The red hills run into the mountains, and the mountains run about twelve miles or so from Lafayette. A red clay road leads off another road called Cusseta—and Cusseta leads to the Buckalew Mountain section—and that's about where I was born on May 13, 1914—Alabama.

I was the seventh child of the Barrow family. You know old people always say there's something lucky about seven, and I believe it. I was a healthy boy, weighed about eleven pounds at birth. Momma was a big woman, my father was a big man. We come from big people, mostly blacks, some whites, and a few powerful Indians; put that all together and I guess you get something.

It wasn't much of a house we had when I was young. I guess we didn't have a proper "living room." We lived all over the house. With eight or nine people in a couple of rooms, you just lived in it.

You know that red clay country was hard soil to till, but we Barrows were hard-working people. We tilled the soil, grew the cotton, picked it, packed it up, and sold it. I didn't know we were sharecroppers, I just knew we were farmers—like everybody we knew. Except of course like the teacher and the doctor. Even the minister was just like us, except on Sunday. I didn't figure on anything except I'd be a farmer, a husband, a father, and that's about it.

But you know my momma told me lots of things, and I still think about it. She told me my great-uncle, Peter Sheley, ran the farm, because my daddy couldn't make it. I was too young to understand the frustrations of a black sharecropper trying to raise a family in that hard, red clay country. I guess it makes a man feel bad not to be able to give his family more, especially if you can see beyond the cotton balls and those hard red hills.

My father, Munrow Barrow, was six-feet one and weighed close to two hundred pounds, but he wasn't strong enough. So when I was about two years old, they put him in the epileptic ward of Searcy Hospital for the Negro Insane in Mt. Vernon, Alabama. The years of strain and hard work was too much for him. Just the same he was always "escaping" from the hospital and coming back to visit with his family. One time he escaped for a little over two years.

I know my daddy tried. Momma always told me he wanted to be a good family man. In 1910, four years before I was born, he rented the 120-acre farm thinking he could make it. Momma always said he wanted the best for his family. Maybe it don't matter, but thinking and being able to do are two different things.

People tell me that my father was the son of Lon and Victoria Harp. Both of them were slaves on a plantation owned by James Barrow, a rich white man. They say my father's mother was a full-blooded Cherokee Indian; that's good, I guess. But you know for sure I'm mostly of black blood, and I'm proud of that.

Sorry to say, I didn't know my father at all.

My momma was Lily Reese before she got married, from Chambers County, Alabama, and she was, for those days, a big woman—five-foot six and 170 pounds. Her face was honey-brown, sweet, and pleasant. When she had the time, she was a loving teacher. Of course time for her was hard to come by. My father was taken away, and there she was with eight children to raise on a back-breaking piece of land. She worked as hard, and many times harder, than any man around. She could plow a good straight furrow, plant and pick with the best of them—cut cord wood like a lumberjack then leave the fields an hour earlier than anyone else and fix a meal to serve to her family.

God! I loved that woman.

Don't get me wrong, though, Momma could mix it up some, too. She could be tough. You stepped out of line with her, and she'd put your head between her knees and whip you with a strap. One thing, though, nobody around could say the Barrow children were wild or bad or didn't have any manners.

Momma got a lot of her inspiration from God at the Mt. Sinai Baptist Church, about three miles from the house where I was born. Momma was very religious, and when she could spare the time from work, she'd fix all the boys up in clean overalls and we'd go to Mt. Sinai for a day of worship. It was good for all of us. It seemed to renew her for the hard struggles she had to endure the next week.

I hope they're still making women like my momma. She always told me to do the right thing. She always told me to have pride in myself; she said a good name is better than money.

When I was just a little boy, I always wanted my momma to smile on me. Sometimes I'd run off and try to sneak away from my chores and play, but lots of times I'd scrub all the floors in the house. When Momma came home and saw what I had done, she'd grab me up and give me a big kiss for it. Then I could have floated clear up to the sky.

Now when I look back on things I can realize how hard it must have been. But to me everything seemed fine. I had my brothers and sisters: Susie, Lonnie, Eulalia, Emmarell, De Leon, Alvanius, me—Joseph Louis, and Vunice. Seems to me I always had enough to eat. No fancy food, but plenty of corn and potatoes, pork chops and chicken, good fresh farm-grown food. In fact, I had so many pork chops in those days, I haven't eaten one since I was a young man.

Except for me and my baby sister Vunice, everybody

was up and out of the house by sunup. They seldom came home until sundown. I had plenty of time to go exploring, fishing, and, in good weather, learning to swim in a nearby pond. Sometimes I played with the other neighbors' children, but most times I liked to be by myself. I'd even get annoyed when Momma made me move over to make room for my brothers in the bed we shared.

There were games I remember that I liked to play. One was called "Skin the Tree." It was a country kind of hide-and-seek. One boy would be It. He'd have to close his eyes and count to ten. The rest of us would then shinny up a tree and hide in the branches. You usually picked a tree that was a slender sapling, so it would bend. If the fellow who was It found you, he had to tag you by climbing the tree. If he got near you, you'd get a good hold on that sapling and bend it down 'til you dropped to the ground. Sometimes we'd just swing in the trees like little Tarzans. It sure was good for the development of shoulders and arms.

One time when I was a little kid, I found a half bottle of White Lightning. Of course I drank it, and of course I got drunk. I wandered around stumbling until I fell asleep under a tree. Momma found the bottle and me under the tree, asleep. She didn't spank me, but, worse, she gave me a lecture on the evils of drink. She won. It was many decades before I touched a drink of alcohol.

As I was getting older, I got a few more chores to do. Momma had fixed up a lunch basket and told me to bring it to the fields where they were working around high noon. It made me feel real important. I got me a big-time job. I sat there and watched the sun and when it was nearly overhead, I picked up the basket and headed on out to do my job. Only thing, I got too curious—I peeked in the basket. Right on top was a baked chicken leg. Now, what can I tell you? That golden-brown drumstick looked so good, my stomach started crying for it. I just sat on the road and ate that and something else, I can't remember.

When I finally got to my folks in the fields, the basket was light. Oh, let me tell you, I got one hell of a whipping. I cried some mean tears, but my stomach was happy.

When I got to be older, my sister Eulalia would take me and my younger sister Vunice to school at the Mt. Sinai Baptist Church, a big, one-room church school. Just plain boards, no paint. There were two windows that did not have glass panes. They were called batten windows, something like shutters. There was a big iron stove for heat on cold days. Everybody brought their lunch, and school started whenever you got there. Some kids rode on mules, if their parents could afford to spare the mule or the child that particular day. There weren't any desks as such, just pews with a slate board for writing.

All the black kids from seven to seventeen went there—if they went at all. The school term was from October 'til April, to coincide with farm planting and harvesting.

Well, for sure, I didn't like school. Maybe because I stayed so much by myself and maybe because everybody was so busy working, no one had the time to teach me to talk properly.

I stammered and stuttered, and I guess I was so plain nervous that the other kids laughed at me. So when Eulalia walked back home to get us younger kids, Vunice would go into school, but I didn't. Why should I stay in school and be made fun of, when there were snakes to catch or a cool spot under a shady tree where I could watch the clouds change shape?

My father stopped escaping from the Asylum; somebody told Momma he was dead and she believed them. At least he was dead to her. You know, you wonder how people could think that way. But now is now and then was then. Then meant hard times, no telephones, poor transportation, eight kids to raise on a poor-land farm.

A lot of people were real nice to us. They knew Momma

was a widow with a big farm and a lot of children. People would send me on errands and give me pennies and sometimes nickels. I'd give it all to Momma. Even though these were real poor people, they'd share a little bit of food with us when the crops didn't come through like they should.

Somehow Momma met up with a man named Patrick Brooks, a sharecropper around our parts who was a widower with eight children. So, here's Momma with eight kids, and here's Pat Brooks with eight kids, and they up and got married.

Patrick Brooks was all the father I really knew. He was a good stepfather who worked hard and did the best he could. He was always fair and treated all those sixteen children as equally as a man could. His kids and my brothers and sisters fit in like one big family, but we were too much for his little house or the one Momma had. So we moved to a larger house in Camp Hill, deeper into the Buckalew Mountains.

We still weren't too far from the Mt. Sinai Church and their school, and I still wasn't going to it. All in all, we didn't have much in Alabama. I didn't know anything about life then, but it seems we kept happy.

My stepbrother Pat Brooks and I were the same age, and we got along well. Of course we did have disagreements sometimes. I remember one day we had a fight. He took a brick and hit me in the head—I still have the scar. Another time I'd fight was when I played marbles with the other kids, but only if they bothered me. Then sometimes if somebody bothered my sisters, I'd fight. There was another fighting game we played, called "Knocking." I was only about eight years old, but I'd put a chip on my shoulder and dare bigger guys than me to knock it off. If they did, we would fight. Most times it was more noise and running and throwing a few stones than anything else.

I usually didn't fight because I didn't get into a situation where it was necessary. I was always quiet and liked to be alone a lot.

Funny thing, you know, people are always asking me about Alabama: "Those crackers must have given you a hard time." "Did the Ku Klux Klan bother your family?" To tell the honest absolute truth, there didn't seem to be anything bad between blacks and whites in Lafayette, Alabama, but you have to remember I was a little boy. There were other things that I did not take a hold to. I remember black people getting together and talking about how much white blood they had, how much Indian blood they had, but hardly heard anybody would talk about how much black blood they had. I didn't know too much, but I could easily see that all these white-blooded, Indian-blooded black people lived a damn sight worse than some of the poorest white people I saw. I knew there was a difference, but it made no difference to me.

My folks seemed to get along with the white people in the area. Maybe it was because, "You got your place, and I got mine." Probably we never crossed the line to cause the angers and hurts and lynchings that took place all over the South. Another funny thing, I never heard about lynchings; nobody white ever called me a "nigger" until I got to Detroit.

Thinking back, I remember the white Langley family around Camp Hill. They owned most of the land around there. The father ran the country store and was very nice to us. His sons James and George and I would play around with each other. Generally I met them on my way to the Mt. Sinai School and we'd fool around chasing each other, or playing marbles or something. They were on the way to their white school. Since none of us probably wanted to go to school, it was a good interruption.

Well, anyway, my family made me go to school some, and I finally gave in to learning a little reading, writing, and arithmetic. But it was more fun when they were taking the cotton to the cotton gin in carts pulled by mules. Pat and me would lay on the cotton and bounce up and down on those dirt roads. When we got the cotton to the cotton gin in Camp Hill, we'd love to watch the machine suck it off the wagon.

As the years go by, I often reflect on the things that influenced me. Sometimes I look and think, "How come me?" "How come I'm a world champion? How come I've got all the responsibilities it carries, when I only looked forward to a simple, poor country life?" I guess it has something to do with a strong mother, a good stepfather, and a special, God-given talent.

Life to me seemed fine, with plenty to eat, a warm place to stay, and loving relatives. I knew big responsibilities were coming because I was a boy and an extra-size big boy, but the little chores didn't bother me. Only thing, I had to go to school—when they caught me and carried me there. But my older brothers and my stepfather didn't feel the same way; they wanted more because they said we didn't have enough. My stepfather was getting dissatisfied having to scratch a meager living out of the earth. His older children were getting married and having babies. The family was multiplying flesh but not the means to care for them.

Some of Poppa Brooks's relatives came to visit for a while. They were from Detroit, Michigan. I guess that's the first time I'd ever heard of Detroit and it didn't mean a thing to me, but to my momma and stepfather it seemed like another world. All of a sudden, everybody was talking about cars, factories, jobs, and money. There were jobs that didn't depend on the rainfall or the boll weevil. You got paid every week. I heard about stone sidewalks, movies, and electricity. Of course I knew about electricity, but I'd never seen it at home. Seemed like everybody I knew saw by kerosene lamps that smoked and smelled all over the house. What do you need electricity for when practically everybody was going to sleep by sundown?

Pat Brooks made the decision that we couldn't do any worse, so why not try to do better?—and plans went ahead for moving to Detroit. They said the Ford factory didn't mind hiring Negroes, and for once we'd have hard solid money we wouldn't have to share with the landowner.

So my stepfather and mother and older brothers made arrangements to go there and look before they uprooted the whole family. My mother's brother, Peter Reese, took the place of my stepfather for that year, until they could save enough money to bring us up. My older sisters and stepsisters took over the care of the younger children, and they did a good job, but I missed my momma and stepfather. It was a strange and distant feeling I had. It seemed like a hundred years before I would join them.

Reports kept coming back to us that everything was fine in Detroit; that we'd do better, have better opportunities. Well, by that time the bug really bit me. All of a sudden, I was not as happy catching snakes, shooting marbles, fishing, and playing Skin the Tree.

A lot of our other relatives would come by to talk about the big move. Some were glad, glad to see us getting away from a "no-place-to-go" world. Some said we were making a big mistake. They said, "White people up North didn't understand Negroes," said we weren't "ready" to live in a city. Best we could do was to stay on the farm and organize ourselves better. I only knew one thing—we were going.

Now I started taking interest in more things. When we went to town, I still bounced up and down on the piles of cotton, but I started looking at more stores and trying to figure out how many there were in a big city. I started wondering how it felt to ride in one of those locomotive trains that puffed all that steam up. For the first time, I started to wonder what would happen to me. Wouldn't be a farmer when I grew up—guess I'd wear a suit like the preacher did (on Sundays). Yeah, but what would I do? Would I have to go to school? If I did, I didn't know what to expect. Down home everybody said, "Negroes up North are smart." Shoot! I didn't feel smart down home.

Finally the day came when we were supposed to leave. All week long, everybody was washing and ironing the few clothes we had. My sister Eulalia took me and baby sister, Vunice, down to town to get new shoes and some new overalls for me. There was a whole lot of chicken-frying and ham-baking—we had to take plenty of food for the trip. In those days black people weren't allowed in the dining car, and even if we were allowed, there was no way we could have paid for it. Besides, this way seemed more fun to me—more like a picnic. We wrapped up everything in old shoe boxes, baskets—whatever we could carry was filled with good country food. Momma had sent instructions to bring some country-cured sausage and ham; seems that was hard to come by in Detroit.

Well, with all the excitement and such, once I got on the train and started eating some of that good food, I promptly went to sleep. When I woke up, it all looked the same as back home—the trees, the fields, and for the first time I saw some chain gangs. Those prisoners actually had on the striped uniforms that you see in the movies. Their legs were chained up four or five together, and they had a big iron ball at one end. They smiled and waved as we clickety-clacked by on the train, and I waved back and grinned. I thought real deep about things my momma told me about being good, and after seeing those men all latched together, I thought to myself, "I ain't never doing nothing to be chained up like some penned animal."

As the train kept going north, the cities kept getting bigger, the houses were taller, and I knew I wouldn't be seeing any more red clay hills and cotton fields.

1926

DETROIT

Now, take me, a twelve-year-old country boy, in Detroit for the first time. You can't imagine the impact that city had. I never saw so many people in one place, so many cars at one time; I had never even seen a trolley car before. There were other things that I had never heard of—parks, libraries, brick schoolhouses, movie theaters. People dressed different, and then I realized that even with those brand-new overalls and country shoes, I wasn't dressed right. But one thing I knew, Detroit looked awfully good to me.

Arriving was great. It's good to know somebody's glad to see you. Momma nearly squeezed me to death. My stepfather was so proud to have his family together, and proud to have been able to get us out of Alabama.

We moved in with some kinfolks who lived in a gray wooden frame house on MacCombs Street on the east side of the city. The house was crowded there, but I was used to being crowded and didn't know that there were more private ways to live, and it seemed fine. How could I notice, anyway, when I had electric lights to pull off and on and a toilet indoors that flushed and flushed when I pulled that chain string? But we soon moved to a place of our own, another frame house on Madison Avenue and Mullick Street.

There was something else I had never seen or heard of before—gangs. Near us was the Purple Gang, a mostly Jewish gang of real tough guys. They only used colored people to help them do the real dirty jobs. Their connections went all the way down to Louisiana and out to Al Capone in Chicago. They operated from the Detroit River. We'd see the police stop trucks—bootleg liquor and stolen goods. Sometimes we saw the police take bodies away after a murder. Hastings Street was a bad street.

One thing I knew, I didn't want any part of people like that. Maybe it was Momma, maybe it was the church, but I knew I would never, ever try to do nothing to hurt somebody. When I heard some of those murder stories, my stomach would just twist around. No way anyone was going to get me in bad trouble.

Of course Momma had us signed up at Calvary Baptist Church, and we went there every Sunday.

For a while, we had money in Detroit because my stepfather worked for the city as a street cleaner. My older brothers all worked at Ford. I remember when a relative drove us around the town and showed us the Ford plant. My God, it was bigger than a cottonfield and a cornfield combined, bigger than some cities we had passed by on the train. I was impressed. Ford paid more on the job than you'd ever get on the farm. I thought we were doing pretty well, and I looked forward to working in the plant when I got older.

Finally, we got some "regular" clothes—knickers, sweaters, shirts, and Momma registered me in the Duffield Elementary School; they put me in the third grade.

Of course, Duffield was nothing like Mt. Sinai School. There were a whole lot of classrooms, children, and teachers. Tell you the truth, it was too much for me. They had all kinds of routines I didn't know a thing about— assemblies, fire drills, and stuff like that. So I kept myself quiet. It bored me. Most times, I'd just look out the window. I'd be lying if I told you I remembered what I was thinking about, but I guess I'd probably be thinking I'd rather be at the movies or playing ball. All I can be sure about was that I'd rather have been anyplace else than in that classroom trying to listen to something I didn't understand.

JOE LOUIS: MY LIFE

The teachers liked me, though. I didn't give them trouble. Only time I shined was when they had assembly—I carried the flag. That was supposed to be some kind of honor job. No way I could mess that up. I was tall, strong, and they tell me I was a nice-looking kid. Those assembly days, Momma made sure I had a clean, starched white shirt and a blue tie. That's the only thing about school I liked.

In the meantime, I started to make friends. My first, my best, and still my buddy, was a little skinny guy named Freddie Guinyard. First time I saw him was at Calvary Baptist Church. He was always so neat and looking around all curious like. Then I used to run into him at the Eastern Market, vegetable and produce center where young kids used to hang around trying to see if they could get a job moving vegetables or helping out in any way. Well, I'd see Freddie there and just admire him. For all his skinny little self, he was tough and slick—he'd get jobs just on his mouth alone. I was glad when Freddie started talking to me and taking me around (don't forget I was a pretty big kid for my age); work started happening. We made a good team.

Freddie was a warm, friendly guy. He'd really make me laugh. I remember the time they sent him home from school: The teacher had said, only to the colored kids, that if they made good grades she would see to it that they were rewarded by getting a chance to shine shoes in J. L. Hudson's department store on weekends. Freddie jumped up and said, "Why would you need to have good grades to shine shoes?" And they sent him straight home. It was the first time I started thinking about racial matters.

When I was about thirteen or so, and while we were doing all right at home, things started happening to the nation. Funny thing, I'll bet you can predict a depression just by seeing how many black people are starting to lose their jobs—it takes a while to get to the top. Anyway, one by one, my brothers and stepfather started losing their jobs. For the first time in my life I remember being hungry. At one time I didn't have shoes to put on to go to school. Some of my teachers gave me clothes to take home for my family. I was never in trouble in school; those clothes were my only reward.

I couldn't keep up with the class. I was bigger than anybody and couldn't seem to get past the sixth grade. Fact is, my youngest sister, Vunice, caught up with me and passed me by. She was the smart one.

There was a nice teacher named Miss Vada at Duffield who figured out that I had better educate my hands instead of my head. So they transferred me to Bronson, an all-boys vocational school. I was pretty good there. I made tables, cabinets, shelves, and stuff like that. When I finished them off, I took them home to be used in the house. It helped. Furniture was the last thing we needed to buy.

Eventually, we went on the soup line. Momma had to go down to the relief place and wait in line to get us some money every week. I think, all told, we got something like four hundred and some odd dollars, but I'm proud to say that after I fought Charley Massera in 1934, I paid back every cent.

Everything costs a lot of money when you haven't got any. Everybody in the family was trying as hard as they could to get food to put in our stomachs. Me and Freddie, when we were about fifteen or sixteen, got a job together on an ice wagon. I guess you have to go back some to remember that there were no refrigerators or freezers in those days, at least not for poor people. Everybody was dependent on the iceman to keep food from spoiling. We didn't travel around in some big truck that needed gas and fixing up. We used a wagon with an old horse pulling it. We'd put thick wraps of brown burlap over the ice to keep it from melting too fast. Anyway, when it came time to deliver, Freddie stayed downstairs watching the horse while I carried fifty to sixty pounds of ice up a couple of flights. Freddie thought he was tricking me into doing all the heavy work, but I knew he was too small and skinny to carry the weight, anyway. I didn't mind, though. Hard work never bothered me, and it built me up for my profession.

My sister Emmarell had married by then, and sometimes I'd help her by scrubbing her floors on Saturday. She'd give me a quarter for this. Other times me and Freddie delivered groceries and worked in the vegetable section of the Eastern Market.

But it wasn't all hard work and scraping to get by. I had good times, too. When we were younger, I used to tease Freddie about his sailor cap with a silk ribbon hanging down. I'd wear a skull cap because nobody was gonna put that funny hat on me. We also had to wear short pants or knickers. I hated them. One time I saved my pennies and nickels and dimes until I had enough money to buy some cheap long pants. But I had to roll them up since Momma would have had a fit to see her baby boy wearing man's clothes.

On Saturdays we used to go to the Catherine Theater. We'd be at the Eastern Market at five and work until seven, come home, wash up, then go to the movies. We'd do this before school, too. I loved the movies, and still do. You can't see those like they made when I was a kid. Those cowboy movies really thrilled me. My favorites were Buck Jones, Tom Mix, Ken Maynard. Can't remember exactly what I actually thought, but I guess I wanted to be the big, strong, good guy and help those poor defenseless folks who needed it.

We'd stay at the movies all day. You had to make sure you got there before twelve so you could get in for five cents. Sometimes for the fun of it, or when we didn't have enough money, one of us would go and pay to go in the show and push the side exit door open so the rest of the guys could get in. Sometimes one of us would distract the cashier so others could sneak in. We thought it was real funny. With the money we saved, we'd buy candy, sodas, all kinds of junk food.

Oh, and the girls. I always loved beautiful girls, and I had me one, too, a real pretty girl named Bennie Franklin. She was the only girlfriend I had in Detroit from the time I was fourteen till I was practically married. Now, I won't say there wasn't a little fooling around here and there, but Bennie was special. In fact, she was too special. She was one of my older sister's stepdaughters. Although there was no blood between us, we both knew the family wouldn't approve of our going around together. Some kind of way we kept our feelings for each other a secret from the family.

Bennie'd come up from Alabama about the same time I had. She was a small brown-skinned beauty with long shiny black hair. She was kind, sweet, and smart. The two of us would sneak around to the movies, and I'd visit her practically every chance I got. No one noticed because it looked like I was going to see my older sister. When we got a chance we'd go to Belle Island up between Canada and Detroit. It was a kind of amusement park and lovers' lane. On good days, we would go picnicking. Everything was good about our relationship, and it was as close as a relationship could get.

When I had my first amateur fights, Bennie'd be out there rooting for me with her face all lit up. I deeply regret breaking her heart, and I know I did when I called her from the training camp in New Jersey the day before the Baer fight. I told her I was getting married to a girl named Marva. She couldn't believe it.

When you're twenty-one, you may be strong, you may be clever, but you're not too wise. I wish I had broken up with her in a nicer, kinder way.

You know, you often have to wonder about things like

fate or luck. Sometimes you think about things that turn your whole life around; like Momma marrying Pat Brooks; the move to Detroit; the transfer to the Bronson School; and then, funny enough, violin lessons.

Things were picking up a bit at home. A lot of my older brothers were getting married. They were getting good jobs, or at least they could take care of themselves. My baby sister Vunice had started talking about wanting to go to college when she finished high school. Emmarell had some kind of plans for going into business and here I was—seventeen years old—just making cabinets at the Bronson School. Momma wanted me to be something—anything besides hauling ice and coal and making cabinets.

Somewhere, somehow, Momma heard about this music teacher on Warren and Woodward Streets. So she sent me to take violin lessons at fifty cents a class, plus additional money for the rental of the violin. Me, who couldn't even play the mouth organ. I did not like the violin—it felt funny in my big hands, and when I played it—horrible.

Well, here I was, six feet tall, big as a light heavyweight, going to Bronson Vocational School, carrying this little bit of a violin. You can imagine the kidding I had to take. I remember one time some guy called me a sissy when he saw me with the violin, and I broke it over his head.

There was one guy at school, though, who didn't out and out laugh at me. His name was Thurston McKinney. He was a real good-looking guy with beautiful brown skin. Everybody was wild over him because he had just won the 1932 Golden Gloves in Detroit for the 147-pound division.

We were just nodding friends because he was a year or so older than I was. One day, he saw me with the violin and talked me into going to the gym with him. It made me feel real good that he would ask me to go. I skipped music, and Thurston, me, and the violin went to Brewster's East Side Gymnasium.

JOE LOUIS: MY LIFE

Funny thing, a good friend, Amsey Rinson, and me used to spar around my backyard every time we got a chance. He'd said that if we went over to the gym, maybe we could borrow some boxing gloves. We just never got around to it, then. So when Thurston asked me to go with him, I knew where I was going, but I didn't have any idea of what to expect. Of course I knew about school gyms and stuff like that, but this was really different.

It was my first time in a professional gym. I looked at the ring, the punching bag, pulleys, exercise mat, and it was love at first sight. I watched Thurston box with a sparring partner and real equipment. I liked what I saw. So, I just right away took the fifty cents my momma had given me for violin lessons and rented a locker and put the violin in first. Thurston loaned me some trunks and found me some old tennis shoes that would fit, and I started punching the bag.

And that's how it began.

Amsey Rinson, Thurston McKinney, and me would go regularly. After a little while, Atler Ellis, the man who ran the gym, said he would show me how to box if I came by often enough. And I did.

One day, Thurston asked me to be his sparring partner. That was a real honor to me. Well, he beat me all over the ring. He hit me with a right to the jaw that almost dropped me. I got mad. I let go my right. It caught him on the chin. His eyes got glassy and his knees buckled, and if I hadn't moved fast to hold him up, I would have knocked him out—and he was the Golden Glove Welterweight Champion of Detroit. I remember Thurston shaking his head and then grinning at me and saying, "Man, throw that violin away."

You can't imagine how I felt. I don't know how to describe it. It was like power pumping through me. Maybe it's something like people getting religion. I don't know, because I'd been in some street fights before, but this was different. This was not like fighting because you mad at somebody or because you were defending somebody. You were doing it because there was something professional about it.

That was the first time I knew what I really wanted to be. At last there would be something where I could be an individual. I wasn't thinking about being a world champion. I wanted to be a Golden Gloves Light Heavyweight Champion.

But there was still a problem to solve with the violin lessons. I was taking Momma's fifty cents for the gym locker, but I needed a little more for other fight stuff. I finally confided in my sister Emmarell. Emmarell was an ambitious woman, and I don't think she thought too much of me. But when I told her I really wanted to do something for the first time, she'd give me a little change. She promised she wouldn't tell Momma till I worked something out about this fighting business.

As it turned out, I didn't have to work out too much. One Saturday I got home from the gym, and the violin teacher was there talking to Momma. Well, Momma just looked at me real hard and asked me for my lesson punch card, but I had torn it up and thrown it away. I knew there was no backing down at this point, especially with the man there and Momma looking me straight in my face. I told my mother I didn't want to play the violin—I wanted to be a fighter. The teacher helped a lot too; he told her I didn't have any talent, and despite the Depression, he didn't see any need for Momma to waste money.

After the teacher left, Momma and I had a good talk. At first she looked unhappy, but she said that if any of us kids wanted to do something bad enough, she'd try to see that we got a chance at it. "No matter what you do," she said, "remember you're from a Christian family, and always act that way." My stepfather wasn't enthusiastic about it, but he went along with Momma, and at least they let me keep on training.

Me, Thurston, and Rinson became close friends as

fighters. Thurston used to show me magazines about fighters. I remember him showing me pictures of Jack Dempsey, Jack Johnson, and Kid Chocolate. He said these guys made a lot of money. That really triggered me—the idea of big money almost busted up my head. I had told Momma I gave up the violin to be a fighter, but I really hadn't thought that deep about being a heavyweight contender, much less a champion. Money can motivate you a lot.

When I wasn't in school or working part-time, I was in the gym. I'd started to get more respect from people in the neighborhood. People around there always knew I could fight because of my stepbrother Pat and the Catherine Street Gang.

Pat and I went to the Bronson School together. I'll never forget how Pat would get into an argument, and I'd have to fight for him in school. One time I was in an alley coming home from school; Pat came running after me, wanting to know where I was going. When I told him I was going home, he said, "No, you can't do that—you gotta fight somebody for me." This happened often. Sometimes when these guys saw me, they wouldn't want to fight. Whenever I fought, I won.

Now, I'm not trying to say I was a goody-goody boy or a momma's boy, but I'm not saying I was bad. The Catherine Street Gang in our neighborhood must have had maybe fifty or more members, and they fought all the time. Neither me nor my brothers were ever members of this gang. They were rough guys. I'd occasionally fight with them when they were supposedly trying to protect the neighborhood. We just fought with our fists in those days, at least I know I did. I got a reputation as a good hard puncher and they were always after me to join them. I didn't want to because those guys would play some pretty bad tricks on people.

You know something, I never was a leader. I always followed other people, but I never followed anyone doing something I knew was wrong or doing something I didn't want to do. I was a stubborn kind of guy—I never led anyone anywhere, but I only did what I wanted to do.

Between what I wouldn't do and chance, there came a man named Ben Turpin. Ben Turpin was a black cop, a quiet sort of man, about five-feet eleven, real dark-skinned, and tougher than anyone in that Catherine Street Gang. He used to keep me out of trouble. If he caught me out at night, he'd run me home or take me home himself. He had a lot of respect for my family. When he patrolled the neighborhood, he used to hang out in a restaurant across the street from the Catherine Theater. He knew I was training to be a fighter, and he didn't want anything to happen to me.

One time the gang tried to get me to hold somebody so they could rob him. I told them "no," but they kept trying to convince me. Ben Turpin was around that night. Thank God, he had some kind of policeman's instinct, and he chased me away from the gang and took me home. I'll never forget the thankful look my mother had on her face that night when he pushed me through the door.

Most of that gang wound up in jail.

But soon I was too busy with fighting to be bothered or concerned about gangs. I had better things to do with my fists than to be involved in street fights, plus I had Bennie Franklin, and that was enough for me—at that time.

Did you ever have a goal and still not know where you're going? Story of my life—plain and simple. I knew I wasn't going to stay where I was, but I wasn't sure just where I was going. Most likely, though, my destination was going to involve fighting. So I left school at about seventeen to spend more time in the gym. I had the body, the weight, and there was nothing else I could see that I could do as well. I was determined that this time I'd do it right.

When I quit school, I didn't feel guilty because even though I was still hauling coal and selling vegetables, I could say out loud, "I'm going to be a fighter. I'm going to be somebody." It gave me a sense of pride and dignity to at last want to be something. Got to admit I strutted a little.

I even had a reputation—little kids on my block followed me around all the time. There was one kid in particular who seemed to know my schedule. He'd be there, Johnny-on-the-spot, asking to carry my bag. I felt embarrassed and silly and proud, but anyway I let him carry it to Brewster's Gym for me. When he moved to New York, I missed him. He was a real nice kid. His name was Walker Smith. Later they changed his name to "Sugar" Ray Robinson.

Atler Ellis, the man who run the gym, was becoming very interested in me. He got Holman Williams, a black middleweight, to help train me. Holman was just a couple years older than me, but he had some experience. He was already an amateur fighter who later turned pro.

Atler and Holman would take turns training me. It was hard, but I got better as I went along.

I was hustling little jobs all day. Came home at five, ate dinner, and headed for the gym. I knew I needed more time in the gym, but I had to work to help the family out. My stepfather tried talking to me about getting a steady job because he didn't see any future to boxing. Sometimes when I just felt like a punching bag in the gym, I agreed with him. Other times, though, when I was knocking down other fighters and I knew I was sharp, I disagreed. My momma said, "If you want to be a fighter, be one," but what Momma said and what she meant were probably two different things. Anyway, I tried to convince my stepfather that there was something to boxing. I brought Thurston up to talk to him. He told him about the merchandise checks you get as an amateur boxer. Those checks were from seven to twenty-five dollars, whether you won or lost, and you could take those checks and buy food with them. Well, with my stepfather out of work, the idea of boxing and those checks seemed more appealing to him.

Punch. I could punch you and knock you out, if I could catch you. I had a lot to learn—there's no such thing as a "natural." A "natural" dancer has to practice hard. A "natural" painter has to paint all the time, even a "natural" fool has to work at it. I had the God-given equipment to be a professional fighter, but I had to train at it, and train damn hard.

Holman Williams encouraged me a lot. I respected him. He was a beautiful boxer. He told me I had the stuff to be a champion, and I knew he was serious. My ego soared up there and I was hungry for my first amateur fight. I told Holman and Atler Ellis I was ready.

Ellis said he could match me with Johnny Miler, a white fighter who had been on the Olympic boxing team in Los Angeles in 1932. He was experienced and tough and maybe the best in the light heavyweight amateur division. Holman wasn't too keen on the match. He said I was in over my head. Holman knew Miler because he had had several bouts with him. He said he didn't know if I was ready for him, but my mind was made up.

I had seen a photograph of Miler, and there was something about the way he posed that convinced me that I could beat him. I knew it. This was going to be the start of a successful career. But I didn't want my family to know anything about it yet, so before I boxed Miler I decided I'd drop the name Barrow and just be plain Joe Louis. That way, if it got into the papers, Momma wouldn't know the difference.

I entered the ring at the Naval Armory in Detroit, feeling good. This was going to be my day. I had Thurston, Holman, and Atler Ellis, and my regular buddy Freddie Guinyard with me—my own rooting crowd.

It was scheduled for three rounds. Miler knocked me down seven times in two rounds. He won. I lost. He was too far ahead of me in everything. Holman and Atler reassured me that anybody who can get up seven times has something. They said: "The next time, jab with your left before shooting that right hand."

In sparring sessions I was able to drop opponents with my right hand, so I had been set to knock out Miler with one punch. I hit him all right, and I stepped back to let him fall. Instead he came at me with both hands flying.

My friends didn't say a word to me about my defeat. I just kept talking and talking and talking about how determined I was to go back in the ring and to train more and beat him the next go 'round.

All that was easier said than done. I had to go home, Momma never saw me look so bad. Me, who'd never in my life had anything more serious than an earache—I looked like something the cat dragged in. She cried and said I better find something better to do—after all, I was her baby boy. I gave my stepfather the merchandise check for seven dollars. He didn't say anything—then.

Next day, I went back to the gym. I tell you I was sore and aching, but my pride hurt more. When I got home, my stepfather sat and had a long talk with me. He told me he was getting to be an old man and, except for marrying my momma and getting out of Alabama, he hadn't accomplished much. I was young, he said, and maybe I should just try to get a regular job, settle down, and marry some nice girl.

Well, the way I ached and the way my feelings hurt even more, I went out and in a few days I had a job at the Ford factory at River Rouge for twenty-five dollars a week. I didn't go near the gym for two months.

This was my first time at a regular job putting in a certain number of hours and getting paid a certain amount each week. I was the newest there, and I got, I think, the hardest job. My job was pushing truck bodies to a conveyor belt, and it wasn't my idea of fun. Sometimes after work my back would hurt me so much I couldn't straighten up. But since my stepfather was out of work, I knew I had to do this.

Eventually, I couldn't stand it anymore. I figured, if I'm going to hurt that much for twenty-five dollars a week, I might as well go back and try fighting again. I covered myself, though. I asked my boss for a six-month leave of absence. I could come back to the factory if things went bad in the ring.

I left Ford in January, 1933, and I never returned.

When I walked back into the gym, I wondered why I ever let my stepfather persuade me to stop. I knew that I wanted money, big money—but big money to me was sixty or seventy dollars a week. With enough work I could get it. My trainer, Holman Williams, worked even harder with me because he knew I had the ability.

This time Momma went along with me wholeheartedly, especially since I had just taken a six-month leave of absence from Ford. She knew there was something to fall back on. I trained more seriously. Didn't bother with Bennie, didn't go out running around with Freddie and my stepbrother Pat. I ate as well as I could, slept well, and trained all day. I was learning fast.

Although Holman was training me, Atler Ellis was still watching me. He saw I had a strong right hand, but he also saw I wasn't using my left hand as well as I could. One day Ellis said he wanted to try something. He tied my right hand to the corner of the ring so I'd have to use my left. He put Thurston McKinney in with me. Thurston beat the hell out of me. I yelled to Ellis, "Tie me loose" but he just laughed and made me practice that way. I learned the importance of using my left hand—I had no choice.

Holman got me a three-round amateur fight with Otis Thomas at the Forest Athletic Club in Detroit. When I climbed in the ring, I had Miler on my mind. Would this guy knock me all over the ring, too? I promised myself,

"Not this time." I beat Thomas, K.O.'d him in round one with a left hook and a right to the jaw. I'd scored my first official knockout. I was on top of the world.

After Thomas, I knocked out thirteen more opponents in a row. My confidence was growing; around amateur circles, fight promoters were beginning to give me a second look. Promoters began asking for me more and more. Those twenty-five-dollar merchandise checks kept coming in.

By now, with so many fights behind me, Thurston encouraged me to go into the Golden Gloves. I got the application form from the *Detroit Free Press*, who sponsored the Golden Gloves in Detroit. I knew this was something big; I wouldn't be getting merchandise checks any more, but trophies and medals instead. My next step after the Gloves would be to turn professional.

I didn't have the courage to tell Momma right away, so I hid the application in the light globe over the dining room table. Of course Momma found it, and, with a little sigh, she told me to fill it out and send it in.

Now I was a Golden Glover. That's what I wanted. My world was getting bigger and deeper. The *Detroit Free Press* sent me to Chicago to fight Clinton Bridges, a heavyweight. He beat me on points. Then I was in Boston and was outpointed by Max Marek in the National Amateur Championship. Marek was the star of the Notre Dame football team, but he hadn't knocked me out. Then it was six victories in a row in the National Amateur Championship Tournament. These were really tough guys, and I was winning more than I was losing. I defeated guys like Ario Soldati of Chicago, Bud Schildknecht of Kansas City, and Hugh Rogers of Jacksonville, Florida.

For the first time in my life, I was away from my family. It felt strange, but I liked it; it was like being in a new family. You knew all the guys in the amateur circle, you'd eat and sleep together, and you became friends.

Going to places like Boston and Toronto opened my

eyes. I saw things I wanted that I had never really known about. I met important people, and I wanted to be important, too. Doctors, lawyers, big time gamblers would come up and talk to me and encourage me.

About this time, Holman Williams decided that I was going too fast for him, especially since he was fighting, too. So Holman recommended a new trainer for me— George Slayton. He ran the Detroit A.C.

December of 1933. I was nineteen years old. There was another young black heavyweight who was becoming popular in Detroit, Stanley Evans. He was strong, but Slayton thought I was ready for him, and I did, too. Slayton booked the fight. Well, I wasn't ready. Evans taught me some things I didn't know existed—he didn't knock me down, but he sure the hell outpointed me. Slayton still had the faith in me, though. Otherwise he wouldn't have introduced me to John Roxborough.

Slayton brought Mr. Roxborough to my dressing room. This man had real class. He was a very light-skinned black man about six feet tall, and he weighed about 190 pounds. He didn't seem flashy, but stylish and rich-looking. He had a gray silk suit, the kind you don't buy off the rack. It made me look twice. His attitude was gentle, like a gentleman should be. Mr. Roxborough told me he liked the way I fought and he was interested in me. I couldn't understand why—hell, I'd just lost the fight. He told me to drop by his real estate office within the next couple of days.

Well, in the next couple of days, I found out a lot about Mr. Roxborough. He had a reputation for helping a lot of people, he even sent some through college. Roxborough had a real estate office, but that was just a front. He was a big-time numbers man. Now, you have to think back some. In those days it was hard living if you were black, and it was harder still because the Depression was on. If you were smart enough to have your own numbers operation and you were kind and giving in the black neighborhoods, you got as much respect as a doctor or lawyer. It was a kind of a charge to me to know a man like him was interested in me. His brother Charlie was a lawyer and politician and a big wheel in the Urban League and the Young Negro Progressive Association. So Mr. Roxborough was well encased in dignity and legitimacy.

He had a long talk with me. He knew I was hurting financially and knew I needed things for my career. I'll never forget the day he took me over to Long's Drugstore and told the owner to give me anything I wanted and charge it to him. First time I ever had so many clean bandages, rubbing alcohol, and such. He even gave me some of his old clothes, shirts, ties, everything except shoes—my feet were too big.

Sometimes he'd invite me to his house for dinner. It was a beautiful house, and he had a good looking and gracious wife. I loved it. I never saw black people living this way, and I was envious and watched everything he did.

I remember the day he gave me a pair of brand new professional boxing gloves. Well, with my new clothes and my new professional gloves, I went over to the Mt. Olivet Church gym and showed the guys. Their eyes nearly popped out of their heads, and I proudly told them they needed a backer, too. The next day eleven guys showed up in Mr. Roxborough's office pleading their case. Mr. Roxborough told me not to do that any more, and so I never bragged about him again.

I was still training regularly, and Mr. Roxborough was giving me pocket money. My reputation was growing bigger, and I had an important match coming up in Chicago. It was a Golden Gloves light heavyweight fight.

I'll never forget it. I was in Chicago, early in 1934, for a Golden Gloves fight, all primed up sitting in my dressing room waiting to go on. All of a sudden, there was a lot of pushing and excitement, and a gang of detectives barged in and told me I was under arrest and they were taking me to the Eleventh Street Police Station. I was scared shitless. I couldn't think of anything I did or had ever done wrong.

After I heard the charges, I wanted to bust out laughing, but I was too scared. They said I was being held on the charge of murdering "my wife" in Gary, Indiana, in 1929. I was trying to tell them that I was only fifteen years old at the time. They finally released me, but too late for the fight I was scheduled to appear in.

Mr. Roxborough found out later some Chicago "fight fans" had been watching me while I was training and probably thought I would win. They had this whole murder thing trumped up to put me out of the way so that their man would have a chance.

After that Chicago incident was explained to me, I took on a greater sense of my own importance—I was a threat to other boxers. Well, in my on-again, off-again training schedule, I determined that I would work harder for my next fight with Evans. I cut down again on fooling around with my out-of-the-fight-game buddies and settled into a real rhythm of training. Later in 1934 I fought Evans again, and this time I beat him to win the light heavyweight crown for the Detroit Golden Gloves.

My last amateur fight was in Ford Field, Detroit, an intercity light heavyweight competition. It was over in less than two minutes. The guy I fought was Joe Bauer. I knocked him out on June 12, 1934. After that Mr. Roxborough came over to me and said, "I think you're ready, Joe. Time to turn professional." This was it. I knew it and Mr. Roxborough knew it, but my momma and stepfather had to know it, too.

I think it was the next day or so that Mr. Roxborough had me in his office talking to me. He said he wanted to send me to Chicago to live and train. He said he had great faith in me, and for that reason I'd do better in Chicago with his friend Julian Black—both of them would be my managers. At first I was confused; I'd come to depend on Mr. Roxborough, not only for the money and clothes he gave me, but for the honor of his friendship. He assured me he'd always be around, and I could contact him any time I wanted. Then he told me a little bit about Julian Black. Seems like a few years earlier Mr. Roxborough was in financial trouble with his numbers business and Julian Black had bailed him out with a lot of money. Now that Mr. Roxborough was doing well again, and as he never forgot a favor, he wanted to return one. That was one reason. Another reason was that Julian Black had a stable of black fighters in Chicago, and plenty of money because he too was a big-operating numbers man. I learned a lesson here, too—you can't ever really be a big success without having money, or having someone to give it to you.

We talked a few days later. Sometimes I'm a little hardheaded and need a lot of persuasion, but this time I was scared to tell my momma and a little nervous about leaving home and my friends. Mr. Roxborough was a patient and kind man. He told me about the fate of most black fighters, ones with white managers, who wound up burned-out and broke before they reached their prime. The white managers were not interested in the men they were handling but in the money they could make from them. They didn't take the proper time to see that their fighters had a proper training, that they lived comfortably, or ate well, or had some pocket change. Mr. Roxborough was talking about Black Power before it became popular.

I took another gamble and told Mr. Roxborough, "OK, I'm ready, but you have to tell my momma."

Next day, I told Momma Mr. Roxborough was coming by; she wanted to know why. She, like everybody else, respected him and appreciated everything he had been doing for me, but I held out and told her to wait and see.

Mr. Roxborough had the charm and intelligence to know how to convince people. He told my momma and stepfather all the things he had talked to me about. Finally, Momma said yes, if he would make sure that I lived well and led a decent Christian life. My stepfather thought some and said, "Well, fighting was all right when he used to get those merchandise checks, but who can eat all those trophies he's bringing home now? Might as well try to make some money."

I could go now. I would have anyway, but now I could go with an easy conscience.

It was hardest on Bennie. Six years is a lot of time to be in love and keep it a secret. I told her it was going to be great, I would make the money and then we'd tell the world and nobody could do anything about it.

Like leaving Alabama, I felt happy and scared, but what the hell—Chicago, here I come.

1934
CHICAGO

SINCE I'D BEEN TO CHICAGO PLENTY OF TIMES BEFORE, I knew what to expect from the city, but the thing that had me in suspense was what Julian Black would be like.

When Mr. Roxborough and I got off the train, Mr. Black met us. He was a fine-looking man about five-foot ten or eleven, a little stocky, straight hair, light-brown complexion, and he had a slight limp. He was friendly enough to me, but I knew he was basically a tough guy.

They took me over to an apartment building on Forty-sixth Street. I was to take a room in an apartment owned by Bill Bottoms, who was to become another important person in my life. Bill was a chef. When I started training in camps, he ran the kitchen, and he continued for the rest of my fighting days. He was something. Not only did he cook well, he made sure I had all the kind of food that I needed. A good friend, Bill Bottoms was.

Mr. Roxborough and Mr. Black helped me settle in and showed me my room. First time in my life that I was going to have a room all to myself. First time in my life I was really going to know privacy and learn to love it—and, sometimes, hate it. The two of them talked a lot of business that I did not quite understand, maybe because I was too busy trying to adjust myself to a different way of life. I looked out the window and I saw Washington Park, where I would have to do my roadwork every morning for almost a year.

Mr. Black looked at me hard. He told me my first professional fight would be in a little over a month. He was making a big investment in me and expected me to make a big investment in myself. Training would be hard and long so I would be ready. But he was going to drop most of the other fighters (about four or five) and just concentrate on me.

Two days later I met the man who was going to be my trainer during the best part of my career, and my friend the rest of his life. I met him at Trafton's Gym on Randolph Street. Jack Blackburn was a wiry, strong-looking man, bald-headed and with a mean-looking scar down the left side of his face from the corner of his mouth up to his ear.

Now, let me tell you what I know and remember about this man who, with his superior knowledge and God-given talent, was to make me the first black world heavyweight champion since Jack Johnson in 1915.

Blackburn was born in Kentucky in 1893. He'd been one hell of a fighter himself. In twenty years he'd had over one hundred fights as a lightweight and had won most of them. He was rough-talking; I suppose anybody who'd been in and out of prison—he had served five years for murder—would talk rough.

He wouldn't let me in the ring for the first week I knew him, but made me hit the punching bag over and over. He'd hold the bag and give me instructions on how to throw punches. I did this morning, noon, and night till I could have sworn the bag was punching me, too.

After a while, he let me box for him. He saw my faults right off. I was hitting off-balance. He started correcting this by showing me how to plant my feet and punch with my whole body, not just by swinging my arms. He said people going to fights don't want to see a dancer or a clincher—they want to see a man who goes for the guts. He said that I had strength and that I could beat or knock out anybody I wanted to if I planted my body in the right position.

One day while I was resting up some, he said, "You know, boy, the heavyweight division for a Negro is hardly likely. The white man ain't too keen on it. You have to really be something to get anywhere. If you really ain't gonna be another Jack Johnson, you got some hope. White man hasn't forgotten that fool nigger with his white women, acting like he owned the world. And you got to listen to everything I tell you. You got to jump when I say jump, sleep when I say sleep. Other than that, you're wasting my time."

I looked at him, told him that I'd promise him and myself there would be no time wasted. With a little tight funny smile he said "OK, Chappie." I smiled and said back to him "OK, Chappie," and from that time on that's what we called each other.

First time in my life I had so much routine. At six A.M. I ran six miles—twice around Washington Park. Punching the bag, boxing with sparring partners, jumping rope, and Chappie all the time telling me how to punch with my body properly.

Sometimes I'd laugh when he told me about how black fighters were permitted in the ring just to make the white fighters look good. They let you put up a good fight, but you dare not better look better than some of the worst white boxers you were supposed to be fighting.

Another time he told me he wore a size eight and a half shoe, but when he was fighting he had to put on a size ten before the fight. He made sure he got paid his gold pieces in advance. He'd put his money in his shoes—otherwise the promoters would take off without paying.

Most importantly, he told me that sometime, someplace, somebody was going to try to get me to throw a fight. He told me about all the pitfalls. I remember him looking me dead in the eye and saying, "I've done a lot of things I haven't been proud of but I never threw a fight, and you won't either 'cause I'll know, and then it's going to be you and me."

Well, the fight was almost there, and the contract was worked out. I was to get fifty percent of the purse, and Mr. Roxborough and Mr. Black were to get fifty percent.

Expenses came out of their share. Seemed fair enough to me, and it was.

A little before the fight night, it was just me and Chappie talking while he was giving me a rubdown. He kept telling me that the cards were stacked against me because I was a black fighter opposing white fighters. He told me that I could not win on points alone. I had to go for the knockout, so there'd be no doubt. His words were "Negro fighters do not go to town winning decisions."

Chappie said it was real nice that I was easygoing, but that wouldn't help me in the ring. Even with my sparring partners, I'd have to get some blood in my eyes. He said when you get in that ring, you go for the kill—let your right fist be the referee.

On July 4, 1934, me, Chappie, Black, Roxborough, and Freddie Guinyard headed for the Bacon Casino on the South Side of Chicago at Forty-seventh Street. Because of my Golden Gloves reputation, I never had to fight preliminaries when I started. This was the main event. My first professional fight, and I'm up against Jack Kracken of Chicago. Chappie talked to me all the way there. I was worried because of the number of rounds involved—I was used to fighting three rounds, as an amateur. Now I was scheduled for ten rounds, and I wasn't sure I could make it.

Chappie told me not to worry about it—if you can go three, you can go six. If you can go six, you can go ten. This talk was fine until I got in the ring. One thing for sure, Jack Kracken didn't look like an amateur. He was white and had on white trunks, and he looked older than me. He had black hair and weighed about 175 pounds, but I weighed 181. Thing about him, though, he didn't look the least bit concerned about me. He looked like he had it made, and that bothered me a lot.

Chappie could see I was nervous. He kept talking, "Remember everything I taught you." "You get in there and knock that guy out as fast as you can." "One clean

punch is better than a hundred punches." "Bide your
time." "Place your punches and knock your opponent out."
I looked at Kracken again. He was the top Chicago heavyweight, that was sure enough.

When the bell rang, I did just what Chappie told me. I
went straight to the body. When he dropped his guard, I
gave him a left to the chin, and in less than two minutes
I knocked him out. The fight was over—I won.

You know, I believed it and I couldn't believe it. I knew
that I'd always do exactly what Chappie told me. Freddie
and me were jumping around hooting and hollering. I
was happy and proud of myself.

Thing is, though, Chappie and Mr. Roxborough and Mr.
Black weren't all that happy. Of course, they were glad I
won, but they said I looked sluggish. I couldn't think of
any reason until Chappie asked me about what was I
eating. I got real indignant and told him I stuck to my
diet, " 'cepting for the dozen bananas I ate before the
fight." They just looked at me, shook their heads, and
sighed. After that, everybody watched me like a hawk
before every fight.

Well, when I got that first check I just couldn't believe
it. Fifty-nine dollars. It looked pretty good to me for two
minutes of work. When Mr. Roxborough gave me the
check, he told it was all mine and to send it to my mother.
I protested a little, but Mr. Roxborough just smiled and
said when you get to the real money, then we'll honor the
signed contract. I didn't know managers were like that.
Other fighters always told me that managers always take
over half your money and then make you pay your own
expenses. Mr. Roxborough was a real gentleman and I've
always appreciated that. I sent most of the money home
but kept a few dollars for me and Freddie to celebrate a
little. Celebrating was going bowling and eating junk
food.

Besides my momma, Mr. Roxborough, Mr. Black, and
Chappie Blackburn were my teachers. Seems like simple

things they taught me, now, but then there were a lot of things I never had known—proper methods for washing my ears, combing my hair, and general grooming; how to hold a fork. Chappie took care of teaching me the fighting end.

There was more though, much more. My backers were not about to let their investment in me be messed up by any kind of scandal. They told me I had to live my life both professionally and personally a certain way. They remembered how Jack Johnson had ruined boxing for blacks, especially for black heavyweights.

They did not set down in writing any particular rules and say, "Now this is what you have to do." No, just in day by day talking I knew what they wanted. They never told me not to go out with white women—they said don't ever get your picture taken with one—that would be the end of my career.

One time we were talking about these little black toy dolls they used to make of fighters. Those dolls always had the wide grin with thick red lips. They looked foolish. I got the message—don't look like a fool nigger doll. Look like a black man with dignity.

They told me that I was going to be big popular man and people would always be watching me—and not always in admiration. They told me not to travel around alone much, and never to go in a night club by myself—that didn't bother me too much, since I'd never been in one and had no particular desire to go in one.

They said they saw my potential and they wanted a good image of me for the public.

If anybody tried to fix one of my fights, I was to tell them. There were to be no easy fights.

Seems like I had barely turned around, because when I looked up my next fight was there, against Willie Davis, a colored fighter, right back at the Bacon Casino, July 11, 1934. Knockout in the third round. Willie was a friend of mine, but in that ring he was tough enough. This time I got sixty-two dollars—my manager gave me the whole check.

Next fight was scheduled for July 29 at the Marigold Gardens, an eight-rounder with Larry Udell. They booked Marigold because I was getting a following. The promoters were looking real hard at me. Knockout second round. Winner's check, $101.00. All mine and Momma's.

Since my last fight was a sellout, the Marigold Gardens booked me again for August 13. This time they put me against Jack Kranz, who was a tough fighter coming along the same way I was. It was a six-rounder, and we both lasted it through, but I won on points. That night I took home $125. Well, by this time even my stepfather was getting enthusiastic—I was sending home more money than the whole family made, put together.

I was working hard and never even had a couple of hours to myself. Sometimes Chappie would break down and let me go to a movie. This was a serious business, but I was used to the amateur clubs and all the fellows. We'd kid and clown around a lot. When I got a little tired of working so hard and got a little bored, I'd play little tricks. Black and Roxborough used to caution me to stop playing and to be serious. "You're in man's game now." I'd try to calm it down—but I was only twenty.

What did make me get serious was my next fight, on August 27, with Buck Everett of Washington. I K.O.'d him in two rounds and the check was for $250. All mine. That was sobering. I had been content with the little bit of money I was making, but now I saw there was even more to be made, and I meant to do it. And I was beginning to cause a flurry in the papers.

Roxborough and Black decided it was time to go back home for the big kill. Some sports editors of the *Detroit Times* made arrangements for me to appear at the Naval Armory in Detroit. I had built up a good following there from the days when I was an amateur and had fought in the Armory, but this time I was going back as a Pro, and I wasn't going to let my home folks down. September 11, I was put up against Alex Borchuk of Canada, another real tough guy.

Everything seemed to be going all right till they called Mr. Roxborough down to the Michigan State Boxing Commission. When he got back he told us that Bingo Brown, the Commissioner, and a couple of white fight managers, and Eddie Edgar, the sports editor of the *Detroit Free Press* were there. Seems like Bingo Brown was trying to guerrilla Mr. Roxborough into taking on a white comanager, and when Mr. Roxborough said no way, Bingo Brown said I couldn't ever fight again in Michigan. Mr. Roxborough took the chance, said if that's the way they wanted it, then it would have to be that way.

I think about it now and get even madder. Those white people couldn't stand to see a black on the rise, and if you were moving up, they wanted a piece of you for free. Mr. Roxborough held his ground; and that gang backed down.

The night of the fight, they had to call out the police reserves to handle the overflow crowd. Momma wouldn't come, but practically all the rest of the family was there with my friends and Bennie Franklin. I felt the confidence, I knew I was going to do it.

But Borchuk was tough. At the end of the third round, I was very discouraged. He hit so hard he chipped one of my back teeth. I beat him, but I feel lucky to have won that fight. I told Chappie that I had hit him with everything I had and he kept coming back stronger. Chappie told me I wasn't seeing right, that I had him. I told you before, I always listened to Chappie, and in round four—K.O.

That night I was the toast of Detroit, and I earned it.

I can't remember how much I made that night, but by now anything over two hundred dollars made me feel rich. Roxborough and Black let me stay over a couple of days with my family—I treated all my friends to bowling games and bought some clothes for some of my family. Two hundred dollars in those days was a lot of money.

Couple of days later, I get a call saying Chicago wanted me back to fight Adolph Wiater from Green Bay, Wisconsin at the Arcadia Gardens. Wiater had whipped Johnny Risko, and Risko was an outstanding heavyweight contender.

The fight was scheduled for September 25. I started training as soon as I got back. One day I walked in the gym, and Chappie had a red brick in his hand. He raised up his arm and it looked like he was going to hit me with it. I did what anybody would do, I ducked. Chappie laughed. "See what I'm trying to teach you? Pretend you have a brick in your fist. Naturally the guy's gonna duck, then you hit him with the other hand."

The night of the fight, Wiater hurt me some and stood his ground. He was a crowder, the first man to bring blood to my face. I decisioned him, though, and won three hundred dollars.

Next day in the gym Chappie showed me how to beat a crowder like Wiater. Catch him under the arm, spin him around, and bang him in the jaw. Nobody crowded me much after that.

The promoters were ready to set me up for another fight October 24 with Art Sykes of New York. Roxborough asked for, and got, $450. It was a hard fight, and Art Sykes had a lot of heart, but in the eighth round I got in a powerful right to the jaw. K.O.'d him so hard they had to drag him to his corner, and his seconds couldn't revive him. Later on they had two physicians trying to get him together. I was scared. If I had killed him, I would have given up boxing. So, I never felt so good as when I got word a few hours later that he was recovering in a hospital.

I was fighting so often and training so much I didn't even get a chance to spend my money. Every time I could, I'd buy some really fine clothes. Thanks to my managers,

JOE LOUIS: MY LIFE

I knew how to dress well; all I had to do was copy them. Sent my family a fistful of money and they looked fine too in new clothes. No more welfare, no more worrying about simple things like food. Even my sister Emmarell was busting with pride.

Mr. Roxborough and Mr. Black were so proud of me they let me buy my first car—a black Buick with whitewall tires. Me and Freddie and Thurston would ride around in that car for hours, but we'd only go around the same four-block area. All the girls would smile at us and we'd invite them in. There was nothing I could do since I was training, but some of my other friends had a lot of new dates. Got so the mothers would tell their daughters, "I better not see you get in Joe Louis Barrow's car." After a little fun, it was back to Chicago.

Mr. Roxborough and Mr. Black had a talk with me. They told me my name was getting famous all over the country but that a lot of promoters thought that my managers were getting me easy opponents so I would look good. So now it was time for me to fight an unquestioned, nationally known heavyweight from some big arena like Madison Square Garden. We had to prove that I was the real thing.

They found me Stanley Poreda, the heavyweight champion of Hoboken, N.J. He was a hot name in the East and had a national reputation. The fight was set for the Arcadia Gardens, Chicago, on November 14. I knew it was important for my career to beat this man, and important for the dignity of my managers, too.

K.O., round one. One of the easiest fights of my career.

Well, still a lot of the promoters and journalists had doubts. Could I do it again? They came up with the next toughest fighter they could find—Charley Massera (of Monongahela, Pennsylvania, near Pittsburgh). They called him a knockout artist. All the papers in the East were raving about him. I was looking forward to proving myself.

The first time I ever broke training was in Chicago before the Massera fight. One of the ladies in the building I was living in had a daughter who was much older than I was. About ten days before the Massera fight, she talked me into going to bed with her. The next morning when I got up to do roadwork, I felt so guilty that instead of running five miles, I ran ten. I just ran, ran, ran. Instead of boxing three rounds, I'd box six. Chappie Blackburn said to me, "Chappie, what the hell is wrong with you?" I told him I felt good. I didn't tell him what I'd done. It worried the hell out of me. Here I am getting ready for a big fight, and already I was fooling around.

On November 30 at Chicago Stadium, I K.O.'d Massera in the third round. Despite the K.O., I didn't feel like myself physically, plus I felt guilty even though I received my biggest check yet—$1,200. This fight business was all I had and I was good at it, and I promised myself I wouldn't fool around again.

While I was training hard, I followed the ball games. Loved baseball, always did ever since I was a little kid. Kind of had a hankering to become a ball player; I remember I told Holman Williams that maybe I just should try out for a team. "My friend," Holman said, "you don't want to do that. A colored ball player has the cards stacked against him and he can't even get merchandise checks. At least at fighting you might make a few bucks." In those days a black man couldn't even dream.

Anyway, my last fight in 1934 was with Lee Ramage of Los Angeles. He was considered just as tough as I was. He'd never been knocked out, and he was supposed to be very smart. The promoters were having a field day trying to get me in their arenas. Mr. Black was a hard bargainer and finally let the stadium in Chicago promote the fight when they finally offered me $2,750.

Then something happened that changed my life all around. While I was training in the Chicago gym for the

Lee Ramage fight, a lot of people came in to watch. Out of the corner of my eye, I saw the most beautiful girl I'd ever seen. She was about five-feet six-inches tall and well dressed. Pretty hair, pretty complexion, classy-looking. The only reason, I found out later, she came to the gym was because an insurance executive friend of hers had promised to introduce her to "the next Heavyweight Champion of the World." She saw me work out but I didn't get a chance to meet her.

As fate would have it, I had an interview with a sportswriter, Al Monroe, at the *Chicago Defender*. She was working there as a secretary. I found out her name was Marva Trotter, and I knew where to find her. But if fate hadn't been kind, I would have used all the power I personally had to find her.

December 14—me and Lee Ramage. They were right, he was smart. He knew all about boxing. I knew my only salvation was to back him in a corner. Finally I got my chance—the third round I got him in the corner and gave a left to the body and a right to the jaw. K.O. I'd finished my first professional year as a fighter. My record for twelve fights: All wins. Ten K.O.'s. Two decisions.

Soon after the fight I decided to have a party. I was staying at the Grand Hotel in Chicago. "Chappie," I said, "I'm having a party and I want you to invite that girl Marva that came to visit the gym." She came to the party with her sister Gladys. I liked her; she was a real lady. She was born in Muskogee, Oklahoma, and at the age of five she had came to Chicago with her family. We sat there talking about things we wanted to do in life. She was attending the Vogue School of Designing in Chicago and wanted to be a great designer. She was also taking part-time courses in English at the University of Chicago and working as a stenographer. Marva was the first real ambitious woman I had met, and she was only about eighteen years old.

When we parted, it was understood that we would see each other again when I got back from Detroit. I was looking forward to that.

I left Chicago and went back to Detroit to spend the Christmas season with my family. Must have been the best Christmas we all had. Money didn't mean a thing to me. I spent it on my family and my friends. I was happy and they were happy. I knew there was no place for me to go except up.

1935

NEW YORK: CARNERA AND BAER

M R. ROXBOROUGH AND MR. BLACK LINED ME UP for two fights in January. Roxborough thought I was ready for the really big time and asked Chappie what he thought. Without batting an eye, Chappie said, "Yeah, he's ready for New York, but New York ain't ready for him." But they decided to try it, especially since I was such hot property.

They called James J. Johnston, the boxing promoter at Madison Square Garden. His answer went something like this: You're a colored manager and so's your fighter— you're not going to make the same money as the white boys and your boy is going to have to lose a few. Johnston didn't feel that colored fights would be a draw at the box office, and he would be taking too great a risk. In the end he turned the deal down. Chappie laughed and said, "I told you so."

On January 4 I fought Patsy Perroni from Cleveland at the Detroit Olympic Arena for a scheduled ten-rounder. He was tough. I dropped him three times during the fight, but he wouldn't stay down. Perroni staggered me several times throughout the battle, but I won a ten-round decision. Now people knew I could take it as well as give it. Made $4,000 that fight.

Met Hans Birkie at the Duquesne Garden in Pittsburgh on January 11. I was heavier now, about 194. He fought well, but I knocked him out in round ten. I received $1,900 for this.

My managers were still grumbling about not being able to get me into New York, and about wasted talent, and, especially, about not getting top dollar. But everything was fine as far as I was concerned. Almost $6,000 in seven days went far beyond anything I dreamed of making.

Lee Ramage was asking for a return match in Los Angeles, California. Some people were saying that I shouldn't go there because that's Ramage's home town and I might not get a fair shake. Didn't bother me. I was concerned about the money, and, besides, I had already beat him once. The fight was scheduled for February 21. That gave me some free time. As soon as I could get there, I was in Chicago to see Marva.

She was glad to see me. I met her family. Very nice, warm, decent people. She had seven sisters and three brothers. Then she introduced me to her friends. I loved taking her out and having a girl I didn't have to sneak around with. I still talked to Bennie in Detroit, but there was nothing much we could do. My managers were cautioning me about being alone or in places where I didn't belong.

I was proud to be seen with Marva, and I think she felt the same way about me. People recognized me in Chicago and crowded both of us. It felt good.

On February 21 I knocked Ramage out with a left hook to the jaw in the second round. I made a little over $4,000.

The papers went wild. I kept winning. They started coming up with all kinds of names for me: The Dark Destroyer, Alabama Assassin, Detroit Destroyer, Michigan Mauler, Sepia Socker, and the Brown Bomber. The Brown Bomber was the name that stuck the rest of my career.

Then I started noticing some things I thought was strange. A lot of black people would come to me and want to kiss me, pump my hand. I thought they were congratulating me on my fighting skills. Now they started saying things like "Joe, you're our savior," and "Show them whites!" and sometimes they'd just shout, "Brown Bomber, Brown Bomber!" I didn't understand, then.

While we were getting ready to leave for Chicago, we received an offer to fight Donald "Reds" Barry in San Francisco. We took it because everybody thought he'd be a pushover. I knocked Barry out in three.

The fight was funny, though. I could have put him away anytime I felt like it. But, you see, I'd met this San Francisco sportswriter, Harry Smith. When he interviewed me, I told him I'd stop Barry in the third round. Smith printed this up as his own prediction. I really liked the guy and so I didn't want to disappoint him by knocking Barry out in the first round like I could have.

Chappie don't know what was going on and he give me hell. After the second round, Chappie decided I was crazy, but I told him to cool it and explained what went down with Smith. Chappie gave me that funny grin and said, "Well it's round three coming, so don't fuck up now." And I went out and K.O.'d him.

Everything was going on as usual. My managers had signed me to fight Natie Brown out of Detroit on March 28. Of course, he was a hard fighter.

Now again people came into my life and changed it. The change started with Nat Fleischer the sportswriter and owner of *Ring Magazine*. Fleischer loved heavyweights and he had been following my career since I turned pro. One of his best friends was Mike Jacobs, a true hustler, but a damn good man—and he changed history. Mike had just organized the Twentieth Century Sporting Club, and he was going head-on against the promoters who controlled Madison Square Garden—the ones who turned Mr. Roxborough's offer down because they didn't believe in black fighters.

Mike Jacobs didn't feel that one organization should have control of everything—especially heavyweights, as that's where the big money was. Everybody could or should have a little piece. Mike didn't have any big office, just a smart brain and the goodwill of the William Randolph Hearst sportswriters, and that was a whole lot.

Another piece of the puzzle: The Hearst Milk Fund staged fights at the Garden for the purpose of obtaining milk for poor kids. The promoters at Madison Square Garden kept raising the rent whenever the Hearst Fund had an affair. Of course, they didn't like this, especially since a good portion of the gate receipts went to charity.

Mike Jacobs approached the Hearst Fund people, telling them that if they would support his opposing club, he would not only charge the Fund less rent, but he would give a portion of the gate to the Fund. The top Hearst sportswriters all over the country liked Mike. It was a risk, a daring one, and it worked.

Anyway, the night after I beat Barry, Mike Jacobs called Roxborough and Black from New York. He told them about his newly formed club and that they wanted to sign me to fight former heavyweight champion, Primo Carnera. Roxborough jumped sky-high, but Black stayed calm. Mike Jacobs said he was coming out to Detroit to see the Natie Brown fight and had taken a special car on the train to bring out a lot of sportswriters.

Right away, Chappie started some really serious training even though I was well primed up from so many fights.

I wanted to make a good impression, but I was nervous and overanxious. That March 28 was some trial for me. Natie Brown was what you call a spoiler. He was trying to show me up, and I could hardly get through his guard. I had him down in the first round, but he stuck it out for the limit. He was clumsy and had an awkward style that would make anyone look bad. I decisioned him in ten rounds, but I didn't feel happy about it.

After the Natie Brown fight, Mr. Roxborough and Mr. Black took me and Chappie to the Frog Club (a colored place) and met Mr. Jacobs. When I started talking about how bad I looked, he just dismissed it. Then he told me that there was a kind of silent agreement between promoters that there would never be another black heavyweight champion like Jack Johnson. He told me how Jack Dempsey had run all over the country to avoid fighting Harry Wills, a black fighter. And he wanted me to fight Primo Carnera. If I could fight, he'd get me a shot at the title, and he'd make a lot of money for me.

When my managers asked me how I felt about it, I told them they were the managers and what they said was fine with me.

There was a big noisy victory party going on for me in the club, so we all went in the men's room to sign the contracts. The contract said that Mike Jacobs would be the sole promoter for my fights for the next three years—with a renewal option. A lot of people get things mixed up. Mike Jacobs was the promoter, Roxborough and Black were the managers, and Chappie was trainer, and that's the way it stayed.

It was a very long time before I figured how important a move this was. Jacobs was depending on me to be the next world's heavyweight champion. This scared a lot of people in the fight world. They started running around to find white contenders to stop me, covering the whole world looking for a "white hope" even before I got started.

Mike Jacobs always had a plan. With the contract in his pocket, he told my managers to set up a string of fights to keep me in the public eye, while he made arrangements for me to fight Primo Carnera.

Then Jacobs turned to my manager and said he'd arrange for an advance. They said no thanks. I think that shook Jacobs up. That's always been the problem with Negroes or poor white managers—you get trapped taking that promoter's money because then you have to fight the way the man tells you. If he tells you to lose the fight because he's got a heavy bet on, you have to lose the fight. Of course, I don't believe it was that way with Mike Jacobs. He wasn't interested in that two-bit game. He was

going for the big casino. Besides, by my managers refusing that advance, they demanded of Mike that I get
37½ percent of the gate instead of the usual 12½ percent.

The first fight was with Roy Lazer of Chicago on April
12. K.O., round three. The funny thing about that fight,
though, was that the gate paid $42,000. My managers
hadn't realized how many people were coming out to see
the fight, otherwise they would have asked for a percent-
age instead of the $10,000 guarantee. This never hap-
pened again. April 22 there was Biff Benton, Dayton,
Ohio—K.O., second round. April 27, Roscoe Toles, Flint,
Michigan—K.O., sixth round. May 3, Willie Davis, Peoria,
Illinois—K.O. May 7 Gene Stanton, Kalamazoo, Michigan—K.O., third round.

I really stormed the country; there was hardly anyone
who hadn't heard of me. Somehow, in between times, I
managed to buy a house for my mother and surprise her
with it on Easter Sunday of 1935. This was what the game
was all about. The house was at 2100 McDougal Avenue
in Detroit. It had two bedrooms downstairs and two upstairs. Momma couldn't believe it when I showed her the
house.

I paid $9,000 for the house, cash. No bills for Momma.
That was one time I had saved up my money. I was
prouder of this than anything I had ever done. And soon
after, I bought Momma a chicken ranch on the outskirts
of Detroit.

I had a little time, and I started thinking about Marva
Trotter. I wanted her to meet my family. I had never
really invited a girl to my Momma's house. So she had to
be something special for that. I asked Marva to meet me
in Detroit to see a tennis match.

She showed up alright and, as usual, with a sister.
Shoot! Wasn't I ever going to see that girl alone? I
thought, "My God, I may have to marry her to get her by

myself." Then I thought twice, maybe that's not such a bad idea.

Marva and my family hit it off right away. Momma and Marva started off acting like mother and daughter.

The Primo Carnera fight was set for June 25, 1935, at Yankee Stadium, New York City. I was itching for this bout. Never was the least bit worried. From what I'd read and what Chappie had told me, I didn't fear anything.

Carnera had won the championship from Jack Sharkey and had defended his title twice before being defeated by Max Baer in 1934. Old Chappie said that there was always a cloud over his ability, but that Carnera was the gateway to the championship.

We left Detroit around the middle of May. Mike Jacobs and some people picked me up along with Chappie, Mr. Roxborough, Mr. Black, and Bill Bottom at the depot station. We went straight to Mike Jacobs's office and had a press conference.

The conference scared me. There were so many reporters, and cameras flashing, newsreels running. If I hadn't had my managers and Mike Jacobs there, I would have looked funny. I couldn't talk as fast as those reporters were talking.

Anyway, I was sure glad when it was over and I had time to go and see New York City, and especially Harlem. In Detroit they talked about it like the streets were made of gold. We got in a car and went through Central Park. When they told me we'd be on Seventh Avenue and in Harlem, I was thrilled. But it looked like any other big city I had seen. In those days, though, the streets were clean, the buildings neat, and there were trees growing everywhere. The avenues were broader than in some places I'd been, but that's about all.

We went up to 381 Edgecombe Avenue, where Lucille Armistead, a school teacher and an old friend of Mrs.

Roxborough, had a beautiful apartment. It had been arranged that I'd have a room there—I could see Yankee Stadium from my window. 381 Edgecombe Avenue was a good building, and it wasn't long before Duke Ellington took an apartment there. It was his home base for many years.

I had a while before I had to report to camp and I began to find out what everybody was talking about when they said the word Harlem. First off, for promotional purposes, Mr. Roxborough and Mr. Black had me booked at the Harlem Opera House on One hundred twenty-fifth Street between Seventh and Eighth Avenues. I did a boxing skit with Dusty Fletcher, a well-known black comedian. He was so funny that sometimes my poker face would split into a grin. Then I skipped rope and punched the speed bag while the band played "Anchors Aweigh." As a finale, I punched the bag into the audience. There were four shows a day, the last one at midnight. The house was always jammed. The people cheered me and when I was hitting the bag they'd yell out, "That's what you gonna do to Carnera."

Chappie didn't like this at all; he was always sulking around and mumbling under his breath, but the man who owned the theatre, Frank Schiffman, kept everything together. I must say here Frank Schiffman was a beautiful man and perhaps the nicest white man I'd ever been associated with outside of Mike Jacobs. Of course I hadn't met that many white people at the time.

One day, while I was in my dressing room after the show, I heard a big ruckus going on. I heard this man's voice saying to my manager, "You got to let me see Joe. I got this friend of mine who wants to give him a real beautiful hat for free. All Joe has to do is pose in the hat." Roxborough and Black were busy trying to get rid of this guy. I said to myself, "What the hell, the man is only trying to make a living." So I went out and told Roxborough and Black to let the man in. He was probably the only man in New York who wanted to give me something for nothing.

Well, that was the start of a long friendship. The super salesman was named Billy Rowe, a columnist for the *Pittsburgh Courier,* who was trying to do a little public relations work on the side. We hit it off right away. He was my kind of guy. Smart.

Seems like the Negro press couldn't get ringside tickets for the fight like the rest of the press could get. The promoters did not right out say they didn't want no niggers in the press section, they just said it real polite: "Sorry, no ringside tickets for the weekly press." Well, that automatically eliminated all the Negro press. Negroes can't afford to support a daily press. Billy taught me a lot of things real quick. Like how the Negro papers couldn't make money because big-time stores and people who manufacture things didn't even try to advertise to the Negro market.

Me, I'd never thought about it, but I figured that was a damn shame. Negroes go to stores to buy their clothes and whatever else they want. So, anyway, I went to Mike Jacobs and told him the problem. It was something he never thought about either. That's the trouble, nobody thinks about the other fellow.

All this got to be a big thing. Hype Igoe, a white writer for the *Journal American,* really went out to bat for the Negro writers. After all the noise I and Igoe and Mike Jacobs were making, the promoters decided to set up an auxiliary press. So Billy Rowe and Chester Washington of the *Pittsburgh Courier,* Al Monroe of the *Chicago Defender,* and Rowen Dougherty of the *Amsterdam News* and a whole lot of other Negro guys who were reporting got a chance to get a little farther up front and report the fight to the Negro papers. This was a first-time deal, and I'm glad I had something to do with it.

After the week at the Harlem Opera House was over, I'd stay in the house in the daytime but I'd get out at night. Now, the first place in Harlem you had to go was Small's Paradise on Seventh Avenue at One hundred thirty-fifth Street. I saw the show and met a lot of people.

I felt great. Can you imagine people I always admired were seeking me out? Bill "Bojangles" Robinson, the dancer, took me around one night. He introduced me to a beautiful girl, one of the most beautiful I have ever known. Her name was Marion Eggberg. She was a chorus girl at the Memo Club on One hundred thirty-third Street and Seventh Avenue. I went with her for years. I was crazy about her. Later on, she'd meet me all over the country when I was fighting.

Second day I was in New York, I met a guy named Owney Madden. He was the owner of the Cotton Club on One hundred fortieth Street and Lenox Avenue, smack dab in Harlem—but black people couldn't go there. It was for whites only. The Club featured black entertainment and some of the most gorgeous black women that could be found. There were dancers, singers, and a lot of black male comedians working there, and bands like Duke Ellington, Cab Calloway, Claude Hopkins, to name a few.

Well, anyway, one night after a show was over he brought over three girls: Edna Mae Holly (later she became Sugar Ray Robinson's first wife), another girl, I can't remember her name, and Lena Horne. Madden told me, "Take your pick." I took Lena.

But then I had to head for Pompton Lakes, New Jersey, to take care of important matters.

Before I left for camp, my momma sent to me the biggest Bible I ever saw. Reporters made such a to-do about it, wanting to take my picture with it and so forth. My momma sent it to me for a reason, and I intended to honor the reason. Every night before I went to bed, I made myself read a bit of it.

I knew I had to make a big hit with this fight, and I trained hard. I was fighting a giant, and so Chappie searched for and found some of the biggest guys he could for my sparring partners. I always did like to fight big guys, anyway. They gave me a bigger target to punch.

We set up training at Pompton Lakes, New Jersey. A Dr. Joseph Bier, a dentist, rented us his place. There was an old colonial house with several cottages around it on the border of the lake. It was beautiful and peaceful. They converted an old barn into a bar, and between four hundred and five hundred people a day would come up. For a small town of about two thousand, we sure increased their income. At first my managers thought we might have some trouble with so many black people coming out to an all-white town, but the only color those people saw was green.

I donated a couple of days' proceeds from admission receipts at the camp toward the Pompton Lakes First Aid Fund. In fact, that's when the organization got started. Anyway, we had the goodwill of the town.

The crowds got so big that they had to hire extra security guards. My biggest thrill up there had been to meet the last black heavyweight champion, Jack Johnson. I liked him. He never mentioned the problems he was having and never asked for any money or anything. He was an impressive-looking guy and a good talker. He told me I was going to run into every kind of situation possible, and he warned me to keep my head at all times.

My days were very routine. I'd be up before six and run at least five miles before breakfast. Come back, eat a big hunk of cheese, and drink some fruit juice, take a shower and a short nap. Get up and have a big breakfast, oatmeal, half a dozen eggs, ham steaks, bread, and milk. Dinner time, I'd eat a three-pound steak and salad. Bill Bottoms would see to it I got a dish of black-eyed peas whenever I wanted it. He made sure I had plenty of protein. Loved ice cream, usually ate a quart a night.

I knew that when I got past this fight, I'd want to meet Max Baer. My managers didn't think I was ready. I didn't say anything to anybody then, but I knew after I saw a movie of Baer beating Carnera that I could take him. Mr. Black and Chappie said I was a kid and Baer was a killer. Hell, I'd beaten every leading heavyweight up till now, and I had all the confidence I needed for Carnera.

Anyway, while we were at Pompton Lakes, I told my trainer that Baer was going to defend his title against Jimmy Braddock on June 13, so we went to ringside and I watched closely. Baer kept swinging at Braddock and kept missing him all night. Braddock won the championship. Now I was really mixed up. I asked Chappie and my managers, "How come not me? Hell, I'm ready for that kind of fight right now." They told me there's a whole plan worked out for me. I was still young and still black. I had to wait my turn.

Meanwhile, all kinds of noise was being made about this Carnera fight. Funny thing how a lot of trouble brewing in Europe could affect us. Mussolini had started threatening Ethiopia. So here you had a black man and an Italian man having a fight. The whole world was looking. Lots of black groups came up to camp telling me that I represented Ethiopia. They talked to me about Marcus Garvey, who I hadn't even heard of. They told about his plan for black people to go back to Africa. They put a heavy weight on my twenty-year-old shoulders. Now, not only did I have to beat the man, but I had to beat him for a cause.

The Hearst people were getting nervous about the tension that seemed to be coming from this Italian-Ethiopian affair and thought about canceling the match. Mr. Roxborough talked them out of it, and I promised to contribute 10 percent of my purse to the Milk Fund. They decided to go ahead with it all.

We broke camp two days before the fight, and I went back to Lucille Armistead's apartment to rest up some.

I called Momma, she was all excited. I had made arrangements for a seven-passenger limousine to bring along my sisters Susie, Emmarell, Eulalia, and Vunice as well as my brothers Alvanius, DeLeon, and Lonnie. Momma and Pat Brooks were going to stay home and take care of the little ones—my nieces and nephews.

Momma said that all the reporters in Chicago must have been to the house. DeLeon and Eulalia were telling the reporters that I was definitely going to beat Carnera because when the family got there, they were going to make me mad. Told those reporters that they'd tease me about how the giant would squash me, and I'd just tear out of my corner so mad I'd beat him. Momma and me laughed, she knew I didn't need that kind of encouragement. She knew I would do it on my own. She said, "Son, you know I'm prayin' for you, but anyway don't get hurt."

The weigh-in at the State Office Building was almost a riot. Mounted policemen had to clear a path for me and Carnera to enter. Finally we got in and went through the usual routine, and when it came time for the actual weigh-in, I really looked close up at Canera standing there in his boxing trunks. He was a huge hunk of man— six feet five and three-quarters and 260 ½ pounds. I was six feet one and a half and weighed in at 196. For all his big self, I wasn't the least bit intimidated, although Carnera kept making faces at me, saying all kinds of silly things. He looked foolish to me.

On the night of June 25, when I climbed into the ring to fight Carnera, I was, well, awestruck. I never saw so many people in my life. Sixty thousand were in Yankee Stadium ball park. It was the largest number of people to see a fight in New York City since 1927. Me, Joe Louis Barrow, from a little rag-tailed farm in Alabama—sixty thousand people waiting for me to beat up this giant, or for me to get my ass kicked.

While waiting for the bell, Chappie kept talking to

me—hypnotizing me with his tactics and reassurances. Chappie told me to work on Carnera's body till he dropped his guard, and then go to the head.

I was nervous, my nerves always came on when I was in the ring. The referee called me and Carnera to the center of the ring to give us our instructions. Sitting there waiting for the bell to ring, I knew deep down that that jittery feeling would go away as soon as I landed my first punch. So I was even nervous waiting for the bell to ring so I could get started.

I got in some hard punches in round one. He just moved around and flicked out a jab. The first thing that shocked Carnera and the audience was that instead of him handling me like a baby, I handled him. They were looking at his size and not his talent. I moved him around easily.

The fight moved along smoothly for me. I remember in the fifth round we clinched, and I picked him off his feet. That's when he spoke to me the only time in the fight. He said, "Oh . . . oh . . . oh. . . ." His eyes bulged out in surprise. Then he said, "I should be doing this to you." I was just as surprised as he was at the ease with which I moved him around. Carnera had nothing. He couldn't punch, but he had a pretty decent jab. He pushed with his right and he was awkward. Mostly he tried to scare me with his weight.

It was hard to get under his guard at first, but Chappie had told me to pace myself and the openings would come.

Just before the bell rang for the sixth round, Chappie said, "Go get him." I hit him with a right, and the blood spurted from his mouth. I knocked him down the first time with a right to the jaw. I put him down again with another right to the jaw. Then I finished off with a left-right combination. He went down for the third and last time.

He never hurt me once. I felt ready for any heavyweight in the world—Jimmy Braddock, Max Baer, any-body.

Made it in New York City—the Boxing Capital of the World. Now there was no question about my fighting ability, nor my ability to draw a crowd. I had $60,000 to prove it, and that was after my managers, for the first time, took their share and 10 percent had gone to the Hearst Milk Fund.

There was a lot of dickering about where I would fight next. Some cities were even offering their stadiums free. Finally Mr. Roxborough and Mr. Black convinced Mike Jacobs that it should be where I started my professional career—Chicago. They all figured the best card would be Harry "Kingfish" Levinsky. He had a reputation of being a strong hitter and he would be able to prove the one thing that didn't show in the Carnera fight—that I could take punishment.

The fight wasn't scheduled until August 7. I wasn't training or preparing for training, and I remembered some of those sweet, beautiful girls I had met. It was a round of Small's Paradise, the Memo Club, and some I can't remember the names of. I wasn't drinking and even if I had been, nobody would let me spend any money. For the first time, I was beginning to feel itchy about being some kind of hero.

One of my greatest thrills in New York was meeting Duke Ellington. I know why they called him "Duke"—he was royalty. Good-looking, dressed like a king, and easy-going. He could just as soon talk to the King of England as he could talk to some little jive hustler. I'd just lean on the piano and listen to his mellow tones. Our friendship continued throughout the years.

I can't remember whether it was Duke, but somebody told me about Billy Taub, a tailor located on Fortieth Street and Broadway. About 90 percent of his customers were sports celebrities, people like Kid Chocolate, Dizzy

Dean, and Babe Ruth. He had a card: "By Special Appointment—Tailor to the Royalty of Sportsdom." His clothes weren't flashy, they were stylish—high-stylish and expensive. I must have ordered a dozen suits and slacks and jackets.

And the people, God, the people—black people, white people always crowding around me. It made me nervous for a long time, but I never minded it. These were the people who were making me rich. I loved them then and I love them now—but I wasn't yet used to it.

Ah! New York was beautiful, but I had to leave. It was already the end of June, and I knew I only had a short time before I went back into training. I had about twelve days to take care of a lot of important business. First off, even with all the fooling and funning I was having, I knew now I was in love with Marva Trotter. Something would have to be done about that. Oh, I was crazy about those sweet beauties, but I loved Marva. I had to get back to my family in Detroit and share with them and my friends some of all this big money I still had.

I was going to stop off in Chicago first and I telegraphed Freddie Guinyard to meet me at the Grant Hotel with my car. Planning to court Marva Trotter—seriously.

Marva was some glad to see me. I was loaded down with all kinds of fancy, expensive things. I don't remember what they were. Marva told me how proud she was of me and how she was looking forward to seeing me, and why had I taken so long to get back to Chicago? Of course, I couldn't tell her why. We went around some and, again, the crowds were there, but it was exciting. Only thing, so many people were around all the time I didn't get a chance to talk more to her about the things I was thinking about. It was time for me to go to Detroit, but it was understood that we were going to be more serious the next time I saw her. Now to Detroit and Momma for a few days.

I arrived home looking like Santa Claus. Momma and

my family were about to bust with pride. You would have thought I was a king holding court. Come Sunday, Momma was busy bustling around. We all went off to Calvary Church to give thanks to the Lord. When I walked in that church, you'd have thought it was the second coming of Christ. The Reverend J. H. Maston preached a powerful sermon that day, and it was about and around me. He talked about how God gave certain people gifts and that these gifts were given to help other men. My gift was fighting, and through my fighting I was to uplift the spirit of my race. I must make the whole world know that Negro people were strong, fair, and decent. Through fighting, I was also supposed to show that the Negroes were tired of being muddled around in the ground. He said I was one of the Chosen.

I thought to myself, "Jesus Christ, am I all that?" After that I thought many times of my responsibilities and I worried. I just wanted to fight and make some money and have some fun with pretty girls. Now I knew there was more.

My managers were calling me to the training camp to get ready for the fight with "King" Levinsky. Despite Levinsky's reputation as a tough puncher, I wasn't worried about this fight. After all, the Reverend had told me I was one of the Chosen Ones, and I really felt I had it.

During the training sessions, Chappie was behaving strangely. I found out that he had been drinking a lot. Ordinarily Chappie never drank during training periods, but off times I knew he was a hard, heavy drinker. At that time I didn't want anything to do with alcohol. I knew I needed Chappie more than anyone else. So I went to Mr. Roxborough and Mr. Black and asked them to close down the bar while I was working out. Well, they couldn't quite do that, but at least it was closed when I was training. I don't know what private things were bothering Chappie, but I knew they shouldn't interfere with the training.

Another time, at camp, some fellow come up to me

about endorsing cigarettes (I don't remember which ones). My manager said I'd make a lot of money doing this, but I wouldn't do it because I didn't smoke and didn't approve of smoking.

On the way to the ring at Comiskey Park, Chappie said to me, "Man, I don't feel good, been drinking too much." I said, "You just walk up the steps with me one time, that's all you have to do." Then I said, "Chappie, if I knock him out in the first round, would you quit drinking for six months?" Of course he said, "OK, OK." I didn't use more than ten punches in the first round. When I looked around Levinsky was sitting on the bottom strand of the ropes yelling at the referee, "Don't let him hit me again. Don't let him hit me again." Knockout—round one.

When I got back to the dressing room, Chappie said to me, "Chappie, about that drinking, would you let me off the hook?"

I knew my next fight would have to be soon. Mike Jacobs and my managers wanted to keep me in the public eye as much as possible. Besides, I was giving boxing a shot in the arm with our large gates. Funny thing about the Depression, people who may need a pair of shoes would rather spend that money on a movie or a fight. I guess, especially in a fight, a person can work out a lot of the things on their mind.

They got a hold of Max Baer from Livermore, California—he was six feet two and a half, weighed 220 pounds. Baer had won the heavyweight crown from Primo Carnera in June, 1934, but he lost the title to Jimmy Braddock one year later. Baer had a reputation of being a hard puncher, and that's why they called him the "Livermore Larruper." Max thought a lot of himself; he was a real egotistical glamor boy and lover. He was just as anxious for this fight as I was. He figured if he won it, he'd be on the road back to the championship. I figured if I won it, that would mean I'd have beaten two exchampions, and then the door would soon open for me to have a crack at the title. The fight was scheduled for September 24 at Yankee Stadium. I had a nice break here, so I took off.

When I got back to Detroit, I had a lot of things to do, but after hanging out with my friends for a few days, I was depressed. None of them seemed to be going anywhere. They were talented guys, but they didn't have the luck I had. So I decided to make some luck for them. I took twenty-two of them, including Thurston McKinney, and we organized the Brown Bomber Softball Team. Always loved baseball, especially the Tigers. Now I could afford the opportunity to get into a game that really appealed to me. I'd told the guys that I would be able to play with them on occasion and that this would boost the ticket sales. You can't imagine how happy those guys were. They'd be doing something they loved and could do well.

After they were organized with grey and red uniforms and a big, brightly painted bus, the team was on its way. Later on, whenever I got the chance, I'd meet them in whatever city they were in. I'd play first base and then go to bat at least once. Then I'd coach from first base or direct play from the bench. I was a switch hitter, but preferred batting right-handed, and, got to admit it, I was a damn good hitter.

Of course, Chappie, Mr. Roxborough, and Mr. Black didn't approve. They were afraid I'd get hurt. And, in a way, they were right; I did injure my ankle slightly one time in Pittsburgh. But I was getting to be a big boy, and I was determined to do something I really wanted to do.

While we were getting all this idea of a softball team together, I did a whole lot of soul-searching about Bennie Franklin. Of course I'd seen her, but again in the company of the family—couldn't get away with her because I was too well known. I should have told her then about Marva, but for the first time in my life I backed down. But there was no way it could have worked for us. In the last year

I had grown in so many ways, and as a result of those ways I grew away from her. Probably if I had stayed at Ford, we might have found a way to get around to being married, and that would have been all right with me. But, you see, I didn't stay at the factory and I was pushed in all kinds of places and situations I never would have dreamed of. My needs were for another kind of woman now, and I had made up my mind.

You're never going to catch me in this bind: I always believed that women should have their fair share. I've always enjoyed being generous to women, and I knew women should have the same privileges as men. There have always been liberated women. Sometimes you just have to search some to find them. Some are liberated because they demand it, some just because they can afford to be. Well, anyway, I found one at the Buick showroom in Detroit.

I decided I wanted a new fancy car. So I took myself down to the showroom to look things over. The salesman rushed over to me and gave me the royal treatment—he showed me this car, black, with white-wall tires and a mahogany bar built in the back. That bar intrigued me. I didn't drink, but it looked first-class to me.

Anyway, while I was fooling around the car this salesman asked if he might be excused for a minute and rushed over to a real good-looking white woman with blonde hair. He talked with her for a while and then came back to me. I told him I liked the car and wanted to buy it. He said, "The lady has already purchased the car for you." My mind immediately flashed to Jack Johnson and my managers warning about "having your picture taken with a white woman," and I tried to get out of it. But what the hell can you do when the lady is insistent and charming as hell? I took the car and promised her two ringside tickets for the Max Baer fight.

I got a new Buick every Christmas for the next five

years. The lady was a very important white woman and I was a very important black man. She taught me the word for many of the things I'd been doing all along. The word was "discretion." And we were "discreet" the several times we met during those five years.

When I got to my training camp at Pompton Lakes, there was a welcome surprise for me. Mr. Roxborough and Mr. Black had hired a secretary and tutor for me. Mail was coming in by the ton. A lot of the letters came from my people praising me, and telling me how much better they felt about themselves because of the way I was fighting and acting. The letters I really loved were from black kids—and a few white ones too—wanting to know how I trained and wanting to be like me. It was these times when I wished I could talk and write letters; I wished that I hadn't stayed in my own private world while I was going to school.

Mr. Roxborough and Mr. Black were smart business-men. They knew I was meeting all kinds of important people and I'd have to do more than stand there with a poker face mumbling something nobody could under-stand. So they hired Russell Cowans to be my secretary and tutor. He was a short man, about five-foot five, and a college graduate. He was a sportswriter for the *Detroit Chronicle* and so was ideal for the job. While I was train-ing, he'd spend about two hours a day, usually after my road work, teaching me grammar and arithmetic.

Cowans had to send out written stuff about my life to papers all over the country. He was constantly talking to me about things I thought I had forgotten. I could see myself in relation to what I was doing, and in relation to what I might mean to some people. That was the big thing Cowans did for me. And he did little things. He told me what to do when I was introduced to important people, how to speak properly, and general etiquette. He stayed with me until 1938. I'm very thankful to Russell Cowans; he had a hard job.

We used to get the major papers every day and read the sports sections together. The reporters were saying all kinds of things about me: they called me "a born killer" and wrote things that were untrue about my family and mother, and stuff like that. I'd get real mad, but Roxborough and Black told me to keep calm and to be glad that I was important enough for people to talk and write about. That meant they'd be spending their money to come to see the "born killer."

One item in particular, though, really upset me. One paper reported that Jack Johnson said I was just a flash in the pan; that at his age of fifty-seven he would have done just as well against me as Carnera and Levinsky. He said my stance was all wrong, and pointed out other faults I had. I couldn't believe this. I respected this man; he had come to my training camp and all. It really disappointed me, but I decided I wouldn't believe all I read in the papers.

But you know, on the other hand, there's always more than meets the eye. Later on I was talking to Chappie about what I had read in the papers. Chappie gave me his little slanted grin and said it had to do with me being a well-liked Negro heavyweight, unlike Johnson. And there was one other thing that happened before I was even born. Seems that in something like 1908, before he was champion, Johnson was training in a gym in Philadelphia and he needed a sparring partner. Chappie was there and he said he'd go a few rounds with Johnson, even though Chappie was only about 135 pounds. I guess Johnson figured Chappie was no threat, being all that much smaller than him. So they went at it and Chappie bloodied up his nose, making Johnson mad—he kept trying to put Chappie out, but couldn't do it. Johnson was embarrassed by this little guy giving him a hard time.

Later, when Chappie got out of jail, the fight-crowd people were giving him a benefit so he could get started again, and they asked Jack Johnson to participate. Johnson called Chappie all kinds of sons-of-a-bitches and let this information get around.

Now, in the meantime, I was getting real popular as a fighter and a personality. I didn't know till later that when I was preparing for Carnera, Johnson went up to Mr. Roxborough and told him—mind you, he didn't ask him, but told him—that he would be willing to be my trainer and to throw Chappie out. He shouldn't have said that to Roxborough. Roxy is a loyal man. He cursed Johnson out, told him how he had held up the progress of Negro people for years with his attitude, how he was a low-down, no-good nigger, and told him he wasn't welcome in my camp anymore. I didn't see too much more of Johnson after that.

That's when Johnson started going to the papers telling them all kinds of bad things about me. It didn't do him much good; he was working as a strong man in Robert Ripley's Flea Circus, and by my standards that ain't shit. And the black people who were rallying around me put him down for talking against me.

Any fight and every fight is important. I knew Baer was no pushover and that he was as hungry as I was. I trained hard, but something was wrong. I was poky and depressed. Mr. Black sat me down one day on the porch of the training cabin and asked me what was wrong; I was doing all the right things, he said, but something seemed missing. I told him I didn't know what was wrong, although deep down I did. I found it hard to express myself. Finally, Mr. Black looked at me and said, "Man, you're in love with Marva. Marry her." For some reason I was shy around her, and she was the same around me. So about a week before the fight, Mr. Black told me to ask Marva to come to New York.

Well, you know, you can be very brave on the telephone. I called and, real easy, I said I wanted her to come to the Max Baer fight and for us to get married. Hot damn! She said "yes." When I told Mr. Black, I think he was happier than I was. He'd seen the women coming after me like Grant storming Richmond. He was very concerned about my "image." Marva was pretty, intelligent, and came from a fine family—and she was black. No Jack Johnson problem here. There was nothing anyone could say bad about her; in fact, he was so happy he told me not to worry about a thing, he'd take care of all the arrangements. All I had to do was continue training with my mind at ease.

Mr. Black made sure everything was going just right. He got some good friends to let Marva stay in one of the best parts of Harlem—Sugar Hill, 409 Edgecombe Avenue.

Marva arrived a couple of days before the fight with her sister Novella and her brother, the Reverend Walter C. Trotter, and they stayed at 409 Edgecombe Avenue. I was still living at 381 Edgecombe Avenue.

We had planned on getting married shortly after the fight, but the situation was fidgety; Marva was too beautiful and sweet. I told Julian Black I wanted to get married right away. After the fight I wanted to come home to a bride. Of course he said I was crazy, but he'd fix it up somehow.

I woke up to a beautiful day that September 24, 1935. I was confident about the fight and anxious to get married.

I weighed in at 199 ¼ and Max at 210 ½. But life is full of hassles. Baer and his manager said they were going to call off the bout because they wanted to use a special kind of glove and the State Athletic Commission said they couldn't. Baer had a customized glove with a raised cushion on the side of the forefinger, extra padding to close the gap between the thumb and forefinger. Baer said he had already worked this out with my managers weeks ago. He claimed he needed that extra protection for his thumbs.

Finally my side OK'd his gloves on the condition that I

be allowed to use twelve feet of bandage instead of six, and two-inch width of bandage instead of one and a half. The tape I used to hold the bandage in place would be six feet in length instead of two. After all, I had to protect my "thumbs" too. The Commissioner OK'd both requests and we continued the examination.

After the doctor examined my heart, I asked him if I could fight tonight and he laughed and said, "Twice, if you want to."

About six or so I got up from a nap, showered, put on a dark grey business suit and a white-on-white shirt, and forgot the damned tie. In the meantime the streets and hallways were starting to get crowded with fans. They didn't know I was getting married. The apartment where I stayed, Mrs. Armistead's, wasn't big enough for the ceremony, so we went downstairs to the apartment of Mr. and Mrs. Vernon Porter. Marva and her sister had come over earlier through the fire escape.

When Marva came out, my blood started throbbing. She looked like something you'd see in a fairy-tale book, with a white silk velvet gown, a long train in the back trimmed with ermine, and a bunch of little white flowers in her hand.

We didn't have time for cake, flowers, music, and decorations. The chief city clerk had come uptown with a blank marriage license, and Julian Black and his wife witnessed the signing of the license. Roxborough, Chappie, and a few other close friends were there too. Marva's brother, Reverend Trotter, performed the ceremony; Novella, her sister, as the maid of honor; and Julian Black was the best man. The wedding was at 7:45. I left for the fight at 8:00 P.M.

It was hell getting out. Seemed like all of Sugar Hill and every newspaper sports reporter was standing in the halls and the streets in front of the house. When they found out I had just gotten married, they really got excited. They had to get a police emergency squad to clear a

path so me and my people could get to the car waiting
for us.

They say there were over 95,000 people at Yankee
Stadium that night. When I climbed into the ring, I
spotted Marva at ringside. I wanted this to be a quick
fight. I wanted to start being a married man as soon as
possible, but I put all those thoughts out of my mind and
concentrated on Baer. He looked in good condition and
had Jack Dempsey in his corner. That didn't bother me.

When the bell rang for round one, Baer came out of his
corner like he was scared to death. Chappie told me to
wait for an opening. He said he was depending on me to
beat Baer to the punch and get off first.

I knew I had Baer when I hit him with a left uppercut
in the first round. After that, I just jabbed him with my
left until I found openings. The only time Baer hit me
hard was at the end of the second round. He'd hit me with
two rights on the head, but they didn't hurt. He couldn't
hit as hard as I thought he could, yet he was a better
fighter than Carnera. I hit him several times and I could
not feel him give. But I knew he would eventually. In the
second round, I had him bleeding from the nose and
mouth. For a while, I think he tried to throw the fight. He
just wasn't right. I don't know what happened to him that
night. I felt he wasn't the fighter he should have been.

I remember when the bell clanged for the end of the
second round, I dropped my hands and the son of a bitch
hit me with a left hook and a right hand to my jaw. I
stared at him and I said to myself: Kick his ass now.

In the third, I put on some steam. I banged him with
rights and lefts. He looked lost. As the round was coming
to the end, I hit him on the chin with a right hand and
down he went for a nine count. I got in another right and
a left hook, and he went down again. At the count of four,
the bell saved him.

He came out weak in the fourth round. I hit him with a
hard left hook and a hard right to the head. He went

down to stay. He was on one knee when Referee Arthur Donovan counted him out. I had beaten the Great Lover; I'd knocked out my second exheavyweight champion. I've always considered the Baer fight my greatest. I've never had better hand speed; I felt so good I knew I could have fought for two or three days straight.

When I knocked out Max Baer, I knew in my head that this was the turning point. He was a popular exchampion and a good puncher. All my fights had meant nothing until Baer. I said to myself, "Maybe I can go all the way."

After the fight I could hardly wait to get back to the apartment. We didn't have a big celebration, but everything was the way I wanted. All during our marriage, Marva saw to it I would always have the rest and peace I needed after a fight. Just my managers, Chappie, Marva's family, and the few friends whose apartments we shared got together. I was a very happy man that night. I had more than I had ever expected to. I had a wife who was a dream, I had money, I had fame.

But I was disappointed in Baer. The next day I read in the papers that Baer said that I was just lucky and I had no business being in the ring with him. He said some bad things about my race and my personal life. We got in the ring as equal as possible and because I beat him, he looked outside the ring for ways to hurt me. I was thrilled to have won, but disappointed that he took it that way.

Marva and I stayed in New York a little more than two weeks. We didn't have a lot of people in. It was some hard job trying to show Marva the city—people followed us everywhere we went. If we went to the movies, we'd have to leave before it was over; if we went to dinner, we'd have to leave before dessert. Attention is nice, but it gets in the way sometimes of just enjoying yourself. The girls were still coming at me as if Marva wasn't there. They'd just push her aside; crowds would mess up her hair and clothes. We had to spend a lot of time just in the apartment, but then that's what you're supposed to do when you've just got married.

Bill Robinson had heard about my marriage, and he invited Marva and me to come to Hollywood to watch him and Shirley Temple make a movie. That sounded great to us. Me, Marva, Roxborough, Black, and my group of friends all headed out there.

My God, it was some good time. All the guys I admired on the screen admired me in the ring. Remember Ricardo Cortez? He was my man. He showed me all kinds of places I knew nothing about. George Raft, a real regular guy, Victor McLaglen, Dick Arlen, Bert Wheeler, all saw that we were entertained.

Marva was really excited. A Hollywood makeup man did her face. I always knew she was beautiful, but now she looked fantastic. Swore she wouldn't wash her face for three days. And when Bill Robinson took us out in his big, tall, brown Dusenberg with that little green-velvet rug that the chauffeur let down before you stepped in, I knew we were living.

But it was time to head back to Chicago. Julian Black and his wife had gotten us a five-room apartment where they lived, in the Rosenwald on Forty-sixth and South Michigan Avenue. This building was the most fabulous building black people could live in at that time. It covered a whole block. Doormen, porters, elevator operators, all kinds of special service.

Everything was just fine. Momma was glad to see me settled down with a girl like Marva. My friends started visiting me, and for a while it was alright. I bought Marva all the beautiful clothes and furs and jewelry I had promised her, and that made me feel like a king. Marva designed a lot of her clothes and had some fancy dressmaker make them up.

On October 31, 1935, me and Marva went to St. Louis to see John Henry Lewis win the light heavyweight title from Bob Olin in fifteen rounds. This was a very important fight. John Henry was a black man; Bob Olin was white. John Henry was managed by Gus Greenlee, a black Pittsburgh numbers king who owned the Pittsburgh Crawfords baseball team in the Negro National League.

John Henry Lewis, a black man with a black manager, in 1935 was the only black holding a boxing title in the world. Maybe things were breaking through. Maybe that dream about me being a heavyweight contender could happen. It was an exciting thought.

By this time me, Black, Roxie, and Chappie wanted a chance at the heavyweight title that Jimmy Braddock held. Times were opening up; I might make it. They figured if I could get through the heavyweights standing between me and Braddock, the fight would have to go on, and I'd have proved my right for a shot. Right after I'd beaten Hans Birkie and Lee Ramage in January and February, 1935, Max Schmeling, the former heavyweight champion, made it known that he was ready to shoot for the title he'd held from 1930 to 1932.

In March of 1935, Steve Hamas, who had beaten Schmeling decisively in 1934, went to Hamburg, Germany, to fight him again. Schmeling figured if he looked good in this fight, he would definitely try to regain the heavyweight crown by working his way into a challenger's position. Hell, let me tell you, Schmeling looked spectacular when he knocked out Hamas in the ninth round.

Then in July of 1935, in Berlin, he beat the hell out of Paulino Uzcudun in twelve rounds. Now, because of these two wins, Schmeling had opened the door to come back to America. My managers and Mike Jacobs then offered Uzcudun $19,000 to come from Spain and meet me in Madison Square Garden. They wanted me to do Uzcudun in more quickly than Schmeling. Uzcudun said yes, and the fight was set for December 13 at Madison Square Garden.

JOE LOUIS: MY LIFE

When I talked to Marva about the fight and my hopes to become heavyweight champion, she seemed a little depressed. She said that after I got the championship maybe I could retire and we could live a good life together. We'd have plenty of money and could do more interesting things. Of course I agreed with her, but I knew I wanted even more money. I still wanted to help my family and provide for my old friends from Detroit. Hell, I was only twenty-two years old. I was beginning to really feel my oats. Who retires at twenty-two or twenty-three? I was feeling so good, I felt I could go on forever. So I patted her arm and told her after we made some good investments I'd retire.

Before you could turn around good, it was time to head for Pompton Lakes and heavy training. Got Chappie and my crowd together, and it was strictly serious time. I was following my usual hard daily routine, and one day I saw Schmeling watching me train. He was about my size, six-foot one and 196 pounds. I looked at him, he looked at me, and I said to myself, "I'll take him."

After the training session, I heard that Schmeling told reporters in the gym, "I see something. He hasn't forgotten his amateur mistakes. He drops his left after a lead and tips his head back at the same time. He can be hit with a right hand. I have a good right hand. I will beat him with my right." Russell Cowans and I read that in the papers the next day and we laughed. Shit! That guy was at least eight years older than me. And I had conned myself into thinking nobody is stronger or better than an American. I wasn't the least bit worried.

I was determined not to let anything stand in my way of being champion. So on December 13, when I stepped out at the bell, I knew Uzcudun was all mine.

Uzcudun came out of his corner in a low crouch, he stooped over and lunged forward. His face was hidden behind his gloves and crossed arms. Chappie had told me to be careful. He didn't want me to possibly break my hands on Uzcudun's head. So all I did was jab, jab, jab, lightly and carefully, until I could get through. I knew after the first round that Uzcudun was just in that ring to stay—I'd wait for the opening. In the fourth round I hit him with a right to the jaw. He countered with a left hook. I banged a right over his left, and he went down for an eight count. When he got up, I hit him with a left and right to the jaw, sending him up against the ropes. I could see his face split open and some of his gold teeth sprinkle down on the canvas. Donovan counted him out on his feet at two minutes and thirty-two seconds. It was my twenty-sixth straight victory as a pro.

After the fight, trainer Whitey Bimstein, who worked in Uzcudun's corner, told me that he never saw anybody hit a man as hard as I hit Uzcudun that night.

It was an easy fight for me. The only guy that gave me less trouble was Levinsky.

I was ready for the world. I had beat Schmeling's record. It took him twelve rounds to beat Uzcudun; I did it in four. Me and Schmeling were even-steven for the heavyweight. Even-stevens don't make it, though. It had to be me and Schmeling in the ring. Mike Jacobs started his negotiating for me to meet with him. Everybody figured it would be an easy fight for me, and, when I beat him, that would take care of any foreign chances at the title. At that time I didn't give a damn whether the man was a foreigner or not, I just wanted my chance.

I had just signed up to fight Charley Retzlaff in Chicago for January 17, 1936, when Mike Jacobs set the Schmeling fight for Yankee Stadium on June 19, 1936.

At the time we signed up to fight Schmeling his manager, Joe Jacobs, said there had to be a clause in the agreement that said neither me nor Schmeling could fight for six months before our meeting at Yankee Stadium. They let the Retzlaff fight go on because the date had been made ahead of time.

At first that clause didn't mean anything to me. No

fights for him, no fights for me. OK. We didn't think about it at the time, but Schmeling's manager might have pulled a fast one on us. Maybe they knew that for me to be really great, I had to keep fighting. I'd been fighting two to three times a month since I turned pro; all my timing, and coordination, stayed honed up that way.

Then, on the other hand, maybe they were just trying to build up the gate, and people would be anxious to see us and pay for us to fight. There's also the other possibility: One of us could be kicked on our ass if we fought before the big match, and we wouldn't draw a crowd.

Anyway, I didn't give a damn then, because I wasn't scared of Schmeling and I could do with a rest.

It was while I was in New York at 381 Edgecombe, before I went into training for Retzlaff, that I met a young sports reporter for the *New York Daily News* named Ed Sullivan. He took a real shine to me and I did the same for him. Ed slowly got me hooked on golf. First he came to the house with some books on golf. Only time I enjoyed reading was when it was about sports. I ate up those books. Then Ed would come by with one golf club at a time. I was swinging, slicing, hooking, and putting all around the apartment. Marva would get a little nervous, afraid I might strain myself, or break up the apartment.

Between my fights and my new passion for golf, I'd finished up one hell of a year.

FIRST SCHMELING
FIGHT

G US GREENLEE HAD A MEETING IN JANUARY WITH
Roxborough. He wanted us to set up a team in
Detroit to compete in the Negro Baseball League.
I loved the idea; if it hadn't been for boxing, I would have
loved to have been a baseball player.

Greenlee was President of the National Association of
Negro Baseball Clubs and he was the owner of the Pittsburgh Crawfords. So he set up a meeting with Ferdinand
Q. Morton, the Commissioner of the Negro National
League. I would have liked the team idea, but it didn't pan
out. I already had my friends working the Brown Bombers
Softball Team, and that was eating up money. Roxborough felt the League was a great cause, but a new
team just was too costly. Marva wasn't enthusiastic
either; bad enough I was always training or going around
meeting the guys in various cities with the softball team.

I regretted the whole thing, but, well, you can't do it all.
Anyway, I got to get ready to meet Charley Retzlaff, on
January 17 in Chicago. Retzlaff was one hell of a
puncher, and was rated high in the heavyweight division.

But the deal wasn't simple. I learned later that Joe
Triner, Chairman of the Illinois State Athletic Commission, told Retzlaff that if he didn't put up a good sincere
fight against me, he wouldn't get paid. They figured King
Levinsky had just been jiving, playing chicken—for
$35,000. I knew this wasn't true. Levinsky wanted the
fight, but he just wasn't good enough. You know, when
you're a black man, you constantly have to prove yourself.

Anyway, Triner made sure that Retzlaff knew he'd be well watched. If he didn't, they'd hold up his purse.

I had just stopped Uzcudun at the Garden two and a half weeks before, and Chappie wanted to make sure I don't overtrain. I ran five miles every morning in Washington Park but really cut down the gym work; for several days in a row I didn't go near the gym. Then Chappie sent me in to spar about four days before the fight.

Chappie told me that Retzlaff was tough. He had trained him a couple of years before for plenty of his matches, and he had been in his corner when he beat Art Lasky the first time. According to Chappie, he was a better boxer now.

I took him by a knockout in only one minute and fifty-six seconds of the first round. Two left hooks and a right uppercut, and the job was done. But damn, in that little bit of time Retzlaff hit me with a right on my chin that really rocked me. Up to this point, it was the hardest anybody had hit me in my professional career.

Well, it was a victory anyway, so me and Marva and my gang went to Julian Black's house. Black and his wife gave me a big cocktail party at the Century Civic Clubhouse on Michigan Avenue. Fredi Washington, who played Peola in *Imitation of Life,* was there. Louise Beavers and a lot of important, and not so important, people were there.

Now I had about four months to myself, and I wasn't thinking or worrying about Max Schmeling. Besides, Hollywood was calling. I was going to be a goddamned movie star. Elliot Shanburg and Leo Golden were going to produce a movie called "The Spirit of Youth," and I was set to play the lead. Me, I've been a movie fan from the time I saw my first movie. Me and Marva packed up and headed for Los Angeles.

We loved it there. I took a bunch of my friends with me, including Roxy and Julian Black, and we had a real good time making that movie. It was supposed to be about a young poor boy who started out as a dishwasher and wound up champion of the world. I guess it was supposed to be something like my life story. Edna Mae Harris was my leading lady. She was a beautiful colored girl who used to play a lot in vaudeville. Black women certainly weren't playing any heroine roles in those days. If you were a black actress who was good-looking, you were lucky if you got the role of the maid. Most times you had to be big, fat, talk with a heavy Southern accent, bug your eyes, and act stupid. You know, though, when you think back, it must have been hard on those actors. Think about those Tarzan movies. Those Africans had been around for centuries, taking care of themselves, but in those Tarzan movies they look like they can't live one day to the next without some strange white man swinging through the trees and screaming like a baboon, coming to save them.

Now, don't get me wrong, I'm not by any stretch putting down black actors in those days. Stephen Fetchit was a funny man. Those black actors who bugged their eyes and acted stupid were funny, and that's alright, to be funny. Look at Jerry Lewis; he acts silly and we laugh, but when that's the only side of a race of people you see, that's bad. When you think of the influence of the movies on black people and white people, it can scare you.

Well, I'm older now, and I can be wise and look at all these things. Then I was just happy to see some black people making money. I wanted a good time and I had it.

I don't know where they get this idea that women are the weaker sex and that they're shy. My God, the women, the starlets, white and black, came jumping at me. I was the weaker sex. I didn't resist one pretty girl who had a sparkle in her eye.

In particular, there was one of the cutest gals I ever met. Her name was Sonja Henie. She was from Norway, and she had won the Women's Figure Skating Gold Medal in three Olympics, one after the other. Now she had come to Hollywood to make pictures. She was a pug-nosed blonde with bright blue eyes, and one of the best sports I've ever known. We had a nice thing going, but she was a smart woman and so kept everything "undercover."

Whenever I felt guilty, I'd go out and buy Marva an expensive present. Sometimes she'd look at me with her beautiful face and say, "Oh, but you didn't have to." But I did.

Enough of the glamor; time to get back to work to have the money for the glamor. We all headed for Lakewood, New Jersey, for training. Personally, I liked Pompton Lakes better. It was quiet, pretty, peaceful. But my manager figured that Lakewood could accommodate more visitors because they had the Stanley Hotel nearby, and a lot of people who couldn't make it to Florida stayed there. The more people you got, the more money you drew. Then, when they told me about the beautiful golf course, they sold me.

May 13 was my 22nd birthday, and so we had a party. Nat Fleischer, editor of *Ring Magazine,* gave me a gold-decorated belt, meaning I'd been picked by the magazine as the Number One Boxer of 1935.

Now, guess who else came to this party? Jimmy Braddock, along with Tony Canzoneri, Tommy Loughran, and Johnny Dundee. Braddock comes over and wishes me happy birthday and says, "OK, Joe, you must be running from me. Why don't you come after me? I mean, I'm the champion and all. Now here I am coming to you." I told Jimmy that as soon as I finished off Schmeling, for him to look out because he's looking at the next heavyweight titleholder. I said this jokingly, but deep down I meant it.

Now, look at me in May, 1936. I look back and get mad at myself. I think I'm Mr. Big Shit. I know I'm going to win anything I want. My record speaks for itself. I married a fabulous woman, I bought a beautiful home for my mother, I'm sending my sister Vunice to Howard University to study teaching, women are running me crazy, big, important people are my friends. Shit! I can't go wrong. I got the money, I got the power.

I took my clubs to training camp with me, and some writers, Hype Igoe and Walter Stewart from Memphis, Tennessee, and me started playing together. They took me on the Lakewood, New Jersey, golf course for the first time. Good God, I was really in love with the game.

When I entered training camp, I had the idea that I was going to do a lot of hard work for nothing. I thought I could name the round that I would knock Schmeling out. Instead of training as I should have, I'd cut my training short and jump in the car and head for the golf course with Stewart and Igoe. Instead of boxing six rounds, I'd box three. Punch the bag one round instead of two.

I'd even sneak off to Atlantic City when I got the chance to see some girl whose name I don't even remember.

Instead of gradually working up to a physical peak, I began bearing down and melting off weight. Could take it off easy enough, but couldn't put it back on. That weakened me.

That's not all that weakened me.

This was the first and only time Marva was this close to me at camp time. I mean, we were real young then— Marva was twenty years old on May 7 and I was twenty-two on May 13. She stayed at the Stanley Hotel, about two blocks from the stucco house called the Alpert Mansion where I was staying. What can I say? I was young, she was younger, and we'd just been married must be nine months. She was having fun at the hotel meeting the people who came there to watch me train. My managers thought she was too much of a distraction, and they made her leave the Stanley Hotel and go back to New York. It bothered me but it didn't bother me.

And the other girls were coming around like flies. I remember one time Chappie actually took a stick and threatened them. I found them anyway.

JOE LOUIS: MY LIFE

When Marva left the camp, I'd wire ahead to the florists at the Theresa Hotel, where she stayed, and have her room full of flowers and champagne and liquor even though she didn't drink. I tried in a feeble kind of way, but I just couldn't seem to help myself. Lord knows I didn't mean to be fresh to Chappie, Roxy, and Black and certainly not Marva. I kept excusing myself because I was twenty-two. People crowding all around me, getting a kind of respect I never anticipated, doing things real grand—like I never expected. Sometimes you have to excuse youth—but it nearly cost me my career.

Well, anyway, I'd still go through the routine. I was on the road at seven in the morning for six miles. I always ran off four pounds. Then I'd drink fruit juices, eat prunes and toast, and go to bed for about three hours of sleep. Usually during this nap I'd get back the weight I lost. But this time it didn't work—those camp-following girls took too much out of me. When I came to the camp, I weighed 216 pounds, and then I went down to 204 two weeks before the fight.

Everybody was upset, Roxy, Black, and Chappie. Two times Roxy chased me off the golf course—I was dehydrating myself under that hot sun. I was acting like a spoiled little boy. When I told him I was twenty-two years old and could do what I wanted, he'd walk away real hurt. I don't know—too much, too soon. Anyway, I took off eighteen pounds in five weeks—that's too fast for anyone.

Chappie kept bugging me about Schmeling's right-hand punch. I told him if that was all I had to worry about, forget it. Chappie kept on warning me Schmeling would probably want me to lead with a jab, hoping I'd drop my left arm and he'd get me with a right. I didn't listen.

I didn't listen to anyone. When Bill Farnsworth, one of the Hearst sportswriters, came up to watch me, he had the nerve to say to me, "I'm betting on Schmeling." Got pissed off with him, too.

The Sunday before the fight I was full of confidence.

Salvatore Ruggerillo, one of my sparring partners who had a punch like Schmeling, quit after one round. The other partners were easy game. I beat all of them. I was hell that day. The only problem was that I had reached my peak—and the fight was five days away.

Roxy, Black, and Chappie were worried. They felt I needed to relax and regain some weight, so they rented a big boat for a deep-sea fishing trip. Seemed like a nice idea at first, but when I got down to the dock, I said to myself, "Shit, I'm in top form, I'm going to play a few rounds of golf." I needed golf that day like you need another hole in your head. My body shouldn't have taken the strain of more possible weight loss, with the dehydration.

The day of the weigh-in was here. We drove eleven miles or so by car to Point Pleasant, New Jersey, and then caught the train. When we got into Penn Station, there was a big crowd there to greet me. If it hadn't been for the police, there would have been no way we could get through.

I remember the Hippodrome, still stinking of the animal odor left over from a big circus show called *Jumbo,* with Jimmy Durante. Schmeling hadn't gotten there yet from Napanoch, New York. It was raining real hard up there, and he was coming by car and it took longer. Shoot, I wasn't going to stand around, so I went into Jimmy Durante's old dressing room to take a nap till Schmeling arrived. Got a good hour's sleep.

When we weighed in, Schmeling was 192 pounds and I was 196. We hardly talked except to say hello. But just as we finished weighing in, the fight was postponed till the next day because of rain. I went to 381 Edgecombe Avenue and just lazed around that day. Didn't bother me.

What did bother me and Mike Jacobs was the box office receipts. He had expected a crowd of 85,000, and five days before the fight less than 50,000 tickets were sold. We found out later that some Jewish organization had sent out a big batch of flyers to storekeepers asking them to boycott the fight because Schmeling "represented" Nazi Germany. The whole thing made me uneasy.

Well, anyway, the day the fight was postponed, Marva was out selling "tags" for the Junior Council of the New York Urban League in front of the Big Apple, a popular bar, on One hundred thirty-fifth Street and Seventh Avenue. The money she got that day would help poor children to go to camp. So the day wasn't really wasted.

I was really looking forward to the fight. But I also wanted it over and done with. Practically my whole family would be out there rooting for me and Momma had come to New York for her first time to see me fight. She and some of the family stayed with some of my friends at 409 Edgecombe. Since she had come in a few days earlier, Marva took her around New York, and she bought a brand new outfit.

The damn weather was frustrating to me. All day it was cloudy and it looked like rain. Finally the sky got blue, but then there were flashes of lightning. With weather like this, I knew the gate would be short.

When we got to Yankee Stadium, Mike Jacobs met us and said there were only 40,000 people there to watch. If it hadn't been for that damned weather, we would have had a bigger crowd.

Schmeling was a ten-to-one underdog, and I felt good.

Before the bell rang, I remember Chappie saying, "Don't go for the knockout yet. Keep jabbing him off balance so he can't get that right in, and for God's sake keep your left arm high." The sound of Chappie's words blurred over. Hell, I knew what to do.

Schmeling was in the ring first, wearing a gray and black robe. I came in five seconds later, wearing a blue robe with red trimming. I felt ready. When the bell rang, Schmeling came out almost off balance, he leaned over so much. His chin was tucked in his left shoulder, and his left arm was stuck up in the air. He was going to use his left to protect his chin, and his right was steady. He didn't come out punching or weaving. I could jab him easy. I jabbed till his eye was almost closed in the first round. When I look at some of those old fight films, I could kick myself. His left was so high that his body was wide open for a right hand. Anyway, he couldn't get a shot at me. I wasn't the least bit worried, and when I went to my corner at the bell, I told Chappie Max was a pushover; I would get him anytime with a left hook. Chappie annoyed me when he told me to keep on jabbing him with a high left and not to drop that arm for a hook for about three or four rounds. God, I wish I had listened to him.

In the second round, I hit him, boom, boom, boom, with jabs. Didn't seem to bother him. Then I did just what Chappie told me not to do, drop in a left hook. As soon as I did, Schmeling came in with a right hand over that got me right on the chin. I thought I'd swallowed my mouthpiece. I was dazed, everything clouded over: I don't know how I stayed on my feet. I kept jabbing till my head cleared a little bit.

In round three, I shook him up with some right uppercuts to the body. I tried like hell to hit him in the jaw, but he fended me off with his left. He barely returned any punches, and he seldom used his right hand in the first three rounds.

I opened up a cut under his right eye with a left hook in the fourth round. All of a sudden, he got in a sharp right to my jaw, and I was down for a two count. I couldn't believe that I was on my ass, and I could've sworn my damn jaw was broken. This was my first knockdown as a professional. To be honest, I never fully recovered from that blow.

Before the fifth round, I remember Chappie saying, "Keep your guard up, keep your guard up." Near the end of the fifth, we were fighting near my corner. Schmeling started a right, and the bell rang when his hand was in midair. As I turned around to go to my corner, I got smashed on the jaw. When I staggered back to my corner,

I didn't know where I was. My ears were ringing, and I don't even know if I knew who I was.

By the sixth, Schmeling kept staggering me with rights to the jaw. I found out later that Freddie Guinyard took my momma out of the stadium during this round. They told me Momma was crying and praying and saying, "My God, my God, don't let him kill my child." The rest of my family stayed. My stepbrother, Pat Brooks, Jr., was yelling to Chappie to throw in the towel. Chappie didn't want me to get hurt, but the towel would be the easy way out. I remember telling him, though, that no matter how hurt I was not to throw in the towel. Just before the end of the sixth round, Schmeling hit me so hard with a right to the head I could hardly make it back to my corner. That punch finished me off for keeps. Everything was in a fog. I was fighting now on pure instinct. I lost my poise so much that when I went to make a body attack, I hit low twice. The referee warned me, and I lost those rounds. This was in the eighth and the twelfth.

When the seventh round started, I moved out quickly to meet Schmeling and shot a right hand to his stomach. I had no power behind it, it didn't hurt him. Then I threw some hooks and right hands. He took them all. I figure Max was just waiting to throw those right hands at me again. When the seventh ended, Chappie said, "Try punching to Schmeling's body," if I couldn't reach his head.

The bell rang for the eighth, and when I came out, my legs felt weak. Schmeling started shooting right hands again. I couldn't shake them off like I did in earlier rounds. He hit me with three solid rights to the jaw as the round ended.

In the ninth, he just kept hitting me with right hands.

By the tenth, I seemed to regain my senses. I began punching out at Schmeling, and when my blows failed to drop him, I became annoyed.

OKeh

Licensed by Mfr. under U. S. Patent Nos. 1625705 and/or 1702564 (and
other patents pending) only for non-commercial use on phonographs in homes.
See detailed trade mark and patent notices on envelope. Made in U. S. A.

6475
(31373)

KING JOE PART I
(Joe Louis Blues) Blues Fox Trot
-Wright-Basie-
**PAUL ROBESON with
COUNT BASIE and his ORCH.**

The challenger for Jimmy Braddock's World Heavyweight crown as seen by *Vanity Fair* photographer Nelson in 1935. (Inset) The 1941 Count Basie recording
featured lyrics by Richard Wright and vocal by Paul
Robeson.

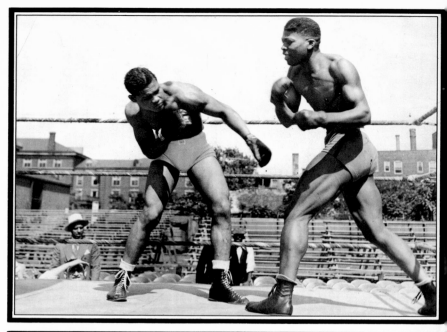

Etig Urso • Tony Bellini • Al Matlow • Phil Kenneally • Danny Farra • Fred Bawino • Joe Louis • Lee Thomas

Chicago Golden Gloves Champions.
1934.

(Top) Louis, at left, conqueror of Carnera in six rounds, in training with Willie Davis for his August 7, 1935 bout with King Levinsky in Cominskey Park, Chicago. (Bottom) Chicago Golden Gloves Champions, 1934. Louis is second from right.

Yours Truly
Joe Louis

Joe Louis, 1934, at the start of his professional career. After his defeat by Max Marek in the finals of the National Amateur Championships, Louis went on to win twenty-seven consecutive bouts, twenty-four by knockout, until his defeat at the hands of Max Schmeling in June, 1936.

(Top) An over-confident Joe Louis and his "Brain Trust" prior to the Schmeling defeat, 1936. Left to right, Assistant Manager Julian Black, Trainer Jack Blackburn, Louis, and Manager John Roxborough. (Bottom) An earlier and more serious Brain Trust at the training camp in Pompton Lakes, New Jersey, 1935, with Russell Cowans at right.

Louis in training at Pompton Lakes: (Top, left) A heavy-bag session for a night bout against Max Baer at Yankee Stadium; (Top, right) Limbering-up with the medicine ball for the Primo Carnera fight; (Bottom, left) Heavyweight Champion James J. Braddock wishing Louis luck in the forthcoming Baer fight; (Bottom, right) boxing impressario Mike Jacobs checking on his charge for the upcoming Paolino Uzcudun contest.

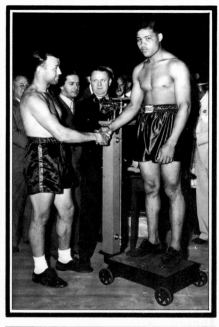

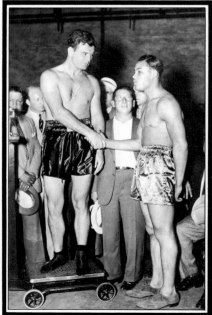

Scowls, smiles, and suede shoes. The very ceremonial weigh-in: (Top, left) Carnera $260\frac{1}{2}$, Louis 196. (Top, right) Former World Champion Jack Sharkey and a poker-faced challenger; (Bottom, left) British challenger Tommy Farr, loser-to-be of a close fifteen round decision to the new champion; (Bottom, right) World Champion James J. Braddock tipping the scales before being dethroned.

WIDE WORLD PHOTOS

BAER		LOUIS	
AGE	26	AGE	21
WEIGHT	210½	WEIGHT	199¼
HEIGHT	6'2½"	HEIGHT	6'1½"
REACH	81½"	REACH	76"
NECK	17"	NECK	16¼"
BICEPS	14¾"	BICEPS	13
FOREARM	14	FOREARM	12½
WRIST	8"	WRIST	7¾"
CHEST	44"	CHEST	41"
CHEST (EXPANDED)	47"	CHEST (EXPANDED)	43"
WAIST	33"	WAIST	34"
THIGH	18"	THIGH	20"
CALF	13"	CALF	15"
ANKLE	8½"	ANKLE	10"

Max Baer, playboy and showman, known as the "Merry Madcap," even had Joe Louis smiling at the weigh-in ceremonies for their September, 1935 bout. Baer's height, weight, and reach advantage were to no avail as he absorbed a barrage of punches before going down in the fourth round.

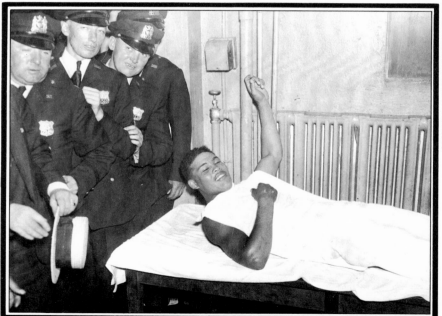

Victory was almost always for Joe Louis. (Top) Ring announcer Hal Totten, at left, and co-manager Julian Black, at right, note that he's just won the heavyweight championship of the world from James J. Braddock. (Bottom) New York's finest help Joe celebrate victory in the dressing room after an earlier Carnera win.

Announcer Harry Balough holds up Joe's fist, symbolic of a non-title victory over Max Baer. (Inset) After twenty-seven consecutive wins, Louis is dazed and helpless in the twelfth round after being floored by Max Schmeling at Yankee Stadium, 1936.

At home in Detroit with his mother and sisters, 1935. Left to right: Vunice, Mrs. Emmarell Davis, Mrs. Eulalie Gaines, Joe, and his mother, Lily.

(Top, left) Joe Louis and Miss Marva Trotter in Washington Park, Chicago, 1935. (Top, right) Joe and his bride of a few hours, Marva, posing for photographers immediately after the win over Max Baer. (Bottom, left) Louis, in training at Pompton Lakes for Tommy Farr, gets some pointers from Babe Ruth, the other "Sultan of Swat." (Bottom, right) The heavyweight champion admiring his recently acquired championship belt.

(Top, left) A pensive champion had almost two years to brood over the Schmeling defeat which radio sponsor Buick (top, right) had billed as the "Biggest Match Yet!" But (bottom) the world really tuned-in for the second Louis-Schmeling fight June 22, 1938, which had become billed as the battle between democracy and fascism.

The world tuned-in, but not for long. It was all over in 2:04 of the first round as Schmeling (top) twisted and turned on the ropes to avoid Louis' devastating attack, but by the third knockdown, he was a battered and beaten hulk (bottom) as referee Arthur Donovan stopped the count at eight, and King Joe had his vindication.

Harlem Madness. Celebrating crowds swarm onto a Fifth Avenue double-decker bus, as Harlem and the nation erupted for the Louis victory. The nation was still safe for democracy.

(Top, left) Joe and Marva, idols of the crowd, as they took one of their many victory strolls down Lenox Avenue. (Top, right) The natty champion and sidekick Freddie Guinyard on Sugar Hill. (Bottom, left and right) Back to Pompton Lakes training where the subsequent taking-on of all comers became known as the "Bum of the Month" campaign.

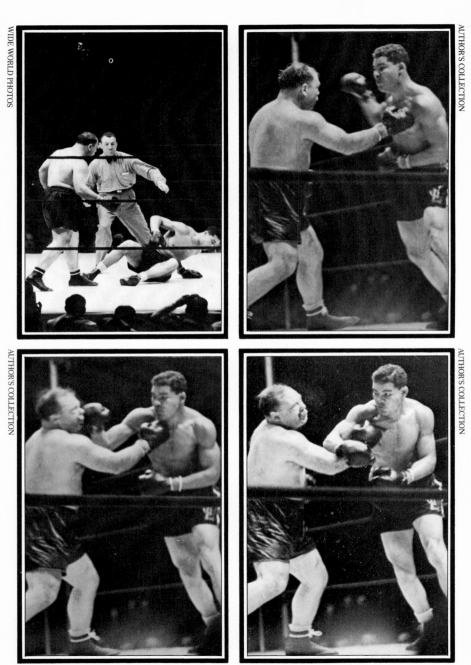

(Top, left) Roundhouse swinging "Bum of the Month" two-ton Tony Galento put Louis on the canvas in the third round of their 1939 bout. The champion got off the deck to severely shellack the rough and tumble ringman culminating in the (above) fourth round technical knockout sequence.

JOE LOUIS: MY LIFE

In the eleventh round, he continued pounding me with those right hands. I just kept on fighting and holding on for my life. Hoping my head might clear up.

In two minutes and twenty-nine seconds of the twelfth round, Schmeling made his knockout. He must have hit me with about fifty right hands that round.

I barely remember being carried back to my dressing room by my attendants and the police. Next thing I knew, I was sitting on the dressing table and crying like I don't think I ever did before. It seemed at that moment I would just die. Chappie, Roxy, and Julian comforted me as best they could. Chappie told me not to worry, I'd do better next time, and that everything happens for the best.

Roxborough and Black took care of the reporters. They told them that Schmeling got me with a "Sunday punch" in the second round, but even with that, it took him ten rounds to take me out.

When I came around, Roxie was talking to me. I asked him what I was doing wrong. I didn't hear a thing he was saying until he said I had hit Schmeling a couple of low blows. That made me feel even worse. I sent Roxie over to Schmeling's dressing room to apologize for me and to tell him I didn't know what I was doing and that I didn't intentionally hit him low. When Roxie came back, he said Schmeling was real nice about it and he understood I didn't and wouldn't pull a low blow on purpose.

When Dr. Chester Ames fixed me up with some first aid, I looked in the mirror. My God, my forehead was swollen down to my eyelids, you couldn't see any lashes, there was a big lump on my left cheek, my lips were swollen, both my thumbs were sprained, and my hands were all puffed up.

I don't care what you heard about me being modest—I wasn't. I was just as vain as Muhammad Ali, I just had to be more discreet about it. No way I was going to the Hotel Theresa that night looking the way I did. I didn't want my wife looking at me or all those black folks who had so much faith in me.

People took the loss bad, too. They say that folks in Chicago's "Little Harlem" rioted that night—people actually stoned streetcars. And in New York a girl took my loss so bad that she attempted to drink poison in a drugstore. She had to be taken to a hospital. Shit!

Somehow, my guys got me to 381 Edgecombe Avenue. I stayed there three days with just the people I needed.

First thing I did was to call Momma like I always did after a fight. I was more concerned about her than about me. I thought she'd be brokenhearted, but instead she gave me courage. She said to me, "You did your best and that's all anyone could ask of you."

I also felt guilty, what with my Momma saying I did my best and it was OK. It was my own guilt that hurt me as much as my body. After that, the other considerations about my race, my country, my wife came in next. I was some sorry guy. Sorry about myself and planning my revenge.

Anyway, after talking to Momma, I called Marva and just told her I'd see her after a while. Good thing I didn't see her, though. I hear she was almost out of her mind, and they had to get a doctor for her.

Well, in those three days I did a lot of reflecting and thinking. It was all my fault, entirely. I was too damn sure of myself. Didn't train properly, and between the golf and the women and not listening to what Chappie said, it's a wonder I wasn't killed in the ring. I let myself down, I let a whole race of people down because I thought I was some kind of hot shit.

During those three days, Dr. Ames spent a lot of time with me. He examined me through and through and finally said I was OK. I sent for Marva and she was loving and comforting to me, staying up practically all day and night giving me hot and cold compresses. When I'd look in the mirror at my face and complexion, Marva would say, "You're a boxer, not a movie star." She knew I had broken training, and why, but she still stuck by me.

The black people, I heard, wouldn't believe what happened. They said I was doped up. They said Schmeling had iron pieces in his gloves. When Chappie took my black bag with my boxing trunks and shoes and stuff, the people around 381 started yelling, "There's the money, there's the money!" I was hurt that anybody would think I'd take that beating for money.

I thought to myself, "Why is everybody jumping on my back?" I got knocked out. I made a mistake. Really, I made a lot of mistakes. Here I was winning all the time and I lost one fight. During that time, I didn't really understand how important I was to so many people.

You say all kinds of things when you don't want to face the truth. I was the only hero they had then, and heroes aren't supposed to lose. But, anyhow, they stuck by me and made excuses for me. Some fans said the powers weren't going to let me reach the championship, that I had gone as far as I could. Some said, "Don't worry, Champ, you'll get him the next time." And I vowed I would.

Chappie and I went over what was wrong; this time I listened. He told me Max was a different kind of fighter for me. He was a counterpuncher. He told me I kept dropping my left hand after a jab, and Max just kept shooting his right hand over it. He said we'd fix that all up.

On top of all of this, I heard that Pat Brooks, Sr., my stepfather, had a paralyzing stroke two days before the fight. Nobody told me about it before because they knew I'd be too upset. They still hadn't told me how sick he was, or some kind of way I would have gone to his bedside.

Well, in a couple of days, like two thieves in the night, Marva and I caught a late train and headed for home. I had the train stop before we reached the station and had a private limousine take us home. I wouldn't go out during the day and made Marva keep all the shades drawn, even though nobody could look in the window. Late at night, I'd let her take me for a drive while my face healed up.

While I was healing, Mike Jacobs, Roxy, Black, and Chappie started working out plans for me to still get to the championship. I had to be resold to the public. It was like I had climbed up a steep flight of stairs and fallen down halfway. I wanted a return match with Schmeling as soon as possible. I could taste the blood, but my managers said no. They wanted a comeback match with Max Baer because I'd already beaten him. They figured if Schmeling came right back in the picture, it wouldn't be good. Maybe they didn't think I could beat him, but I knew I could. On the other hand, Mike Jacobs didn't agree with them. He figured me to fight Jack Sharkey.

Mike is always the businessman. He knew he could get a top price of $11.50 ringside for the Sharkey fight and that it would outdraw a match between me and Baer. Nothing I could do but go along with this. So they made plans for me to meet with Jack Sharkey that August. Sharkey had lost the heavyweight championship to Primo Carnera in 1933. If I could get a knockout over him, combined with my victories over two other titleholders, I'd be heading in the right direction again.

I knew this next training session wouldn't be like the party I was having before. I knew it would be long and hard, and so Marva and I decided to go over and stay a few days with Momma.

When I saw Pat Brooks, Jr. I really got upset. Nobody had explained how bad off he was. That really shook me down some, but everybody, including the doctor, kept telling me he'd be all right in a few weeks. He'd smile at me, because he couldn't talk, and he'd try and raise his fist to encourage me. So at first I didn't feel too bad, and it was great to be with my relatives; they encouraged me and made me feel good. Momma was crazy about Marva and vice versa.

JOE LOUIS: MY LIFE

Everything seemed to be going all right, when Pat Brooks took a turn for the worse. I guess all of us who could fit in the bedroom were there when he died. I broke down and cried and cried. As far as I was concerned, Pat Brooks was my father. I remember all he did for me and the family. I was sorry I ever fussed with him about sneaking around sipping a little white lightning now and then. I was sorry he'd never seen me fight a big-time professional bout, but I was damned glad no one told him about my losing the Schmeling bout. I still miss him.

Marva was real upset. After the funeral, I knew I would have to leave for camp. I needed to get away. I needed to get myself together. Momma would be well taken good care of by my sisters, and Marva stayed on a while to help Momma adjust.

My body was getting better, my mind was set, and my ego returned. Bring on the next fight.

In the middle of July, we headed for Pompton Lakes. Chappie liked this camp better because it was cooler and didn't have all the razzmatazz around it like Lakewood. The public was barred from the camp. Only newspapermen and the general press could come. Chappie didn't let me out of sight. This time he didn't have to worry though. Everytime I fought a sparring partner I couldn't get Schmeling out of my mind. Every partner was Schmeling to me. I wanted that rematch so bad I could taste it. I had been humiliated, and I had to prove to everybody that I was the best heavyweight around.

I didn't know too much about Jack Sharkey, except that he'd held the heavyweight crown for one year and was on the comeback trail. He believed that if he could beat me, he'd put himself back in the thick of the heavyweight action. The Depression was still on, and the money must have looked good enough to him to draw him out of retirement.

August 17. I was ready. Of course my old buddies were

still with me. I told Marva she couldn't come. She was too emotional—she felt every blow that I got in the Schmeling fight. She was still having nightmares about it.

Sharkey was doing a whole lot of talking. He was saying the twelve years difference in our ages didn't make a difference. He was saying he could whip any colored fighter. You know something? If you really listened to all that shit, you could go crazy. It made you wonder if the man really thought you were inferior, or if he was just trying to drum up the gate. If he thought I was inferior, well, I'd feel real bad; if he was trying to drum up the gate, I'd feel real good—more money for both of us.

Anyway, when we went for the weigh-in at the Hippodrome, I came in at 199 ¾ pounds and Sharkey at 197-¼. So I had twelve years and a two-and-a-half-pound edge on him. I was expecting to hear a whole lot of lip from him about how he always had the "Indian sign" on the black boys like Harry Wills and George Godfrey. I was ready for him, but he only said, "How are you, Joe," and I just said "Hello." You just can't believe everything you read in the papers.

When I climbed in the ring at Yankee Stadium, Chappie warned me for the millionth time that Sharkey would use the same tactics Schmeling had. I was nervous and worried when I faced him. This was the toughest time I ever had. My career was at stake. I couldn't afford to lose two fights in a row.

I was extra cautious the first round. I boxed him till I could find an opening. Took special care not to be hit with the sucker punches Sharkey was throwing at me. He got only one good right against my jaw. No doubt about it, I had the first round. In the second round, I hit with a hard right and he went down. After I scored that first knockdown, my coordination was right and my punch had returned. I got him down for a count of nine and another count of eight in the third round. He kept getting up. I remembered him trying to be brave by smiling with all the blood coming out of his mouth. I was giving him everything I had. Then I gave a left to the chin and two short rights to the head. This time he stayed down for the full count.

My morale was sky-high. I couldn't wait till my next bout and I wanted Max Schmeling. But Max wasn't going for it. He told Mike Jacobs he had already beat me and he wanted Braddock so he could get his title back. Even when Mike offered him a $300,000 guarantee, he refused. That man was as hungry for the title as I was.

Mike Jacobs looked around and had no trouble getting me a bout with Al Ettore, the leading heavyweight in Pennsylvania, for September 22. We got the Sesquicentennial Stadium of Philadelphia, where Gene Tunney had won a ten-round decision over Jack Dempsey and the championship in 1926. Mike figured on a big gate, about $300,000, because I was the most popular heavyweight around, and Al Ettore had his own following in Pennsylvania.

Well, with two left hooks and a right uppercut, I knocked out Ettore at 1:28 of the fifth round.

Right around this time, besides wanting another shot at Schmeling, I was still sitting hot and heavy for a fight with Braddock, but it wasn't an easy thing. Back in April, 1935, before the Max Baer-Jimmy Braddock fight for the championship, Braddock signed a contract with the Garden saying that if he won the championship, he would make his first defense of the title under the Garden's promotion.

Then Braddock and Schmeling decided they would fight it out. So Braddock signed another contract with the Garden agreeing to a championship fight with Schmeling in September, 1936. In between all this, I had lost to Schmeling, and I don't think Braddock was too anxious to go against him. Anyway, he had to postpone the fight scheduled for September since his hands were hurting from arthritis. So the Braddock-Schmeling match was postponed until June, 1937.

In the meantime, Braddock got two offers for no-decision exhibition bouts with me. The first offer came from Herman Taylor, a promoter out of Philadelphia. He and Jacobs had just promoted my fight with Ettore. Now Taylor offered Braddock half a million dollars, or 50 percent of the gate receipts. Taylor even heaped on $10,000 for training expenses for Braddock to meet with me in Convention Hall in Atlantic City. He offered me 12½ percent of the net gate. Right then, I could have told him I'd have fought for nothing to get a crack at the championship.

The other offer to Braddock came from a Los Angeles syndicate. They offered Braddock $500,000 for a twelve-round, no-decision exhibition bout in the stadium where the 1932 Olympics had been held. The California Boxing Commission then said that no decisions could be given in a twelve-round exhibition bout. This way, Braddock couldn't lose unless I knocked him out.

Roxie and Black were willing to sign me to fight Braddock anywhere. They figured me to knock out Braddock—forget the no-decision angle. A title is in jeopardy every time that the champion steps in the ring. We hoped to fight Braddock under any conditions so that I could get a shortcut to the title.

Well, nothing was decided or signed, but the idea was building, and I was feeling real good about maybe getting my chance. I wanted to be champion. At this point in my life, I needed that special feeling. Sometimes I think back to what I might have been, a farmer or laborer, and I get nervous. I never asked for this much in my life, but since it was thrown on me, I wanted it.

Meanwhile Mike Jacobs was so happy and wealthy that he rented the Hippodrome on Sixth Avenue in New York for a fight between me and Jorge Brescia of Argentina on October 9. I knocked out Brescia in two minutes and twelve seconds of the third round. I beat him, but he was a tough cookie. He had me up against the ropes at the beginning of the third round and he was really giving it to me until I stopped him.

I was in top form, and my managers wanted to make sure I stayed that way. A series of exhibition tours were set up so I'd keep in shape. The first one, October 14, was against Willie Davis in South Bend, Indiana. It was a knockout in the third round. The same day I fought K. O. Brown (with a name like that, he should have been hell, but he wasn't). I K.O.'d K. O. in round three.

Then it was off to New Orleans. In 1936, Louisiana wasn't the kind of place a black man would go for a vacation. It was alright if you were from there or had relatives, but you didn't just go there—a black heavyweight contender—without some thought. But Chappie knew all about that; he knew all the tricks that could be played on us. So, as a special precaution, Chappie had his gun tucked inside his waistband with his coat over it. But he made sure everybody around saw it. That was the first time I ever saw him with a gun at a fight. When I asked him about it, he said, "Chappie, this is the South, and I'm not taking shit from nobody." When one of the white deputies who knew Chappie's reputation saw the gun, he looked at Chappie nervously and said, "Everything's goin' to be all right, Blackburn. Everything is going to be all right." Only thing was, I was to spar with a white guy—a local promoter had planned the appearance. Well, the people in New Orleans got all riled up at the thought of a black man and a white man in the same ring. The people knew my reputation, and the idea of a white man being knocked around by a black man was more than they could take. So at the last minute they substituted a black fighter.

JOE LOUIS: MY LIFE

Everything was alright on November 20. I knocked out Paul Williams in two rounds, and back to back I stomped out Tom Jones in round three.

I got off the exhibition tour, and I was supposed to meet with Johnny Risko, but he fractured his ribs training. Eddie Simms replaced him, and the fight was scheduled for December 14 in Cleveland. In twenty-six seconds of the first round, I knocked him out. It was my fastest fight—when I hit him with a left hook, he went down for good. I remembered Chappie telling me that when you knock an opponent down, it's like chopping down a tree. You don't need to look because you can feel it in your arms and wrists, and that's what Eddie Simms felt like when I hit him. Funny thing about that fight: I went over to the neutral corner and when I turned around, there was Simms trying to get up. When the referee, Arthur Donovan, counted to seven he was looking straight at me. When the count went to nine he got up. I headed back for him to finish him off. But Simms took Donovan by the arm, and they were saying something. Later, Donovan told me Simms had said, "Let's go someplace. Let's get out of here. Let's go up on the roof or someplace." Donovan said, "Jesus, he's out of it, if he thinks I'm some girl." That's when he announced the fight was over.

I felt good about that fight in Cleveland, though. It was for the *Cleveland News* Christmas Fund. It drew a big crowd, and that meant a lot of poor people would have a nicer Christmas.

In the meantime, though, Schmeling wasn't sitting back there in Germany scratching his back. He wanted the championship again. He must have heard the talk about me and Braddock meeting in Atlantic City, so he got himself on the S.S. *Bremen* and sailed to New York in the middle of December.

He wanted to force a title fight out of Braddock as soon as possible. To make sure of this, he went to the New York State Athletic Commission, saying that Braddock had promised him a fight and then postponed it when he'd gotten arthritis. Schmeling even said that if he beat Braddock, he would come back to America and defend the title. Who the hell would believe that shit? If he won the title, you know it was bye-bye to America for a long time.

The Garden wasn't helping either, talking about stopping the champion from having no-decision exhibition bouts because it would hurt the "prestige" of the champion. I wasn't laughing then, but now, looking back and seeing a lot of things, I get to thinking how come they let Max Baer, when he was Heavyweight Champion, have no-decision exhibition bouts?

I just knew the Commission would mess up. Remember the time Harry Wills, a black boxer, was the number-one heavyweight contender for the title when Dempsey was Champion? The Boxing Commissioner let Dempsey fight anybody but Wills. While Dempsey was making his fortune, Wills was getting the runaround.

The Boxing Commission made it tight. They got Braddock and Schmeling both to put up $5,000 apiece, which they would lose if they didn't show up for the scheduled June match. Also, they ruled out a Braddock-Louis exhibition fight (my first with Braddock) in Atlantic City.

Well, to make everything stronger, the Garden got a third agreement from Braddock saying he could meet any opponent but me before the Schmeling fight, and he could box any number of rounds except fifteen.

Chappie was right. They didn't want a black man to have that title. Looked like the Boxing Commission and the Garden wanted to save that title for Nazi Germany. Here I was, an American, and they were giving Germany a better shot at the title than me. Mike told me not to worry, he'd find a way to get through all this here mess. It was Mike's world, not mine. I just had to go on fighting and trusting Mike.

Anyway, Mike flew out to the coast to talk about a fight between me and onetime light heavyweight champion,

Slapsie Maxie Rosenbloom. Some Hollywood promoter had offered a $100,000 guarantee. Then he planned a Garden appearance for me in January.

1936 had been a rough year for me and worse for Marva. I had some making up to do. Christmas was at hand, and I went home with Schmeling and Braddock on my mind.

1937

HEAVYWEIGHT CHAMPION OF THE WORLD

I WAS REALLY INTO BIG, BIG MONEY, AND I WAS SPENDing it like it'd never stop. Money has always been important to me. Not to save, but to enjoy and give enjoyment to other people. Maybe I felt this way because of all the hard times I'd had as a child. Maybe I'm a damned fool. Maybe I thought the well would never dry up. You tend to think that way when you're twenty-three years old and you've reached what I had reached. Anyway, Roxy and Julian had better sense than I did. Lord knows they tried. They didn't want me to wind up broke, or be some freak like Jack Johnson in the Flea Circus on Forty-second Street in New York.

Roxy planned to have set aside $300,000 in paid-up annuities by January 1, 1939. Shoot, $300,000 didn't seem like a lot to me then, and especially for my old age. I never thought about interest and growing rates and dividends. But Roxy explained that what a fighter earns and what he can save are two different things. When you consider taxes and traveling expenses for that gang I traveled around with, plus what the managers take, expenses for me and Marva, expenses for my family and friends, damn, you don't come out with too much. I had already paid up one $50,000 annuity policy and part of another policy for $100,000. I'd bought a home for my mother in Detroit and a chicken ranch for her in River Rouge. I was paying for my sister Vunice's education and supporting her regularly, and I can't remember how many other people I was supporting or helping out. Then I also had the expense of the Brown Bomber Softball Team. It was a heavy load, but I didn't mind. It gave me pleasure to be able to do it. I had a ball spending money.

Enough of money business for now. I had my own goals: to get to Schmeling, and then to try and get a shot at the championship. Another exhibition tour was set up for January. I met Steve Ketchel in Buffalo and dropped him in two. Ketchel was really a ranking heavyweight and not a part of the exhibition tour, but for what he showed, he might as well have been. Then there was Jack Thompson—K.O., round one; Jack Wright in one; and Tom Jones in two.

As it turned out there was hardly any money coming in on that tour and always some worry about my getting hurt for nothing. There was only one other contender Mike Jacobs was interested in, a New Yorker named Bob Pastor. He had been an amateur boxer when he went to NYU and had also played on their football team. He turned pro in 1935. Pastor had beat up Ray Impellittiere, a 270-pound giant, and had won the New York state heavyweight title. I guess he was known as a clever fighter. In fact, Mike Jacobs only agreed to the match on the condition that his organization, the Twentieth Century Sporting Club, could contract Pastor if he should win. This wasn't a put-down of me, but a Mike Jacobs power play. Pastor was under contract to Jimmy Johnston of Madison Square Garden; if I lost I would still be under Mike, and he'd have Pastor too. Either way he couldn't lose, and he could get control of the heavyweight division.

Well, anyway, we went into training. Later I heard that Pastor's camp was overjoyed when they heard that I had been knocked down in my sparring session by Eddie Malcolm during a last-minute tune-up. They had a good time talking about my not keeping my left hand up and thought they had it made.

JOE LOUIS: MY LIFE

We met at Madison Square Garden on January 27. While me and Chappie and Roxy and four bodyguards were waiting to enter the ring, Jimmy Johnston and four big tough-looking guys burst into my dressing room, yelling for me to take off my bandages. My bodyguards did what they're supposed to—they pulled out their guns; Chappie pushed me behind a locker and stood in front of me to protect me.

I don't know what the hell it was all about. Maybe it was Johnston's idea to rattle me, or maybe he'd been listening to that rumor that I dipped my bandaged hands in quick-drying cement before I put on my gloves. One of my bodyguards said, "Shit, those guys with Johnston are cops." Roxborough told Johnston to get the fuck out of the dressing room unless he wanted a fat lip and no Louis-Pastor fight.

When Roxborough said "no fight," Johnston changed his tune and took his thugs or cops and quietly went away.

When we began to fight, I said, "What the hell is he doing?" Pastor was fighting like Muhammad Ali—jab and run. I couldn't catch him. Jab, run, jab, run. He wouldn't stand still and fight. I was furious; if I could have held him I don't like to think what I'd have done. I felt like a goddamned fool trying to catch this mosquito. Chappie kept telling me to try and trap him in a corner. Impossible. I never fought anybody like him. I was clumsy—when I reached out to give him a good punch, I might just graze him. I didn't get in one crack, except a right to his collarbone. But he bumped me with his head and stuck his thumbs in my eyes. That's all the damage he did. He must have run twelve miles that night. At the end of the tenth round, he run to his corner jumping up and down with his arms raised in the air. I got the decision.

It was a lousy fight. I won but I looked bad. What really made me mad was that this fight had nothing to do with my ability; it had to do with boxing politics. Believe me, those politics are as complicated as the situation in the Middle East. I was the one who was used in the battle between Mike Jacobs and Jimmy Johnston. Johnston wanted me to look bad so that he could hurt Jacobs and his attempt to control the heavyweight division—that's where the big money was.

The papers the next day were saying any "smart boxer could outwit me." Shit! Were they saying I'm a dumb boxer? I knew I didn't finish school and go to college like Pastor, but I've never been dumb. Foolish, yes—dumb, no. I heard that Jimmy Johnston had instructed Pastor's trainer, Freddie Brown, to tell Pastor to stay away from me and run and hold for ten rounds. Never mind the art of boxing; make a political point.

I know one thing, though, the referee Arthur Donovan scored the fight eight rounds for me, two rounds for Pastor. He saw the fight as it was. I was the aggressor; the few punches landed, I landed. In the meantime, Mike Jacobs and everybody were telling me I had to prove myself. For what? I didn't have a fight. Hell, that was a track meet.

No difference, though, I had to resell myself. I know what had gone on, but the people only knew what they read in the papers. They set me up to fight Natie Brown in Kansas City, Missouri, on February 17. I knew Natie well; I had won a ten-round decision when we fought in March, 1935. He didn't bother me, but my manager wanted me to go for the knockout to erase all doubts about the Pastor joke. So I went to train at Trafton's Gym in Chicago, and managed to say hello to Marva.

One interesting thing about this fight was that it was in Missouri. Missouri was a tough state. They had had a law saying it was illegal for whites and blacks to fight in the same ring, but six months before I was to meet Natie, they reversed this law. I don't usually like to speculate or pat myself on the back, but I think that I may have had something to do with this. Boxing was getting to the highest point in years. Despite the Depression, boxing gates were bringing in money. If a black man fighting white boxers could help the economy, well hell, change the damn law.

We fought at the Municipal Auditorium. The first three rounds were easy. Then I cut loose with a barrage of lefts and rights, and in forty-two seconds of the fourth round I had him down. He tried like hell to get up. Finally he grabbed hold of the referee's legs, but in trying to hoist himself up, he pulled the referee down. The referee, flat out on the canvas next to Brown, counted him out.

I was climbing back up the ladder, and I prayed for Mike Jacobs to find some kind of way for me to get at Braddock. Well, it looked like the Lord was looking out for me; there was a group of people I never heard of answering my prayers. They were called the Anti-Nazi League, and they were sending telegrams to the State Athletic Commission and the Garden demanding that the scheduled Braddock-Schmeling fight be canceled. They were some tough people; they threatened to buy newspaper space and radio time to tell everybody in America not to go to that fight because they'd be supporting Nazi Germany. Then they threatened to picket all the box offices. They said they had the support of the American Federation of Labor, representatives in twenty-two countries, and twelve hundred women's clubs in America who would go along with them. On top of all that, Mayor Fiorello LaGuardia was one of its vice-presidents.

With all that power going on, Braddock's manager, Joe Gould, started thinking twice. He got another offer of $500,000 to fight me from Sheldon Clark, President of the Illinois Sporting Club and an executive with the Sinclair Oil Company. Gould knew Clark was for real because he helped promote the second Dempsey-Tunney fight in Chicago in 1927.

Well, Gould put it to Roxie and Black. He said he definitely wanted me and Braddock to meet even if he had to give up that $5,000 check they had given to the Garden guaranteeing a fight between Braddock and Schmeling. No way Gould figured he would fight this boycott coming up. Besides, too, he saw me draw $110,000 in my fight with Pastor, and Pastor was just a two-dollar fighter. He knew if I had the chance to fight Braddock, I'd draw a big gate, maybe over a million bucks. Then too, he knew how bad I looked fighting Pastor. Braddock would probably win, and win big money, too.

That was all well and good, but then Mike Jacobs said, "I got other offers to consider before I agree to the match." Roxie and Black told Jacobs he was full of shit. They said Mike was playing games. See, Mike had a two-year contract with Schmeling, who also owed him $31,000. I still had five years on my contract with Mike. Mike stood to get 50 percent of the title match between Braddock and Schmeling in their June 3 rumble. So he'd tried his best to get Schmeling to let the Braddock-Louis fight take place without much protest, and the winner would meet with Schmeling in Berlin in September.

Schmeling don't want that. Roxie and Black saw Mike hesitating too much, and so they said they would go over his head and bargain for the fight themselves.

Life sure gets more complicated. One day while all these negotiations were going on, Mr. Roxborough was stopped on the streets downtown by some thugs, who told him, "We're gonna take a ride." Mr. Roxborough told me later that he was scared shitless and figured this was his last day on earth. They drove him all around, not saying a thing, and that's even scarier. Well, Mr. Roxborough knew it had to be about the fight, but he didn't know what they wanted. Finally, they stopped at the back door of some night club and he was greeted by none other than Joe Gould.

Joe Gould was acting as if this was what people did every day. He told Mr. Roxborough, plain and clear, that he wanted 50 percent of me, because I was a cinch to win the title. Mr. Roxborough told him he must be crazy, because if I won, why should Gould get on the gravy train? Then Gould said that if he didn't go through with the deal there'd be no fight. Got to hand it to Mr. Roxborough, he held his ground. He told Gould, "That's alright. You're not making any money anyway. You need us more than we need you. Joe can always make a buck and Braddock can't." So Gould said, "OK, let's make it 25 percent." Then he went to 20 percent, and still Mr. Roxborough said, "No deal." Mr. Roxborough knew he had him, and he told Gould he'd better talk to Mike Jacobs, not him.

And slow, easy, and cool, Mr. Roxborough walked out of there, headed uptown, and had a double scotch on the rocks.

But Mr. Roxborough knew something had to be done, so he told Mike what went down. Mike said, "OK, let me see if I can work it out." Gould and Mike got together, and the upshot of it was this: Gould decided that if Braddock lost, he would get a 10-percent cut of the heavyweight money as long as I was champion. When Mike told me this, I blew my top and said "No." But, Mike didn't want to see any kind of good deal go down the drain. He maneuvered like a champion fighter. He knew that if I won this fight, he'd get the big money because he'd have the heavyweight division in his pocket. So he took the long gamble and agreed that if Braddock lost the championship to me, 10 percent of Mike's purse would go to Braddock as long as I was champion. People used to say Jimmy Braddock had a piece of me. No way. He had a part of Mike's purse, not mine.

On Friday, February 19, 1937, Mike Jacobs finally did it. I signed a contract to fight the Heavyweight Champion of the World, Jimmy Braddock. The fight was scheduled for June 22, 1937, at Soldiers Field, but it was changed to Comiskey Park because the Soldiers Field people wanted too much rent.

I was the first black man in twenty-nine years given a chance to get to the top.

My share was to be 17½ percent of the net receipts. Braddock was guaranteed $500,000 or an option of 50 percent of the gate and one-half of the movie and radio rights. He was the reigning champion and that was fair enough—if it had been the end of the deal.

The next day, the President of Madison Square Garden, John Reed Kilpatrick, put in a restraining order with the Federal Court saying Braddock's contract with Schmeling for June 3 had to go through.

Soon after that, Schmeling came in from Germany and offered Braddock $350,000 to fight him in Berlin in the early summer. Braddock wasn't thinking about going to Germany; he had a better deal here in America. So, Schmeling went on back but said he'd return to train in May for what he thought would be the June 3 match.

My last fight was February 17, and it was a long time till June 22. I had to hone down all those rough edges, and it was decided that the best way to do this was to go on a long exhibition tour. It was set up for thirty days, and twenty-one of those days I'd be fighting with my sparring partners. Some of those guys were Seal Harris, Leonard Dixon, Jack Wright, and Eddie Malcolm, all big guys, 200 pounds and over.

Mike Jacobs had made arrangements to hire a private railroad car which attached to a regular train at certain points. Real fancy set up. I felt like a king.

Throughout the early part of the tour, Chappie was pessimistic; he was cranky and irritable all the time. If I had known then what I know now, I'd realize he was just anxious—hoping like hell, but afraid to show it. When everything finally boiled down to a reality, Chappie became a different man; after all, he was going to train the man he considered the next heavyweight champion of the world. He came on tough and proud.

Chappie read me the riot act. I remember him saying

something like, "All right, you son of a bitch, you made it to here, and I'm going to see you make it all the way. When I finish with you, you're gonna be a fucking fighting machine!" I had never heard of a psychologist before, but I know now that's exactly what Chappie was.

First, he told me what was wrong with my fighting: I had a weakness for a right hand; I was always jabbing with my left and dropping it, leaving myself wide open for right-hand punches by my opponents. I had to change my pattern. I was always shuffling in, jabbing with a left and crossing with a right. This made me too predictable. He was going to teach me how, at the right time, to step back, weave, and counterpunch.

The next few months, Chappie and I were almost one person. He was completely devoted to his task, and I was just as blindly devoted to mine. If he had told me to jump off the Empire State Building during this period, I would have done it. I had total faith in him, especially after the Schmeling defeat. Chappie wasn't drinking and I wasn't fooling around. We had to accomplish the biggest goal a black athlete had a chance at.

Chappie made me put into practice all the things he had been preaching. Night after night, he stressed rolling under punches, weaving, stepping back, and countering. During the day, would you believe I was catching flies! Not like in baseball—I mean real flies. He told me not to catch them the same way every time. He was still worried about me dropping my left hand after jabbing. So, catching flies ought to be like picking off punches with both hands. It was good for my reflexes. I laugh now when I think about Chappie and my sparring partners looking all around for a swarm of flies, but it helped me.

But traveling around on tour is hard and boring. Me and the guys would sit around playing cards, telling lies, and listening to music. Man, if it hadn't been for the music, I don't know what I'd have done. I brought my Victrola. Hot damn! Let me tell you, that railroad car was all set up with outlets. They even had standby electricity for when we were parked.

I brought my Duke Ellington records and played my favorites, "Caravan" and "I've Got to Be a Rug Cutter," with my friend Ivie Anderson singing.

Then my favorite, Jimmie Lunceford. When we heard, "For Dancers Only," some of the guys would get up and dance around, and they'd clown around on "Posin'," but when Dan Grisson would sing, "I'll see you in my dreams,/Hold you in my dreams . . ." hell! I'd think of Marva and could hardly wait to get to the next town to call her up.

San Diego was the last stop. I learned more in those thirty days than I had in all my boxing career. My muscles were hard and tough, I had slimmed my waistline, and my reflexes were sharper than they had ever been. I was as fast as lightning (thanks to those flies!).

After the tour I was completely exhausted. I went straight to Julian Black's summer home in Stevensville, Michigan. Chappie and the guys were beat, too. They all went to their various ways until it was time to open camp. The first three days I think I must have slept straight through except to eat. I lounged around a couple of days, and then it was back to limited training, doing roadwork and chopping trees.

Earlier, my managers had made arrangements for me to train in the resort town of Lake Geneva, Wisconsin, seventy-five miles northwest of Chicago. There I was, training for the title, but the Geneva Lake Owners' Association put up such a stink that Julian Black said he wasn't taking me anywhere I wasn't wanted. They finally settled on something better—Kenosha, Wisconsin, on the shore of Lake Michigan. The house I was to stay in was in Chiwaukee, five miles south of Kenosha.

This house was something else again. It was owned by

Fred Fischer, a Chicago bed manufacturer. They say it cost about $100,000. When me and my managers, Carl Nelson my bodyguard, and Bill Bottoms, drove up to it, I laughed. Imagine me staying in a ten-room yellow brick Spanish-type summer home, with all kinds of expensive antique furniture, a pool, and a ping pong table! They had two bathrooms in each bedroom. You have to think back to that old outhouse in Alabama and wonder how sixteen people could use it.

We arrived in camp a few days before my birthday. I received a telegram from Chappie saying he'd be up in a few days, and Russell Cowans also telegraphed that he'd be up soon. My managers rented a small hotel for my sparring partners, and the stage was set.

Until Chappie and the rest arrived, I just did roadwork. Most of my work was done at the Kenosha Stadium. They had a quarter-mile cinder track. Later, a ring was set up in the middle of the stadium and exercise areas were arranged around it. There was a field house with showers, rubbing tables, and other equipment for training. In case of bad weather, they could set up a ring in the auditorium.

You know, during this time Jack Johnson was still running his mouth. I kept thinking back to the man and how nice he'd been to me. Now I read he was offering to be in Braddock's corner the night of the fight. There must have been some jealousy of me combined with his problems with Chappie and his attitude about himself. But you know something, I didn't dislike the man. I understood him and felt sorry.

Anyway he was telling anybody and any paper who'd listen to him that Braddock had everything in his favor, and what he lacked, Johnson'd bone him up on it. He'd advise Braddock from his corner, and this would unnerve me. With all his talking and such, Braddock never hired him. Nobody likes a poor, sore-ass loser.

My twenty-third birthday was May 13 and official training was to start May 14. Bill Bottoms made a great big beautiful cake and baked a bunch of chickens. Bill was telling me to eat all I wanted since I wouldn't start training till the next day. I stuck to my guns and told him I wasn't doing anything to jeopardize my body now. So I ate a regular portion of chicken and it broke my heart, but I only had one piece of cake.

When everybody arrived the next day we thought through the situation. I weighed 208 pounds, and I had to get to 200. I had to lose it slowly and evenly. Chappie wasn't the least bit interested in me boxing so much as conditioning myself. I had had all the boxing I needed on the tour.

There were lots of ways to condition myself: one round (three minutes) of shadow boxing, to start the perspiration flowing; three rounds with sparring partners; one round worked on the big bag; two rounds with the speed bag; two rounds skipping rope; two rounds of floor calisthenics. The purpose of all this was to build and keep up my endurance.

My manager and Mike Jacobs were behind me all the way. They knew the fight had to come off. Of course the Garden was saying, "No, no, no," and they put in for an injunction with the United States Court of Appeals. But Judge Guy T. Fake said the only valid contract was the one I had with Braddock. Maybe public pressure about Nazi Germany influenced him. I don't know. The Garden, of course, appealed Judge Fake's decision, but that appeal stuff takes time.

So, while the Garden was waiting for a decision, Schmeling came on over to Speculator, New York, to start training. The Garden must have thought they'd get their way, because they started selling tickets for the Braddock-Schmeling fight. It didn't work out, though; the Supreme Court upheld Judge Fake's decision. Reporters started saying that Schmeling had just been training for a "Phantom Fight."

Another important thing was that Judge Fake's decision broke up the monopoly the Garden had in the heavyweight division. They weren't all-powerful any more— Mike Jacobs was set up to be the next big shot in the heavyweight division.

When we started the public exhibition bouts about two weeks later, the press gave me a fit. They said I was dull, didn't have any spark, and looked like I didn't care. They didn't know that that was the plan. Chappie was trying to protect my hands from sprains and breaks. I wasn't to punch my sparring partners more than necessary. He had me concentrating on my defense against a right hand. Chappie, Roxborough, and Black wanted me to lay back and not cut loose or I'd get stale, but to let go my last three days of drills. I did not want to peak until the day of the fight.

I felt good. My wind was good, my legs had bounce.

June 22, 1937. I got up before ten and showered. Chappie, Julian Black, Roxy, Russell Cowans, Dr. Chester Ames, and Carl Nelson were waiting for me for breakfast. I came out of my room shadowboxing doing a poor imitation of Bill Robinson. Everybody was glad to see me looking happy and confident.

We were doing the last-minute packing when a car drove up with a special messenger. He had a slim square package in his hands addressed to me. Everybody rushed around and Chappie snatched it from me and tore it open. Inside there's a record. We read the label—"You Can't Take That Away from Me." It's signed, "James J. Braddock."

We jammed into three automobiles and headed for Zion City, Illinois, where a special North Shore Line train was waiting for us. Must have been a thousand people waiting there to cheer me on.

When we got on the train, those damn butterflies

started itching my stomach. I started talking about base-ball. The big series between the Cubs and Giants was opening at Wrigley Field the same day. I was talking, talking, talking; I was nervous as a novice fighter.

Finally, we got to Chicago and the weigh-in at the Auditorium Theater at a quarter to twelve, a little before Braddock. He came in and we were friendly with each other. I kidded him about the record. He looked at my ten-days' growth of beard and says, "Hey, Joe, you need a shave." I looked at him and said, "Hear you had a birth-day, Jimmy, you're thirty-two. I had a birthday too. I was twenty-three!" I weighed in at 197¼—perfect weight for me—and Braddock at 197. Joe Triner, Chairman of the State Athletic Commission, went over the rules. When the press asked how I was doing, I said, "I hope I win." Braddock said, "I'm in shape, Joe's in shape. There'll be a helluva fight tonight."

But his manager, Joe Gould, was acting like a perfect ass. He was trying to get in all the photographs and kept insulting me. He kept going back to that Schmeling fight and saying that I was always complaining about a sneak punch, but tonight Jimmy would give it to me clean, and it would be all over in a few minutes. I learned long ago to ignore this kind of crap; somebody's always trying to scare you. I stayed quiet and cool, although to tell you the truth I would love to have punched that little bastard out. He disappointed me.

Got home. Where the hell was Marva? The maid told me she was getting fixed up real pretty for me at the beauty parlor. At three o'clock, Bill Bottoms prepared dinner for me and my regular crowd. I ate a steak and salad and had a quart of milk and a cup of green tea. Went in my bedroom and slept till seven when Carl Nel-son woke me up. "Time to go," he said.

I liked Comiskey Park, it felt like coming home. Tickets were selling from $3.75 to $27.50 for ringside. A whole lot of black people helped to fill up those bleachers. They must have saved real hard to get that money together. Half of them must have been on welfare, but Lord knows what they sacrificed to see me. I had a responsibility to them. Later, I heard trains, cars and busloads of black people were coming from all over the country. All the black hotels were filled. Black people were sleeping in hotel lobbies, renting space to sleep over in night clubs and cafes. And there was a fair share of black people at ringside, those who could afford it—the gamblers, the doctors, the lawyers, the gangsters. Most of the black folks, though, were sitting around their radios, making little parties, chipping in on beer or booze, and waiting to cheer for me or cry for me.

All kinds of rumors were floating around the day of the fight. I had been picked two-to-one favorite. This was the first time a contender was favored over a heavyweight champion. But a lot of the press and people who had been to my camp were saying that I was acting "indifferent," that I had made all the money I needed. They said my training showed I just didn't care. A lot of other people said it was fixed and I'd never win because they wouldn't let a Negro be the heavyweight champion again.

None of those people knew me. I wanted that championship. I needed that championship. I am not a man without pride and ego; I know that prize money can make life sweeter.

I arrive at Comiskey Park and we headed straight for the White Sox dressing room. The room had been divided by a wooden partition, me on one side, Braddock on the other. I was thinking about the man next door, but I couldn't feel anything at all. I remember walking to the ring with my purple trunks and blue- and red-trimmed robe. Braddock had gone before me. It's usual for the challenger to enter the ring first, but I didn't. Braddock, after standing there for four or five minutes waiting for me, went in. I saw the back of his green robe with a shamrock on it as I started going to the ring. With me were Chappie, of

course, Carl Nelson, Julian Black, and John Roxborough.
We also got somebody special, Harry Lenny, a cut man.
Harry Lenny was a veteran fight manager, and he could
handle any kind of cut or bruise in the ring. People sometimes don't understand a cut man. He's an instant doctor,
and good ones are as hard to come by as a good regular
doctor.

After getting in the ring, Jack Dempsey, Gene Tunney,
Barney Ross, and my friends John Henry Lewis and Sixto
Escobar and some others were introduced. It seemed like
forever. When the bell rang and Jimmy made the sign of
the cross, I probably said a prayer in my head.

I remembered what Chappie had said in the dressing
room: "Don't get careless," "Keep your hands up," "Go get
him right away." Maybe I could get a knockout in the first
round while Braddock was still cold.

My main concern, like in all of my fights, was "How am
I going to start; who's going to land the first punch?"
Braddock came out fighting like he said he would. He
came charging after me, and I had to step back and box
him. I guess he wanted to convince me that he was not
afraid and that he was the champion. Coming out of a
clinch near the end of the round, I had him in the corner
beating on him, when he swung a short right uppercut to
my chin. Down I went. I said to myself, what the hell am
I doing here? I was hurt, but I bounced right up. Blackburn told me later I should have stayed down, to take
advantage of the count. But I guess I was in a hurry. I just
got up and went at it. My head was clear, not like when
Schmeling hit me. Funny, but I'd always wanted to get up
from a knockdown and win a fight.

Braddock thought he'd take me out now and he pushed
me on the ropes. He was a good right-hand puncher. The
knockdown made me mad. I staggered him with a left
hook and a right cross at the bell.

I could have finished him anytime after the first round.
Chappie kept saying, "Wait, wait . . . take it easy. He's

game and he knows a lot. Keep sticking and countering. Don't get in too close. Let him do the crowding. He'll come apart in five or six rounds. Take it easy. I'll tell you when to shoot."

In the second round Braddock brought the fight to me. I always felt he had my knockout by Max Schmeling on his mind; he figured that a few good punches on my chin would enable him to pull an upset. He was jabbing me good in this round. Until I started getting to him with solid left hooks and right hands to the jaw, I don't know what the hell held him up. In rounds three and four I just boxed him and took my time.

I could feel him slowing up in the fourth round. We were setting a terrific pace, and Braddock's age began to tell. Before the fifth, Chappie told me, "Pour it on him a little now. Be careful, and don't shoot all you've got, but let him have a little."

Braddock came out for the fifth round with his eyes puffed and a rip over the left side of his forehead. For a while, he traded me jab for jab.

When I went out for the sixth, Chappie told me to throw my right. So I fooled around and waited. Then I threw everything into the right, and it landed on his mouth, splitting his lip. He reeled but he kept his feet; I knew the end was near.

In the seventh, I kept winging that right hand when Braddock gave me an opening, and each time I put a little more steam on it. I was getting him ready for the kill. My left hook came in handy near the end of the round as Braddock was leaning over to get away from my right. It straightened him up, but the bell rang just as I was getting ready to throw the haymaker.

When the bell rang for the eighth round, he come out wide open. His legs were gone. He couldn't keep his arms up. Joe Gould kept yelling from the corner, "Keep your hands up! Keep your hands up!" But I knocked him out with a punch we called the D.O.A. (dead on his ass) in the gym when I was amateur. It was a left to the body and a right hand to the chin. The punch took him off his feet. He whirled in the air and fell on his face. I knew he couldn't get up.

I walked back to the farthest neutral corner with my back to Braddock. Referee Tommy Thomas counted him out in one minute and ten seconds, as I looked across the heads of the crowd in a complete daze. The one-time cotton picker was now the Heavyweight Champion of the entire World.

I don't remember going back to the dressing room. I started feeling light inside my body, but it wasn't from any blows I got in the ring. I never felt like this in my life. Chappie could see what was coming and pushed me to the rubbing table; I was about to faint. I guess everything came down on me then. I read in the paper the next day that reporters came in and had to "wake me up" because I had just won the heavyweight championship and then had gone to sleep. Damn! What do they think I am? Only thing I remembered saying then was, "Bring on Max Schmeling. Bring him on."

Then the room was filled with reporters and a lot of other people. They tell me that there were governors from all over the country, mayors from all the big cities, society people, movie stars, and baseball players. What I liked more was that I heard that 20,000 tickets had been sold to black people. I thought I was hell before, but this feeling I had now made me feel humble, and I wanted to go home to Marva and talk to my momma on the phone. Through all the fog, though, I remember Chappie saying, "I'm gonna take this right glove. I earned it." I was too tired to argue with him about it, and he was right. He had earned it.

Getting out of the stadium was one thing, trying to get to my home on South Michigan Avenue was something else. I thought all of Chicago was standing outside my house. The cheers, the yells almost had me crying. Marva and I had to come out, I don't know how many times, and wave at the people. Black people were calling out saying, "We got another chance," "Don't be another Jack Johnson," "We're depending on you." Some of the whites around shouted, "Congratulations," and asked for my autograph.

Finally it was time to get back in the house before I collapsed. Marva had a few guests, my sister and her sister and a young woman reporter, and some of my cronies who came home with me were there. She had set up a real beautiful buffet table, but before I could enjoy my guests, I got to the phone and put through a long distance call to my mother in Detroit. Momma was so excited. First off she asked if I had been hurt. When I told her no, she said she hoped to God I hadn't hurt Braddock too much. Then she went on to congratulate me. She said there were hundreds of people outside her home at 2100 McDougall Avenue calling for her. She had to go out and wave to them, and they cheered her. I told her I was leaving Chicago by car with Marva Thursday morning for Detroit and would stay a few days with her. Momma said, "Good. Now I can go to bed."

People all over were celebrating the win—in Chicago they stayed up all night shouting and running through the streets. They burned bonfires on corners, they drove taxis all over; they say that a thousand people were out all night. And in Harlem—thousands and thousands marched up Seventh and down Lenox all night long!

The day after the fight my hands woke me up at six A.M. They hurt so bad I had to soak them in hot water three or four times. Then it was time to get ready to attend a press meeting Mike Jacobs had called at the Morrison Hotel.

When I walked in, everybody applauded. They showed newsreels of the fight and read a batch of telegrams from all over the United States. All kinds of offers were given to me, stage offers, movie offers, radio offers, offers to referee fights at $1,000 a bout. About $500,000 was put up for grabs. And just to think, five years before, I was happy to get those seven-dollar merchandise checks for a fight. Mike Jacobs signed me to a new five-year contract calling for four fights a year.

Life was beautiful, but then I get a real shocker: Some social workers from Lafayette, Alabama, got in touch with me. They told me my father, Munroe Barrow, was alive and had been in their care since 1915. I hate to say this, but it didn't mean too much to me; I never saw him. They told me he was in pitiful condition, and the state had been paying for his keep all this time. I sent my oldest sister Susie down to check all this out. When she came back, she said, yes, he was our father; everybody in the family looked just like him. So I sent a lump of money to the Searcy Institution and agreed to pay the thirty dollars a month that was needed for his care. He died sometime in 1938, and I took care of all the arrangements. But for me and the entire family, Pat Brooks, Sr., was our father.

Marva, me, and Carl Nelson took off for Detroit. My stepbrother, Pat Brooks, drove, as he was to do until the day I retired. This worked out fine, since Roxy and Black had barred me from driving when they heard that me and Freddie Guinyard were seen traveling ninety miles an hour around Chicago.

We sneaked into Detroit that night and into Momma's side door. She and the church sisters had prepared a feast for me. There were chickens and hams, candied yams, macaroni and cheese, salad, collard greens, pies, cakes, and ice cream. I must have eaten a whole chicken and a half and most of the ice cream by myself. Momma was so happy and proud. Carl Nelson kept telling me I was eating too much, and I had to remind him I wasn't in training. With all the activity and such going on around the house, people and relatives coming in and out, the rest of Detroit knew I was there and started hanging around the house. It got so fans would sleep outside Momma's house all night just to get a glimpse of me. Couple of times we had to get the police so I could get out of the house.

Seemed like every time I looked up, Momma was letting somebody in the house who said they were a cousin of mine. I think Momma let anybody in who said they were from Alabama. They came by car, bus, and train. I was beginning to think I'd have to buy Momma an extra house to put up all these "relatives." Most of them were poor black people who needed money. And I had plenty money so I gave it out.

After several days at Momma's, I headed for Washington, D.C., to see my friend John Henry Lewis defeat Willie Reddish. Then I went to New York to talk with Mike Jacobs about my first fight as a champion; Mike told me he was going to try to get me Tommy Farr or Len Harvey in London and have the fight over there. I was excited about the fight as well as the chance to get to England. It boiled down to Mike's selecting Tommy Farr, the Heavyweight Champion of the British Isles. It didn't work out that easily, though. A British promoter, General Critchley, had an agreement for a bout between Schmeling and Farr; the winner of that fight would get to me. Schmeling wanted that fight with Farr bad. He figured he'd clear out the European heavyweight division by beating Farr and get a crack at the heavyweight title he'd lost. Besides, he figured I was easy game. Then, too, if he took on Farr, he'd knock me out of a good money-making deal, and if he won, he'd be in a position to demand a lot of money in his fight against me.

In the meantime, while all these negotiations were going on, Ellwood Rigby, a Pittsburgh promoter, offered me a $450,000 guarantee to meet with John Henry Lewis. I would get $100,000 up front as soon as I signed the contract, plus $1,000 training-expense money. The deal looked awfully good to me, but Mike nixed it. He said two black fighters wouldn't draw a big enough gate. I didn't believe this because in 1936 John Henry Lewis and Al Gainer, a black man, drew a big crowd in Pittsburgh. I figured we'd do well in either Pittsburgh, Chicago, or New York. As a result of Mike's thinking that way, it threw out the possibility of me fighting Tiger Jack Fox, Eddie Blunt, or Leroy Haynes, all high-ranking heavyweights.

Meanwhile, Mike was making trans-Atlantic phone calls and sending cables to London; I don't know exactly what went down, but Mike sent his attorney and cousin Sol Strauss over to London, and when he came back he had a signed, sealed contract from Tommy Farr. He was to meet me anywhere in the United States. They offered Farr $60,000, four round-trip tickets, plus 25 percent of the movie and radio rights. The guarantee doubled the London offer. Farr had told the London papers that I was the real world heavyweight champion regardless of what anyone said, and that's why he wanted to fight me instead of Schmeling. The fight was scheduled for August 26 at Yankee Stadium.

I had a little time before settling into training and so I called Marva and told her to pack her bags and come with me on tour with my Brown Bomber Softball Team. I didn't think she was all that happy about going, but it was one way we could be together. Rough, traveling and living out of a car. She was a game gal, though, and yelled over the phone, "Don't tell me to pack. Don't you know by this time I always have a bag packed? You just tell me where to meet you with it." We met the guys in Cleveland and went on with them to Toledo and left them in Cincinnati.

I had to get my mind back on boxing, and it was too early to open camp, so me and Roxy and a couple of guys headed for Julian Black's summer home in Stevensville, Michigan, to start me conditioning myself to get ready for Farr.

JOE LOUIS: MY LIFE

By the time camp opened in Pompton Lakes, there were some new changes which worked out well. Nobody, I mean nobody, had ever seen Tommy Farr fight. Only thing I knew about him was that he was born in Wales, was twenty-three years old, same age as me, weighed 208 pounds and was six-feet one and a half inches. He'd been working in the coal mines over there since he was thirteen. He was rough. We seemed to be a perfect match for one another. He was probably just as poor and hungry as I had been, and he surely knew fighting was the only way out for him. Another thing we had in common was that we both had beat Max Baer. He defeated him in twelve rounds in London that spring.

It was important that I have the right kind of sparring partners. Mike Jacobs and Chappie felt that most of the guys I had before just couldn't cut it, and that's where Mannie Seamon came in. Jacobs and my managers got Mannie to be in charge of my sparring partners. Some were just big punching bags for me. Mannie had trained Benny Leonard, the one-time lightweight champion.

We didn't know what kind of style Farr was going to use, and Chappie was determined that we'd train for all of them. Mannie Seamon's job was to see to it that I had the right kind of guys to work with. Mannie was an old-fashioned trainer; he believed the only way to train was to box with partners who could fight back. He had them going through the same routines I did. They were up doing roadwork, hitting the big bag, the speed bag, and doing the floor exercises just like me. Hell, they were getting paid twenty-five dollars a day. Believe me, for that amount of money in those days, they really earned it. If they didn't do well, Mannie told 'em it would be nothing to get somebody else.

One of my sparring partners, Marty Gallagher, was the kind of fighter Chappie thought Farr would be and we really used him hard. Gallagher was the rough-tough type. He was always tugging, butting, elbowing and mauling; it was hard to box him at a long range. So far I'd never had anybody who fought me at close range regularly, except maybe Adolph Wiater, who went the ten round limit with me.

I worked hard, and I have many rich memories from that training session. Joe Di Maggio, Jesse Owens, and, of course, my man, Bill Robinson, all came to the camp. I think back now, all those years ago. We were all young men and had so much power, and we didn't even know we had it in its full strength. I remember when Babe Ruth came up. We talked about golf (my managers wouldn't let me bring my clubs up) and what a pain in the ass training can be. He said I should have gone into baseball. It wasn't as dangerous as fighting. There'd be less a chance to hurt your eyes and chin. Once, while I was sparring with Tiger Hairston, I yelled over to Babe and said, "Watch me hit a home run." Then I wheeled around and knocked Hairston flat down. Babe looked at me and said, "Done."

My next-to-last workout, I looked out over the crowd and saw Max Schmeling, whispering to his trainer, Max Machon. They watched me and whispered some more. Max didn't know how bad I wanted him in that ring right then. Later he came over to me and we talked. Marva was visiting the camp that day and I introduced them. When I remembered how upset Marva had been about his defeating me, I didn't know what to expect. But as usual Marva was cool. In fact, later on she told what a gentle, quiet man he was. She understood that fighting is just a business, and was confident enough now to see me fight Farr. Later on me and Max and Mike Jacobs posed for a picture around the pool table. Max and I were talking about things I'd read in the paper about Nazi Germany and the Aryan race being the only pure race. Shoot! Max told me he never said those things and wouldn't think them. I believed him because he's been my friend since then, and we stay, even to this day, in touch with one another. He looked at fighting the way I did. It was just a contest to see who's the strongest, the cleverest, the luckiest, and the best trained.

Still you have to toot your horn. He told the press I could still be hit with a right hand. I told him he'd have his chance, but he said that he thought he could make some money in Europe. Then he said, real disappointedly, "I want the championship and I know I can get it, but they're gonna make me wait another year." I wanted the match too because I intended to beat the hell out of him so there'd be no doubt. But like everything else, you have to bide your time.

In the meantime Tommy Farr was driving Mike Jacobs straight up a wall. This cat was so sure of himself he wouldn't spar with headgear or a mouthpiece. Mike was nervous he'd hurt himself and the fight would have to be postponed. Finally, after the first week Tommy Farr listened to Mike and put on the proper gear.

I have to explain something here. A lot of people thought Mike Jacobs was pushing me into fighting again too soon after winning the championship. Usually a title holder sits tight for a while and can make good money on endorsements and such. Now Mike Jacobs had nothing to do with me fighting Farr so soon—two months and four days after getting the title. It was Roxy and Black who wanted me to defend my championship. I was the first black heavyweight champion since Jack Johnson; I had to prove myself. It works like this: If you're black and at the top, you gotta be superman. You have to be extra, you always have to prove yourself. You have to constantly show the world you're worthy. No way I could have slid by like Braddock, sitting on my championship, for two years. Always had to reaffirm my right to be where I was. I've been all over the world, and believe me America is the greatest country there is, but they still have their hang ups about blacks and slavery. You can't be average or even good to make it; you have to be something special. So when you think about all that, you can understand Roxy and Black pushing Mike Jacobs for the Farr meet.

Anyway, August 26. We go down to the State Building on Worth Street in New York for the weigh-in. Tommy Farr was 207 pounds and I was at my best weight—198. I'm peaking.

The gate receipts were at least $50,000 under what Jacobs expected—another foggy, wet day. Also, the sporting crowd was up at the Saratoga races, which were running through Saturday. Mike checked the weather reports for the next day or so. Not good. He decided to postpone the fight till Monday, so the weather would be better and all the money people would be back in town. I'm not especially happy about this because I remember when I fought Schmeling and we had to postpone the fight because of weather. But what's to do?

We headed on back to Pompton Lakes and I had to hold my peak until Monday. I'd been training hard for a month now. I'd boxed more than eighty rounds and I was down to 198 pounds. Chappie to the rescue—he's got a four-day plan. I box Thursday and Friday to keep my timing up; I get back on roadwork for my legs. Thing is, though, everything has to be cool, I have to avoid overworking.

Monday, August 31. The boxing commission says me and Farr have to weigh in again because there's a law that says a postponement of over forty-eight hours makes it necessary. Roxy was pissed off. He didn't want to tire me out. He figured the postponement alone would get me too anxious. I don't know, what the hell. I was feeling fine and really wasn't worried.

We went back to the State Building and weighed in again.

Chappie had started preaching to me that morning, and when I got in my dressing room, he was still preaching. I remember him telling me not to put my ass on my shoulder—to leave my pride in the dressing room. He told me I'd fucked up in Chicago with Braddock, and he'd remind me of it until the day he died.

I was sitting in my corner getting prepped, and he was still talking about when Braddock dropped me in the first round. He reminded me I'd jumped up like a jackass instead of taking the count so I could get myself together. "False pride" he was softly yelling in my ear, "a younger man than Braddock would have caught you and you'd never be where you are today. If you get knocked down, take the nine count. Remember, I think this guy's a crowder—remember what I told you when you were sparring with Gallagher." Damn it, Chappie is always right.

Tommy Farr fooled me. He was one tough guy, with a peculiar style. He didn't look too effective, yet he was puzzling and his punches were annoying.

In the first two rounds I let him lead and I sized him up, concentrating on jabs. After jabbing him into position in the third, I cut loose with a right, and it landed high, catching his head. I bruised my knuckles as a result and I couldn't use my right hand effectively. If I hadn't hurt my right, I'd knocked him out within five. I just kept jabbing and jabbing and cut his face with the punches.

I took some neat shots from him in the fourth. He really surprised me by rushing out at the gong. But I'd work my left and hold him off.

In the fifth I hit him with a left hook, which to me was the hardest punch I landed all night. I drove it into him with everything I had.

I knew he was hurt and I banged in three more left hooks, one mashed in his body. He grabbed for my arms, and I knew I'd hurt him. It was then and there that I needed a sound right hand. I threw it. But there was nothing on it. I hit him with another left to the body and doubled him up. I was trying frantically to finish him. But he had balls. He seemed to grit his teeth and fight back like a bulldog.

He beat me in the sixth by actually taking the play away from me, rushing out of his corner and punching like a son of a bitch. He hit me with some hard punches that round. He was a good socker.

In the seventh I hurt him again with left hooks, and he was just hanging on when the bell sounded. I hurt my left hand in the seventh, but I don't remember how.

In the eighth Farr came flying out of his corner once more, and it annoyed the hell out of me. He banged me with some good shots.

From the ninth round to the twelfth I just kept sticking and sticking. I had a bruised and swollen eye and I did not intend to take any chances by mixing it with him. Near the end of the thirteenth, I caught him with some good left hooks and right uppercuts. He was hurt. But the round was almost over. I knew it was my last chance to score a knockout, so I just spent the last two rounds boxing him to protect my lead.

Farr stayed the fifteen rounds with me, when everybody thought he couldn't do it. I thought I won the fight, Tommy felt he did. I felt I kept my title by beating him with jabs. Farr was probably the best-conditioned heavyweight to come out of England. He was tough and he had a lot of heart. He took a punch as well as anybody I ever hit.

I was very disgusted with myself as I lay on the rubbing table in my dressing room after the fight. I was far from satisfied with my showing against him. But I won the fight.

Dr. Vincent Nardiello and William Walker of the Athletic Commission and Dr. Chester Ames, my personal doctor, all agreed that I had suffered aggravated bone bruises in the right hand and said I'd have to put it in a plaster cast for about one month. You know me, I just kept that cast on about two weeks. Can't stand being confined or even staying in one place too long.

Caught the two A.M. plane for Detroit to see Henry Armstrong K.O. Orville Drouillard in five rounds.

By this time I was worn out. Me, my managers, and Mike Jacobs felt it was time to take a rest for about six months. It had been a steady grind for me for the last year, and then some. I'd hardly spent any time with my wife, and my mind needed to clear of fighting for a while.

Marva was always after me to save my money, invest, and stop giving so much money away. I told her it was my brains getting rattled, not hers, so it was my money and I'd do what I wanted with it. Anyway, she went on and bought an apartment building at 43–20 South Michigan Avenue for $15,000. She was right when she said there was no point in our paying rent when we could own our own house. Marva set to work decorating this house. I think that made her happy and it kept her busy. She really did a fantastic job; she always had excellent and expensive taste. It was furnished in antiques, beautiful rugs, heavy drapes. It was elegant and I loved it. She even had a special bed made for me. Using antique furniture, she got a carpenter to extend a bed to seven feet and had a special mattress made to fit. You know something? She's still got it.

Meanwhile, the picture I made back in 1936, *The Spirit of Youth* finally premiered at major movie houses. Marva belonged to the Joe Louis Service Guild. They collected money and I contributed heavily to the organization. The Guild made up packages of food and clothing to give to the poor people. Marva got the owner of a theater on Thirty-fifth Street to give all the proceeds of *The Spirit of Youth* to the organization on opening night. He even changed the name of the movie house to the Joe Louis Theater. It was one swell affair and a big financial success. I was proud of myself. Hell, I was a handsome dog in that movie, and I was proud of Marva for getting together such an elegant affair and helping the poor people.

Then a few days after the Farr fight, Mike Jacobs finally got Max Schmeling to agree to meet me. What it broke down to was that Schmeling had wanted 30 percent of the gate and Mike had said no, 20 percent.

Mike told Schmeling to get into line or he'd start a series of elimination tournaments, kicking it off with a Jimmy Braddock-Max Baer match in October, and then he'd throw in Tommy Farr, Bob Pastor, Natie Brown, and Jimmy Adamick. Schmeling would have to wait his turn. After that Schmeling agreed to sign. The fight would take place the next summer. In addition to getting 20 percent of the gate receipts, movie and radio, the contract called for me and Schmeling to have a couple of tune-up fights just before our bout, but not with any real tough fighters who could possibly upset the apple cart.

Now I'm really satisfied—it's finally going to happen.

Got a phone call from Mike Jacobs. He wanted to make sure I was going to attend his "Carnival of Champions" at the Polo Grounds on September 23. He must have known I wouldn't miss that. There were going to be four title fights held that night: the Lightweight Division, the Welterweight, the Middleweight, and the Bantamweight.

He's had the Heavyweight Division—me—and he had the best contenders: Pastor, Schmeling, and Farr. Fifty-thousand people came out and paid $300,000, but Mike lost money. He overpaid the fighters in guarantees, but that didn't bother Mike. He knew what he was doing. He'd been tickled pink by the Farr fight. There was absolutely no bullshit about it and he wanted a return bout with Farr in June, 1938.

JOE LOUIS: MY LIFE

Mike had Yankee Stadium tied up, he had the Garden Bowl in Long Island, and the Polo Grounds. Finally Bill Carey, Commissioner of the New York Sanitation Department and one-time head of the Garden, got Mike and Colonel John Reed Kilpatrick, President of Madison Square Garden, together. Mike was so powerful nobody could ignore him anymore, and he finally gained control of Madison Square Garden. Jimmy Johnston would no longer be the top man in promoting boxing.

Mike got what he wanted, and he got me what I wanted. I helped him make it there, and he never forgot it. Plenty of times later, between fights, when I'd need money—ten to twenty to thirty thousand dollars—he never refused or lectured me. I remember one time I went to see Mike and he was hurrying around trying to get to the airport. I told him I'd drive out with him. I even offered to carry his coat because he had his briefcase and all. When we got to the airport I said, "Mike, lend me $10,000." He laughed as he signed his check and said, "For $10,000 I could have carried my own coat."

God, I was enjoying myself. Me and Marva stayed over in New York. There was the Yankee-Giant World Series. We had a lot of fun together that time. I think Marva bought out Saks Fifth Avenue. Then there were the private parties and dinners. Billy Taub, the tailor, had me looking like a king wished he looked. We didn't go out too much in public, though, because we couldn't have any privacy, and Lord knows, our marriage needed it.

What else do I remember about that year? Yeah! I went around with my Brown Bomber Softball Team. When we got to Philadelphia that October, they had a gigantic crowd. People came out because they knew I'd be playing. There were too many people and the stands collapsed. Nobody was killed, and I took care of the few people that got hurt.

Later on that year, I think it was December, the bus

broke down again in California. The team was broke and Roxy and Black told me to forget it. I'd already lost over $50,000 investing in them.

I felt real bad. Those guys were my friends. So when I got them back to Detroit, I saw to it that I got them jobs at Ford and the Sanitation Department. Those I couldn't get jobs for, I helped support until they could do better.

In the fall of 1937 I got a call from Hollywood asking me to come out and just appear in a Joe Palooka movie. Joe Palooka was a comic strip character who was the portrayal of a heavyweight champion, a white, blond guy. I remember the picture. I was a fighter in the gym punching the speed bag. Leon Errol played the role of Knobby Walsh, Palooka's manager. Anyway, ·in the movie, he walks in the gym and sees me hitting the bag, voom, voom, voom, and he walks by me and says something like, "Give it up, kid, you'll never make it." We had to do I don't know how many takes because we all fell out laughing everytime he said it. Errol was a real funny guy, and I liked Joe Kirkwood, Jr., who played Palooka, very much. I even gave him some pointers for his fight scenes.

It was a ball. John Barrymore and me became good friends. And, oh, the women again. I don't know. You know, there's something about women and men who can't resist each other. Now I'm older, I know it's just an ego trip. A big movie star would see me, the Heavyweight Champion of the World, and wonder how I am in the bed. I'd see a big beautiful movie star and wonder how she is in the bed. We would find out very easily. These were just one-night stands. But we both knew to keep it cool. Neither of us could afford to be found out in America in those days. However, some of those one-night stands went on for weeks. Marva got a lot of expensive presents.

Anyway, while I was out there in California, I was invited by Arthur Stebbins, an insurance executive, to play golf at the Hillcrest Golf Club in Los Angeles. I was the first black man to play there. Usually a member could invite a guest to play once a month, but they told me I could play anytime I wanted to; gradually I made a lot of changes in golf club "rules." But, anyway, there was Jimmy Durante, his partner Lou Clayton (of Clayton, Jackson & Durante), Eddie Cantor, and Al Jolson, who was absolutely crazy and funny. He bet that if he beat you, he'd pee on you. I made sure I didn't lose, because I saw him actually pee on some guy after the guy had lost. Between Durante, Jolson, and Cantor, I nearly died of laughing.

Well, it was time to head back home. When I got there, my sister Emmarell met me; she asked me to stake her to opening up a hat shop in Detroit. I knew she had a good business head and I respected her like my mother. It worked out for Emmarell, and I felt good about it. I didn't forget all those fifty-cent pieces she gave me when I was an amateur fighter and needed that money for my gym locker.

My sister Eulalia was another story altogether. Eulalia was a real good-looking woman. And she was an out-and-out swinger. I had noticed earlier that she had taken to drinking some, but I didn't realize how much. Marva knew more about it than I did. Whenever Eulalia needed money she'd come to Chicago, stay a few days, and head back home. Or so I thought. Later I found out Marva would drive her to the train, put her on, and she'd just ride to the next stop and come back into Chicago. She was hanging out with some bad people. Everything really came to a head when she stole one of Marva's fur coats. Marva had to call down to the railroad station and have them hold the train until she got there. Sure enough, there was Eulalia with Marva's coat on. That almost made me sick. I remember Eulalia trying to take me to school when I was a little boy and being what a big sister should be. I knew Eulalia's husband had died that year, and she was getting more depressed than ever, so I got her into a special private hospital in Windsor, Ontario, just across from Detroit, to try to straighten her out. My mother was sick about it and visited her regular to give her support. While in the hospital, Eulalia studied the Bible, and that saved her. Now she's a member of the Bahai religious sect, and she's been all over the world representing them. I'm proud of Eulalia. Thank God I had the money to help her. That's what money is all about, isn't it?

Family is something else. I remember one day during this time me and my brother Lonnie were at Momma's house. We got to arguing about something silly. Lonnie was a little taller than me, but we were both built the same way. Anyway, we were going at it real strong. Momma says, "Please stop the fussing." She said it three times. Then she hauled off and gave me a right to the jaw that shut me up. She said she didn't care what kind of world champion I was, she was the champion in her home.

In between all this stuff, though, I never forgot Max Schmeling. He was always in the back of my mind. He'd humiliated me. Russell Cowans and I'd read the papers; the war the Germans were pushing was getting bigger and bigger. I didn't like this. Max was taking on the responsibility for what Germany represented. That was too bad, because I knew Max just wanted to be world champion.

Meantime, it's party time. New Year's Eve. I opened up the Chicken Shack at 424 Vernon Highway in Detroit. I didn't need this Chicken Shack, but I was concerned about my friends; it was still 1937 and black people were getting nowhere. Sonny Wilson, a friend of mine, used to have a little bar on Hastings Street, but that closed. He convinced me that with my name, he could run a profitable business. I went along with him on the condition that he hire some of my old friends who were having a tough time, like Thurston McKinney and such. It was a real successful business. A lot of city officials used to come out and have conferences and settle city strikes right there at the Chicken Shack.

I remember the day we opened. It was hectic and haggard. We were looking forward to the big-time New Year's Eve crowd. Man, the people came dressed in white ties, fancy gowns, and all. Lot of famous people I can't remember came, too. Only thing, though, we forgot to order enough chickens. I was having a good time and the people were happy, but at 11:30, I put on my top hat, stepped into a chauffeured limousine, picked up my mother, and went to Calvary Baptist Church to welcome in 1938.

1938

SECOND SCHMELING FIGHT

O K. I'D HAD MY FUN NEW YEAR'S EVE. NOW IT'S 1938 and I was getting myself prepared for my return fight with Max Schmeling. I knew it was going to be almost six straight months of training. This time I didn't care. I could do without the girls, especially for what I knew I could achieve. My head was in the right place.

Only thing I was feeling down about was that my secretary, tutor and friend, Russell Cowans, said he couldn't make it with me any more. He was tired of traveling; after all, he had a family too. And he figured with all the exposure I'd had, I really didn't need him any more. Seemed like he'd gotten a good offer for a newspaper job in Chicago, and that's really what he wanted to go back to. I missed him like hell, but he taught me some good habits. I knew to read the papers every day and at least I had an idea of what was going on in the world besides what's in the funnies.

First tune up fight was with Nathan Mann on February 23 at Madison Square Garden. He was a good opponent for me. He took the first round, because I was trying to feel him out. Then he made his mistake in the second. If I catch you, I have you. He had a hell of a right hand and he did hurt me in the second round, but I dropped him anyway. He took a nine count, and when the third round came up he was still in there. Mann shouldn't have tried to slug it out with me. In the third I knocked him down twice for a two and a three count. Then I hit him with a left hook that put him out for good.

JOE LOUIS: MY LIFE

On April 1 I met with Harry Thomas at the Chicago Stadium. He was a tough guy. It took Schmeling eight rounds the past December to K.O. Thomas. I had a rough five rounds with that guy, but I had him out three rounds less than Schmeling.

Right around this time I felt perfect, absolutely perfect. I was finally the fighting machine Chappie had promised to make me. Schmeling wasn't doing too bad, either. In January he decisioned Ben Foord and in April he K.O.'d Steve Dudas in five. Both his fights were in Hamburg, Germany.

From what I could gather, reading the papers and listening to people talk, the whole world was looking to this fight between me and Schmeling. Germany was tearing up Europe, and we were hearing more and more about the concentration camps for the Jews. A lot of Americans had family in Europe and they were afraid for their people's lives. Schmeling represented everything that Americans disliked, and they wanted him beat and beat good. Now here I was, a black man. I had the burden of representing all America. They tell me I was responsible for a lot of change in race relations in America. Black and white people were talking about my fights; they were talking about me as a person, too. I guess I looked good to them. White Americans—even while some of them still were lynching black people in the South—were depending on me to K.O. Germany.

During this period I had to go to a dinner in Washington, D.C. I had a personal invitation from the President of the United States, Franklin D. Roosevelt. He sent a private car for me, and I met him in the White House. He felt my muscles and said, "Joe, we're depending on those muscles for America." Let me tell you, that was a thrill. Now, even more, I knew I had to get Schmeling good. I had my own personal reasons, and the whole damned country was depending on me.

[137]

Sometime early in May, Schmeling arrived by boat to settle up the contract and start training. Man, did he catch hell. There must have been hundreds of people picketing him on the dock. They had all kinds of signs saying that he shouldn't be allowed in the United States, that he represented Nazi Germany, and that he didn't belong here. And then when Max got over to the Hippodrome to meet with Mike, they had hundreds more pickets walking around in front of the building.

Mike Jacobs was having one hell of a time, too. They had Jewish people on committees threatening Mike, telling him they'd ruin his business. Mike's a smart guy. He got some of the committee people together and had a long set-to with them. He told them that since Max represented Germany, and I represented America, we'd have to fight. He told them that I'd win without a doubt, and then we'd really prove who's the "Master Race." But I don't think he was talking about black or white, rather, America and Germany. He must have done some strong talking because the groups pulled out, and we already had $100,000 advance ticket sales from all over the country.

I damn sure wanted to get to Schmeling. I've been to New York at least five times to try and sign this deal up. If I hadn't have been champion, I don't think he would have come around. I remember Mike offering him $300,000 to fight me in 1936. Schmeling got on his high horse and said he wanted a $600,000 guarantee. This was impossible and Schmeling knew it; he didn't want to fight me again. He'd won, but I looked over those films. For ten rounds I was going around with my hands down. He should have had me out long before. Now, I know Max looked at those films, too; if it took him all that time to knock me out, he was making some big mistakes also. He wasn't that anxious for the fight because he knew that I had defended my title successfully three times.

We signed the necessary papers at the Boxing Commissioner's Office, and the match was set for June 22. Mike picked Yankee Stadium for the fight because it had a bigger capacity than any other well-known stadium in America. Plus, the New York City fans always heavily supported Mike's fights, and he felt they should have the break.

Mike told me all the stuff that was going on around the fight. He had his whole reputation and a lot of money tied up in it. He said he had told those protest groups that I was a cinch to knock out Schmeling and that I'd vindicate the bad things happening to the Jews and put America in line as the top dog in any kind of war. Then he told me that if I didn't win this fight my career might be about over, and he'd be out of business. The last thing he said was, "Murder that bum, and don't make an asshole out of me." I told Mike, "Don't worry about a thing. I ain't going back to Ford to work, and you ain't gonna go back to selling lemon drops on the Staten Island Ferry."

With all that I headed out for West Baden Springs, Indiana, for a week of getting ready to train. Just a lot of roughing around. Chopping wood, running. Getting my sleep and my eating pattern together. Then it was on to Pompton Lakes for the real training, around the middle of May.

My entourage was growing. Seamon, Chappie's assistant, had my sparring partners lined up. Freddie Wilson, John Henry Lewis's former trainer, was in there helping out, too. My managers and my chef were all ready to go now.

Chappie had my sparring partners throwing hard right hands at me. He wanted to make sure I wouldn't be a sucker for Schmeling's right. I just sparred and sparred with my partners, with them constantly throwing those right hands. Got so I could easily block them. In the meantime all kinds of crazy shit was going on. Some Bundists were hanging around. Can you believe, these were white Americans agreeing with what Hitler was doing? The Bund had a camp up at Speculator, New

York, and they'd come to my camp day after day with Swastikas on their arms. They watched me train and sat around laughing like jackasses. But it would have taken more than those fools to unnerve me at this stage. I understood the whole political setup, knew what they were trying to do, but I knew what I had to do. I don't rattle easily.

I heard about Schmeling's camp, too. I understood his trainer, Max Machon, went strutting around in a Nazi uniform, especially after public sessions. The papers said Max was yelling about being a member of a superior race and making some general insults about my race. But Max never talked that shit to me.

Well, anyway, I think every sportswriter was at my camp or Schmeling's, asking all kinds of questions. All bullshit to me. You have to understand how I felt at that time. I knew my body was in prime condition. I knew—I didn't think, I *knew*—I was going to beat Schmeling. The mind is a powerful thing. From the tip of my toes to the last hair on my head, I had complete confidence.

I remember the night before we broke camp, my good friend and a damn good sportswriter, Jimmy Cannon of New York, said, "I'm betting a knockout in six rounds." I held up one finger. "It goes in one," I said.

On June 22, the morning of the fight, they woke me up at nine o'clock. My bodyguard, Carl Nelson, knocked on the door. I went downstairs, and I only had a glass of orange juice. We headed for New York City at ten. Chappie, Roxie, Julian Black, and Carl Nelson were all in the car. Three state troopers escorted us in.

We got to the Boxing Commissioner's office for the weigh-in at eleven. When I got out of the car, there was a crowd of people on the sidewalk. They yelled, "Go get him, Joe," "Good luck, Joe." Schmeling was there, and I weighed in at 198¾ pounds, Schmeling at 193. We just nodded to one another. There were no insults thrown around.

JOE LOUIS: MY LIFE

After the weigh-in, I went to Mal Frazier's apartment at 66 St. Nicholas Place. We had lunch at three o'clock. I ate a big steak and a salad Bill Bottoms fixed. Then me, Chappie, and Freddie Wilson took a long walk down the Speedway next to the Harlem River. Freddie Wilson asked me, "How you feel, Joe?" I told him, "I'm scared." He said, "Scared?" I said, "Yeah, I'm scared I might kill Schmeling tonight."

At seven o'clock we went to the stadium. I took a quick nap. I had to reserve all my energy and make sure I didn't lose any weight. Nine o'clock, Chappie woke me and started bandaging my hands, saying, "Keep cool. It's going to be alright." Mike Jacobs popped in and said, "Joe, I told these folks you're gonna knock that German out. Don't make a sucker out of me, and make it a quick knockout."

While Chappie was bandaging my hands, I said, "In three rounds, Chappie. If I don't have Schmeling knocked out, you better come in and get me, because after that, I'm through." I had made up my mind that for three rounds I was going to let it all go out. I was going to stay on top of him. I meant to put into practice everything Chappie had taught me. Chappie said, "No, it's alright. You can go fifteen rounds." I told Chappie I had no intention of pacing myself; it was going to be all or nothing and I knew my whole career depended on this, right now. Chappie wanted to make sure I was warmed up. Usually I just shadow boxed for ten minutes. This time I shadow boxed a half an hour, right up to the time I went up to the ring. I put on a flannel robe to keep my body warm and, for show, I put my blue silk robe over that.

So when I walked down that aisle to get to my corner and heard all those cheers of 70,000 people, I knew I'd have to make it.

Before the bell rang, I felt like a racehorse in the starting gate. Chappie kept me moving. Kept me dancing. The sweat was pouring, but my body was warm. The muscles were dancing too. I was rarin' to go. In round one I came out of my corner quickly and wasted no time getting at Schmeling. It took me less than five seconds to get myself together. I hit him with two left hooks to the face that snapped his head back, then I banged a right to his jaw. He threw a right hand that I blocked and tried a left to my head that fell short. Those were the only punches he threw. Then I drove him into the ropes with a lot of hooks and right hands. "This ain't like the last fight," I thought. He kept backing up into the ropes, trying to cover up the best he could. But he couldn't seem to lift his hands. Schmeling was completely helpless. He kept staggering backwards like a drunken man. The crowd was in an uproar as I carefully measured him. Max was an open target. His jaw was not protected and it was very inviting. His stomach was wide open. It was time for the kill. I started hitting him with everything I had—about five or six lefts and a right to his chin—and his legs started shaking. He started sinking to the floor and he grabbed the upper strand of the ropes and held on. He was sideways, his eyes were blinking, and his face looked like it was in great pain.

As he hung on the ropes, I hit him with a right to the body. Trying to get away from the punch, Schmeling twisted and took the blow in his lower back. Referee Donovan stepped between us as if he wanted to stop the fight and waved me to a neutral corner. He gave Schmeling a count of one. Then Schmeling got off the ropes, ready for more. I came back as my corner shouted at me, and I hit Schmeling with a right to the jaw. He went down for a three count. When he got up, I tore into him with lefts and rights. He went down again and got up at two. I followed with two hooks and a right to his jaw, and he fell onto the canvas again. His trainer Max Machon threw a towel in the ring, but Donovan tossed it on the ropes and continued to count.

JOE LOUIS: MY LIFE

It was all over in two minutes and four seconds. It was a long time coming, but now I felt like the "real" champion. I'd gotten my revenge. Somebody was counting punches and said I must have hit Schmeling with near fifty blows in the two minutes and four seconds, looking something like a pneumatic drill—and I guess that's what I felt like. God damn it, I won.

Again, the people in Harlem went wild, throwing bottles, tin cans, and cups from rooftops—they had to call the police in to stop them. In Cleveland, they had to use tear gas to stop the rioting. Black people all over the country were out in the streets, celebrating for me. I felt good about the partying, but bad that people would go so crazy over my victory that they'd get in trouble with the police.

After the fight I was sorry to hear they had taken Schmeling to Polyclinic Hospital. I had almost broken his back. He had some fractures of the vertebrae and badly bruised back muscles. Schmeling, or more probably his manager, claimed I fouled him. But I remember when I was giving him my all, he'd turned when I hadn't expected him to, and I had landed that punch on his back because his body wasn't where it was supposed to be. That's perfectly legal; I felt no guilt about it.

I even heard that when the Germans learned how badly I was beating Schmeling, they cut the radio wires to Germany. They didn't want their people to know that just a plain old nigger man was knocking the shit out of the Aryan Race.

Schmeling went on back to Germany, and it wasn't till after World War II that I saw him again. We hugged each other and were real friendly and kept in touch by phone. After all, he won one fight, I won one fight—even-steven. In fact, Schmeling came all the way from Germany to Las Vegas in 1970 to help me celebrate my fifty-sixth birthday. Like I say, to me and Schmeling it was just best man

[143]

wins, but we both knew what was at stake. To the world Schmeling's defeat foretold of things to come for Nazi Germany.

I know now this was the top of my career. I had the championship, and I had beaten the man who had humiliated me. America was proud of me, my people were proud of me, and since the fight, race relations were lightening up—who the hell could ask for more?

Now, for practically six months I'd either been fighting or training to fight. I was tired, I'd accomplished what I wanted to. I went on a fantastic buying spree. It had even gotten so Billy Taub's clothes didn't suit me well enough. I had some ideas of my own. Shoot! I could create my own clothes, and they weren't junk either. I hired special tailors to make suit coats without lapels (always preferred the casual look); I told those tailors to make me a camel's-hair coat and put a piping of leather around the edges. I loved those big-footed slacks, and I'd have them made in two tones. And you know, people were starting to copy what I wore. All in all I must have ordered twenty suits and maybe forty shirts and two extra tuxedos. I was ready for anything. I didn't spare anything on anybody else, either. I think I must have bought two or three houses for my brothers and sisters and as usual gave a lot of money away.

Always tried to spend as much time as I could with Momma. Marva and me would just drop in sometimes. You could always find Momma around the stove. She was one hell of a cook. Whenever Marva and me would get ready to leave, Momma would bake a pound cake, a sweet-potato pie, fry up a batch of chicken, and put all this in a couple of shoeboxes. Well, now I'm world champion, I can't go around carrying these shoeboxes, but at the same time, I want that good food. So, Marva solved the problem. She bought some fancy gift-wrapping paper and ribbons and would wrap the shoeboxes up like expensive presents. As soon as we got back to Chicago and settled down, I'd yell out to Marva, "Bring on the shoeboxes!"

Really living good through this period. Started going out to a place called Spring Hill, about twenty miles or so from Detroit. It was a big four-hundred-and-some-odd acre farm that had the best stables in Michigan. There was a gigantic house on the grounds, and nearly all horseback riders went there one time or the other. I loved the place. It wasn't like any farm I knew in Alabama. Loved horseback riding. Always did, ever since I was a little kid, only I just mostly rode those old mules. So I got all decked out in custom-made boots, custom-made English riding habit, and when I had a free moment, I was there.

Of course when I got all these riding clothes together and was prancing around looking at myself in the mirror and telling myself how good-looking I was, Marva would zap me right down. I had made the mistake of telling her about my hard times when I was at Brewster's Gym years ago and how raggedy my pants were in the back. In fact, that was the reason I had never learned to dance. I used to stand against the wall at the gym watching everybody but didn't dare turn my backside around because of those raggedy pants. So whenever I was getting too proud of myself, Marva'd tell me about myself. And, you know something, she needed to.

All the while I was enjoying myself, I knew Roxie, Black, and Mike were busy looking for an opponent for me. After I'd licked Schmeling, the heavyweight division was cleaned out. They didn't want me to just fight bums.

Gus Greenlee, John Henry Lewis's manager, was driving Mike Jacobs crazy wanting to make a match. Greenlee was saying that I was afraid to fight John Henry. But I wanted the fight; everybody did, only Mike was hesitating about it. Remember, Greenlee's black and so is John

Henry. Mike had no prejudice about a man's color so long as he could make a green buck for him, but Mike had doubts about two black fighters drawing a big gate.

John Henry was the Light Heavyweight Champion and a good fighter. He'd beaten some of the best. Since he turned pro in 1931, he'd had about a hundred fights and only been defeated seven times; three of those defeats came from that cutesie-clever fighter, Slapsie Maxie Rosenbloom. In 1932 John Henry decisioned Jimmy Braddock, but Braddock beat him in 1934. John Henry was a good friend of mine, and I wanted the match. The black press was pushing for it, too. Hell, let some other really good black fighter make some money, too. John Henry, his manager—and everything around him—was black. That means they were almost automatically kept away from the big money. But believe me, now I had got the power and the glory, neither Mike Jacobs nor anybody else was going to refuse me. I told Mike to sign it up, and Mike signed it up.

A lot of people gave John Henry a good chance against me, and, looking at the record, I don't blame them. He was a great long-range boxer and about the best defensive fighter around, but I knew I could take him. I knew I wasn't going to lose nothing and John Henry at least could make a decent buck.

So we signed in November to meet in New York January 27.

In the meantime, I was thinking about a lot of things. There was a night club out in Hollywood called the Rhumboogie; I liked it a lot. Good jazz bands, good jazz singers, and you know good jazz bands and really good jazz singers are black—let's face it. The Rhumboogie was real plush, and I like elegant things. In the back of my mind was always the thought that there should be a place like that in Chicago—a place where plain colored folks could go to enjoy and hear their own music, and not have to wait for "nigger night" (usually Monday when the white folks were too tired after having a ball in some really nice place over the weekend). So, anyway, when my friend Charlie Glenn came up to me and said, "Hey, let's open a real good spot," I was fair game. We opened a "Rhumboogie," which we later called Swingland.

While Charlie Glenn was taking care of opening it, I took off for French Lick, a famous horse riding academy and resort in Indiana. French Lick was a chance for me to rough it up before heading for Pompton Lakes for regular training. My mind was together; I was going to fight John Henry Lewis—the first time in modern boxing history two black men would meet for a heavyweight championship fight. I hear tell that during slavery days black slaves always were fighting in the ring for their masters, and there were big bets. Well, the white man is clever. When they finally realized that all that money was going down, the white man replaced the black man in the ring. Now I felt really good. Here I was, a black man, going to fight another black man, and us blacks are on the money side this time. Jesus Christ, blacks may make it yet.

Must have been just before New Year's, me and my entourage headed again for Pompton Lakes for serious training. Although I felt I could beat John Henry, I wasn't going to take any chances. I was about ten pounds overweight, and I knew I had to get down to my best fighting weight—a little under 200 pounds. John Henry was about 182.

I didn't play John Henry cheap at all; a lucky punch, and it could be all over for me. So Mannie Seamon got me some sparring partners who fought in Lewis's style—fast and clever. The best partners around using this style were Basher Dean and Mickey Dugan, and we worked out just fine.

Another reason I wanted this fight was because John Henry was suing the New York Boxing Commission. They had vacated his title because he refused to fight any of the challengers they had offered. At that time New York State recognized a southpaw name of Melio Bettina as Light Heavyweight Champion. Mike, who was good friends with the guys in the Boxing Commission, convinced them that he could stop the legal action by giving John Henry a money-making fight with me. So it was all green lights for the fight now.

1939-1942
WARTIME

NINETEEN THIRTY-NINE. THE YEAR DIDN'T START out the way it was supposed to. Got a call from Marva. She told me that before she even knew she was pregnant, she'd had a miscarriage. My God, she needed me, and I couldn't be there. It was a frustrating situation, but as usual Marva understood, or at least she said she did. Thing is I had never thought that much about children. Lord knows I love kids, nothing I wouldn't do for a kid, but I was twenty-five and Marva was twenty-three. We're young, I told her, and we've got plenty of time to have babies.

I had to reset my mind on the John Henry Lewis fight coming up. As I said, John Henry's no bum. Then I heard he had a bad eye and couldn't see laterally out of it. Damn, what do I do with this information? The press was constantly on top of us. After all, this was the first major fight between two blacks since slavery. John Henry's my friend, but we're both professionals. He wouldn't expect me to go easy on him any more than I'd expect him to do the same.

On January 25, 1939, we went for the weigh-in. John Henry seemed nervous and drawn; we had just a little light chat. I weighed in at 200¼ pounds and John Henry at 180¾.

When I went in the ring that night, I remember thinking to myself, I'm not gonna punish John, I'm gonna try to get this over in a hurry. I knocked him down three times in the first round, then at two minutes and twenty-nine seconds of the first round, Arthur Donovan, the referee, stopped the fight because John Henry couldn't get up. I wasn't that happy about that fight, but I knew John Henry was on his way out, and at least he'd had the glory of a fight with the Heavyweight Champion—and had made a good dollar.

After I got back to Chicago, I was greeted with a letter from some doctors at the Mayo Clinic. Marva had gone there after the miscarriage. The doctors had also written Roxy and Black. Seems like they felt that maybe Marva shouldn't try to have children. They said that she was unnerved by the helter-skelter way we lived, said she needed more "stability" and more companionship from her husband—if not, she might have a nervous breakdown. This really upset me. I loved Marva. Maybe I did take her too much for granted. Maybe I wasn't home enough. I don't know. I decided to try. The only thing, though, is that I'm a big man; I've got an enormous appetite; I'm a lover. I said I'd try, but I didn't know.

Anyway, me and my manager worked out a plan to buy Spring Hill, that ranch outside of Detroit. We figured it would be a great place to train or at least to rough it. I'd be closer to home, and the ranch should at least pay for itself. I talked to Marva about it and she seemed quite happy. I told her later on she could build a real fancy house on the grounds and maybe when I retired we could live there. In fact, it got so I really liked the idea. Imagine me, a country squire! They must have had almost a hundred hogs there and a big herd of Hereford cows. A man with some money, a beautiful wife, some cute little kids, could lead a good life there. In the meantime they got the riding academy, people always coming around. The idea sounded better and better—so I bought the place for $100,000.

But around this time Marva was a little peakish and the doctors told her she was anemic and prescribed, along with other medicines, a couple of ounces of Virginia Dare wine. I knew she was depressed, so I made sure I measured the amount she was to have three times a day. After all, I didn't want her to become an alcoholic. I laugh now when I think about that. I'm the one, in later years, who had to worry, not Marva.

In the meantime, I still had to work. Mike was looking around for somebody for me to fight and for a good money location. He finally wound up picking Los Angeles. I hadn't been there since I K.O.'d Lee Ramage in 1935. The opponent they set up was Jack Roper, a hell of a left-hooker and we were to meet on April 17.

The fight was over fast, but damned if Roper didn't nearly knock me down with a left hook in the first round. He was a southpaw, but he changed up his style in the middle of the round. First he'd lead with a left and then lead with a right. I said to myself, "Shit, let me get this tricky guy out of the way." So I K.O.'d him in the first round.

I'll never forget Roper; he was a funny man. We were on the air after the fight and when the announcer asked Roper what happened, he said, "I zigged when I should've zagged."

Next thing I know, they've got me scheduled to fight "Two-Ton" Tony Galento of Orange, New Jersey. Tony looked like a beer barrel. He didn't look anything like the athlete you'd expect to meet—five-foot nine and 225 pounds. He was a saloon keeper, and from the looks of him he must have had a drink with every customer. Tony talked about me like a dog before the fight. He even called me on the telephone to tell me about myself. He thought he had me in the bag. At least that's how he was talking. At first he got on my nerves, but later, you know, I got to like that son of a bitch. He had style and what they're calling "charisma" nowadays.

Well, anyway, the fight was scheduled for June 28 at Yankee Stadium. We had a big crowd, must have been 35,000 to 40,000 people. You know, people like a different kind of person, and Tony was it. I knew I wasn't to take him lightly; he was a good street slugger, and his win record showed it. First round, he staggered me with a left. Then he hit me with a right and a left to the jaw. Everything glazed over. I shook my head and got myself together. Chappie was telling me, "He's strong, but a bluff. Box him." I was mad, but I had to sanction what Chappie said. In the second round I hit him so hard that I almost took him off the floor, up in the air. Some fighter; even after I knocked him on his ass, he got up when any other fighter would have stayed there.

Third round, he came out of his corner bleeding from his eye, nose, and mouth. I knew I had him. I got too confident, though, because before I knew it, he hit me with a left hook that set me right on my behind. Now I was really mad. I went after Galento like a machine. He was reeling and rocking, and I kept at him. Finally, after I gave him another heavy barrage, "Two-Ton" Tony fell back and down. Arthur Donovan, the referee, pulled me back, and it was count of ten.

I won, but it was a funny kind of fight, in a way. A lot of people were pulling for Tony. He had a special appeal to a lot of white people. I knew people liked me and were cheering for me, but at the same time, how much did they want to let a black man get ahead? I know when I beat Tony I proved a point.

Funny thing, though, me and Tony are still friends. I used to go to his saloon in Jersey quite a bit, and we'd laugh about all the things we'd been so serious about.

Had a nice break here because my next fight was a return match with Bob Pastor on September 20. Now I'd have some time to be with Marva. She had told me she felt more like a kept woman than a wife.

We spent a lot of time out at Spring Hill, and I was doing a lot of riding. I remember in July, 1938, the First United States Negro Horse Show was being held at the Utica Riding Club, outside of Detroit, and they asked me to be in it. Of course I said yes. I rode a horse called MacDonald's Choice and I took third place, winning a yellow ribbon in the fine-gaited saddle class. The horse also paid $1,500. That was a fun way to make some money.

More important, though, was Marva and me at Spring Hill. It was really beautiful and peaceful. The two of us could walk for hours over all those acres I owned and ride for what seemed like days. I bought two great horses. One was named Flash; he was a demon horse. I left instructions that no one was to ride him but me and the trainer. The other one was Jocko, good horse, more stable than Flash. I even bought a $2,500 English saddle from Bing Crosby. I was really into this thing big. I was staying in good shape, and my wife was happy. Marva looked so cute in her riding clothes, I figured she should learn how to really ride. As soon as I went into training, I sent her to French Lick to learn to master the art. I was determined to make her an equestrian (my new word). She stayed there about six weeks and she learned to ride both straight and sidesaddle, on three-gaited as well as five-gaited horses.

Enough of the good life for me; I had to get down to training for Bob Pastor. This was really going to be some meet. I well remembered how bad Pastor had made me look when he was running all over the ring and he stayed the whole ten rounds. Well, now it would be a little different. Mike set up Briggs Stadium in Detroit. This would be my first fight since I became Champion in my old home town, and we expected a big gate. To make it an extra special event, the fight was scheduled for twenty rounds. First time a heavyweight title fight had been set up for so many rounds since Jack Johnson was beaten by Jess Willard in Cuba.

I found out more about Pastor this time. His trainer, Freddie Brown, had told him before to stick and run because there was no way he could have slugged it out with me. Now Pastor was just as upset as I was with that bad showing we had before. Pastor really was a slugger;

he wanted people to see that he wasn't going to run all over the ring looking like he was scared to fight.

Chappie told me to remember and let him bring the fight to me, cut the ring down, and for God's sake not to chase him all over the place. Turns out I didn't have to. He came straight to me. I knocked him down five times in the first two rounds. But he got in some good punches on me. He was a tough customer until I K.O.'d him in the eleventh. He wasn't on his bicycle in this fight.

Got a nice rest period and headed straight back to Spring Hill for some horse shows. They were exciting affairs. All the big time sports people from everywhere came. I even picked up a few ribbons.

Gave Marva a nice surprise. As nonchalant as I could be, I said, "How about going to Cuba for a little vacation?" and she was as excited as I was trying not to be. Our first big trip out of the U.S.A. together.

When we arrived in Cuba, the crowd seemed even more enthusiastic about me than in America. I never knew there were so many black people anywhere, except in Africa and America. The President, Fulgencio Batista, greeted us. I didn't know about the conditions in Cuba. The only part we saw was the luxury side, and the dark-skinned Cubans we saw looked like they were doing better than a lot of blacks back home. We stayed at El Presidente Hotel—real fancy. Marva and I were getting on real well then.

1940. I had a little bit of time before I had to train for my next fight, with Arturo Godoy. Marva and I had been back a while, and she seemed contented. Hell, why couldn't things stay the way they were?

Lena Horne was in town singing with the Charlie Barnett band. I purposely didn't go to the theater. But one night I went by to visit some friends on Fifty-fifth Street and Lena was there. I hadn't seen much of her until now; I'd heard she was going with Charlie Barnett so I wasn't too worried about talking to her. But, shit, it happened all over again. She was more beautiful than she'd ever been. Nice and sweet, but Lord, she had a filthy mouth. Could cuss better than any sailor wished he could. We started talking and talking; next thing I knew, we were getting real serious. We were planning all kinds of places and ways we could see each other.

Anyway, I had to earn my living. So it was on to New York to meet Godoy. Godoy was a Chilean and I didn't expect any trouble from him, but I was wrong. He made it tough for me because he stayed in a crouch all the time. It was almost like fighting somebody who's on the floor. He went the fifteen rounds, but I won the decision—although it was close. This was the worst fight I ever had. Mike Jacobs figured it would make a good rematch. So Godoy was quickly set up for June 20.

I figured I might as well stay around New York for a while because my next fight was with Johnny Paycheck at the end of March. Hung around a little while with a friend of mine, Dickie Wells. He was a black guy and a real playboy. He knew all the women, all the safe after-hour spots. He's the one introduced me to Lana Turner. Beautiful girl she was, and real likeable.

Then I really got in trouble. One night I was at the Cotton Club downtown and met a dancer there named Ruby Dallas. Of course, she was something else. Fell in love with her, and we saw each other as much as we could. I don't know about me. I knew I had a big appetite. It's like I like steaks, lamb chops, chicken, apples, and bananas. I like each at different times but I have to have them all. It was a bad period; I was going through something like what happens to an alcoholic when he falls off the wagon. I got drunk with all these beautiful, exciting women.

Well, anyway, Paycheck was from Chicago and had everybody saying he was hell on wheels. He wasn't. I could look at him and see he was scared to death. K.O.'d him in the second round.

JOE LOUIS: MY LIFE

After the fight, I headed on home and stayed a few days with Momma. Momma never changes. I marvel at how wonderful and good she is. Then went back to Chicago, and Marva and me entertained some friends and sort of easy like we did fine together. When I was with Marva, she was the only woman I wanted.

Meanwhile the war in Europe worsened. America was uneasy about the invasion of Poland and France, and they knew England would be involved. America could be next. The killing, the bombing, and the gassing upset every decent person. I knew I'd be glad to help defend America. No place else in the world could a onetime black cotton picker like me get to be a millionaire. I love this country like I love my people. Marva and I talked it over, and so I went down and registered at Local Draft Board 8 in Chicago. I'd be ready when they called.

But right now I had to prepare for this second fight with Godoy. He was a hard man and I had no intention of letting him get my title. I headed out to Spring Hill to rough it until we left for Pompton Lakes. I was real busy, riding, walking, chopping trees, and doing some road-work. One day, though, I got back to the big house and there was this great big moving van. I asked Chappie to find out what the hell it was doing there. Chappie checked it out and said "Man, all your clothes, shoes, ties, under-wear, and even your top hat is in there." "Oh, oh," I thought to myself, "Marva's on to something." I got on the phone and before she could say a thing, I acted tough and asked what she meant by sending my clothes up here. I told her I was sending my clothes back home. That's when she hit me the low blow. Somehow she had gotten a hold of a letter Lena Horne sent me and Marva's talking about a separation and divorce. I was embarrassed and ashamed, but I covered up and just said, "I'm sending my clothes back to my home." Well, anyway, it worked out for awhile. I don't think Marva believed me when I told her I had nothing to do with Lena, but at least she let my clothes back in. I had a beautiful Dusenberg roadster car with an all-wooden body that Marva had admired sent along home, too.

Mannie Seamon had gotten me the right sparring partners. These guys all fought low-down all the time. Chappie trained me how to straighten them up with uppercuts. Worked hard till I got the knack of it.

June 20 at Yankee Stadium—and I wanted to see how much I'd learned. The bell rang, and out walked Godoy to the middle of the ring, going down into this ridiculous crouch. I kept sticking him with left hands, left hands. I had him bleeding. Knocked him down in the sixth, but the bell saved him. By the eighth he'd had it. I knocked him down for an eight count and he got up again. Went right into him, and he went down for a two count. The referee stopped the fight after this.

I had about five months all to myself now, and I headed for Washington, D.C., with Marva and my momma to experience the most meaningful thing in my life. My baby sister, Vunice, graduated from Howard University. Hot damn! I'm proud. I helped my sister through college. The President of the college, Dr. Mordecai Johnson, gave me quite a reception. Can you see me, Joe Louis, up there talking to college graduates? I told them how lucky they were to have both inborn intelligence and the intelligence to get their degrees. I also told them to keep getting as much education as they could because our race needed learned men and women to lead them.

Gave Vunice a brand-new Buick, and when she told me she wanted to get her master's degree, I told her, "Go, baby sister, go. It's all on me."

Back at Spring Hill, there was going to be a big horse show, and Marva and me had to get back there. Marva was becoming quite a horsewoman and was beginning to win medals and ribbons; she competed in my show this time.

Got all our new English custom-made boots, riding habits, derby hats on. I was looking forward to this. I didn't know where Marva was, but I knew she was somewhere around the place, probably in the crowds. Then they announced the jumping contest, and when they said the name "Marva Louis riding Flash," the blood drained out of my face. They say I was standing there shouting, "She'll kill herself. She'll kill herself." Flash was the one horse only me and the trainer could ride. But Marva made the jumps like she'd been born on a horse and won the trophy. Later I found out she'd been training on that horse practically every day for months. The trainer had begged her not to, but Marva's a stubborn cuss. Anyway, when I got to her, I told her she needed a good spanking. She told me, "Too late, I did it and I've got the trophy. Besides, if my daddy never spanked me, what makes you think you can?" She looked absolutely gorgeous.

The war was almost worldwide. The Depression was easing up. Some black folks were beginning to get decent jobs because America was starting to prepare for the war. Election time, and President Roosevelt was running for his third term against Wendell Willkie. I didn't know too much about Willkie except that he was running on the internationalist wing of the Republican Party ticket out of Indiana. He was real heavy on civil rights. But you know there was something so sincere and honest about the man that he got my attention. I had started getting involved with politics through Charles Roxborough; he was Roxy's brother. Charles was the first black Senator from Michigan. Sometimes he'd have me appear at political events and sit me up on the dias. When they'd introduce me, I'd just stand up and say "Thank you" and sit right down, but I'd listen. I never supported anybody in politics unless I felt they were giving my people a fair shake.

JOE LOUIS: MY LIFE

Well, anyway, through the years, I had always supported Roosevelt. After all, I knew he was a fan of mine, and thank God for the Welfare Relief programs that he had set up, not only helping my people but the whites, too. The thing, you see, was that I honestly felt Roosevelt was a good human being. You know what I mean?

On the other hand, though, he'd been in office for two terms, and he had helped get the Civil Service going, but things were wrong with this "fair employment" stuff. I talked to too many black people in Washington, D.C., who told me they thought they had good jobs, when, even with "fair employment," they got bumped out of their jobs by white people. There were things I felt the President should have done that he just didn't do. He promised a lot, but he didn't always come through. He wouldn't even sign the antilynch bill.

But when I listened to Willkie, I fell in love with him. He said things like, "Every American is going to have a place in this country." Hell, a lot of people forget black people are Americans, too. We've been here a long time. God bless Africa, but I never saw it. I am an American. I want me and all black Americans to have the same chance in this country.

I campaigned all over for Wendell Willkie, but he just couldn't beat Roosevelt. Roosevelt had that special charm. Never mind, though, I thought Willkie would have made one hell of a President. He made me feel that things would have been better for the blacks.

In between campaigning and Spring Hill, I still found time for my golf. By this time, I was betting heavily on my game, but, damn, I was losing a lot of money. So I got me a black golf pro to show me where I was going wrong. His name was Ted Rhodes, and after I'd worked with him a while, I started doing better and winning some of my money back. Went out to Los Angeles to golf at Hillcrest. Lena was out there, and we started up again. Then I was in New York with Ruby Dallas. In between times, when I was home, I'd be at my club or off to the Chicken Shack to help boost up the sales.

Somewhere in between all this, I'd come home. Sometimes I'd get home at eleven or twelve and I'd see Marva all dressed up sitting in a chair. I'd say, "Where you going?" She'd just look at me and remind me of a date we had to go someplace at six o'clock. I'd clean forgotten. It got so she'd say to me, "Listen, I'm going out tonight and you're going out tonight, but obviously not the same places. I'll make a deal with you. If I see your car parked outside of a club, I won't go in. But if you see my car parked, you're welcome in anytime." I didn't like that, but I said nothing. I wanted Marva, and I wanted the fun I was having. They say you can't have your cake and eat it too. But I tried.

I remember one day Marva told me we were gonna have a dinner party for fourteen early that evening. She had hired extra servants and all. I told her I'd be back in time, just wanted to do some riding at Spring Hill. Well, actually, I'd met a pretty girl and had invited her up to the ranch. Got carried away and forgot my time.

Me and this girl were out riding in the sunset when I saw Marva's car driving up. I shouted to Marva to go back, but she didn't. She gunned the engine, and Flash reared up, missing the windshield by inches. The party was over. I told the girl to cut out and take the horses back to the stables, and I got in the car with Marva. She was mad as hell, and I don't blame her. We got back to the house and the guests were all there waiting for me.

Marva went upstairs with me so we could change our clothes. All the time she was fussing and really going at me. I told her to wait till this dinner party was over and she would get it; I told her that she was never to follow me around. She kept on. Finally, I just took her by the shoulders and gave her a good shaking. Only thing is, while I was shaking her she accidentally bit down on her tongue and started to cry. I let loose of her right away, but I persisted in giving her hell about following me around. I had just taken off one of my beautiful custom-made riding boots and was bending over to take off the other one.

Next thing I knew, I was seeing stars. Marva had picked up that boot and with the force of her 115 pounds had knocked me square in my head. When I got myself together I just looked at her and said, "You're gonna get it later." Of course nothing happened like that. We made up that night.

With all this laying around for five months, I knew it was time to rough it again and start training for my fight with Al McCoy, a good Massachusetts heavyweight. We met in Boston, and I knocked him out in the sixth round on December 16.

1941. This was going to be one hell of a year. I'd always wanted to be a fighting champion, and I was. Only trouble was, who was left to fight? I'd practically cleaned out the heavyweight division. Mike Jacobs lined up six fights for me for January, February, March, April, May, and June. Some smart ass sports columnist called this parade "Bum of the Month Club." I didn't care what the hell they called it. A friend of mine told me that Alexander the Great started crying when he had no more worlds to conquer. Shit! I wasn't gonna cry. I had to make some money. But on the other hand I had some professional pride. I didn't like the "Bum of the Month" bit going around. Those guys I fought were not bums. They were hard-working professionals trying to make a dollar, too. I knew the training they went through, and I knew the dreams they had. No different from me. I respected every man I fought. It's no easy job getting up in that ring; you got to have a special kind of balls. You can get killed, damage your body for life, or you might win the big prize.

JOE LOUIS: MY LIFE

Anyway, my first fight was January 31 with Red Burman in New York City. I'd rate Burman as a fair fighter. It was a K.O. in the fifth round.

Then I went on to Gus Dorazio in Philadelphia, February 17. He was the best Philly had to offer, but I knocked him out in two rounds.

While I was in Philadelphia, some Negro organization wanted to give me a special plaque. I went there with a girl who went up with me to accept it; damn if Marva wasn't there. I thought she was still in New York. Marva walked up to the stage and between her teeth said to the girl, "Bitch, move." She moved. Then Marva graciously accepted the plaque for me, and we went home together.

When we got back to New York to 409, Marva said we had to get a new apartment with at least four rooms. We had gotten tired of hotels and wanted a homelike atmosphere when we came to New York, so we moved to 555 Edgecombe Avenue, the Roger Morris. Only one way to describe the Roger Morris—magnificent. This was the tip of Sugar Hill. From the eighth floor apartment we could look right over the Harlem River and the Polo Grounds— home of the baseball and football Giants. Paul Robeson had just moved out around the corner to a house on Jumel Place. Don Redman, a great arranger and orchestra leader who became Pearl Bailey's music director lived there, too. So did Cootie Williams, the brilliant trumpeter with the Duke Ellington band. Everything was all right for the moment.

March 21. I went to Detroit to meet Abe Simon, a big, strong guy—another twenty-rounder. As big as Abe was, he was clumsy. He reminded me of Primo Carnera in his style. I boxed him and he stayed in quite a while, but in the thirteenth round I knocked him out.

April 8, I fought Tony Musto in St. Louis, Missouri. This was my first match in St. Louis. Tony was strictly a local boxer who was good in his steady way. But he was too predictable. I put him out in the ninth round.

JOE LOUIS: MY LIFE

It was hard going. Maybe a week or two off, and then at it again. Training, training, training. But I didn't let my spare time go by. I let the good times ride when I had the chance.

Just about here in early April I nearly get the shock of my life. Marva served divorce papers on me. I don't know what I expected of her. I know I'd be rough on my woman. Always traveling, half the time training or fooling around with some other woman. My pride hurt—the thought that she didn't want me anymore—wondering and wondering. I thought to myself, "I want that woman." Took off for home.

Marva made it all clear to me. She wanted a husband. She wanted children and a home without all my friends hanging around all the time. And we were hardly ever together. Marva was right. I thought back to all the times I had been going out nightclubbing with Freddie Guinyard and Thurston. I should have been with her. I even remembered the times some of my other friends had been in my house and had stolen her diamond wristwatch and other jewelry. She'd had to call Carl Nelson and tell him what was missing. Carl went out and came back with the stuff. That's no way for a lady to live.

I pleaded my case to Marva like I was a Supreme Court judge. I think then that Marva still loved me very much. She just wanted a normal life. I swore up and down, I'd leave the ring soon and it would be just the two of us. Thank God, she bought it. Since I had two more big fights coming up, I arranged for her to go away with Roxy and Black's wives. They went on a cruise to the Caribbean and I hoped that maybe when she got back, we could patch up.

Between all this hassle I had to get ready to fight Buddy Baer in Washington, D.C. Buddy was the youngest brother of Max Baer. This was no easy fight. I'm sure that in the back of Buddy's head was the K.O. I had delivered to his brother back in 1935. Well, he started with a bang. In the first round he hit me with a left hook that sent me through the ropes onto the apron of the ring. I had to take a four count on that. But he thought he had me; he forgot, I don't like to look like anyone's fool. I was mad and went back to beat the living shit out of him. He was a tough cookie, though, and as stubborn as I was. He even got a mouse going under my right eye in the third round. Opened up a cut under my left eye in the fifth. In the sixth I was giving him my all, and he was right in there mixing it up with me. I knocked him down in this round, but he got up at the count of seven and fell out again.

But this time the crowd was going wild. When the referee started counting, Baer started stirring around about the count of nine. He got up when the bell rang to end the round, but the crowd was making so much noise, hardly nobody heard it. I know I didn't. All I know is when Baer got up I rushed in and dropped him with a right. Well, anyway, Ancil Hoffman, Baer's manager, had heard the bell and was saying I should be disqualified. Buddy's seconds had taken him over to his corner and were trying to get him ready for round seven. When the bell rang, Baer didn't know which way was which way. Hoffman was now refusing to let him start, most of all because he knew I had him, but he was saying I should be disqualified. Referee Donovan was yelling that Hoffman had to leave the ring. Me, I didn't know what the hell is going on. The upshot of the whole thing was that Donovan disqualified Buddy.

In the meantime, Marva returned from the cruise. She looked like peaches and cream. Those worry lines on her forehead were gone and she was almost burnt like an orange. We had a little time together and we enjoyed it. Well, it looked like a Mexican standoff. It was a wait-and-see arrangement. We both knew we liked being together. I had to make the special adjustments. We ran out to Detroit to spend a day or two with Momma, who knew the difficulties we were having. And, you know something, she was strictly on Marva's side. Momma told me about myself and about pride going before a fall, but I told her we were going to be all right now.

We had a lot of fun talking about the trip. In particular, I remember her telling me about Bermuda, which was still a prejudiced place. They got off the cruise ship and went to the hotel they were assigned. Roxy's and Black's wives are so light-complected that generally only black people can tell the difference. Marva's got such sharp features and straight hair, she looks like a sunburned white woman to white people. Funny thing, if she was walking around Harlem, there would be no doubt about her race. But because she was where the white people hang out, they assumed she must be white, too, or else she wouldn't be there. The girls were having more fun laughing at the white people who kept telling them what a terrific tan they had. Some white guys were busy digging them, but the girls kept turning them off. Finally, one day, one of these guys was alone with Marva in the elevator. He told her, "I know who you are." Marva wouldn't listen to his talk, though. So by the time she got to her room, the management was calling up saying she and her friends had to vacate the room.

Now, Marva wouldn't accept anything like that. She said that she and her friends weren't going anywhere. She had paid in advance and the only way they'd leave is if the police dragged them out. Now, that didn't set so well—the Heavyweight Champion of the World's wife being dragged out of a hotel room because she's black! Well, nothing happened; Marva integrated Bermuda.

I knew my next fight would be rough. I was up against Billy Conn, a tough, handsome, arrogant Irishman with all the stuff for a heavyweight champion. He was young, born October 18, 1917, in Pittsburgh, Pennsylvania. He was the New York State light heavyweight champion from 1939 to 1940. I know he was thinking of those other great Irish champions from John L. Sullivan to Jimmy Braddock, and he'd recently vacated his light heavyweight crown to move into the heavies. Now, that's going some. I knew he had the confidence and I knew I had to be ready for him.

I was upset when I found out that Conn was going to weigh in at less than 175 pounds. At that time I was generally coming in at 200, 202, and I always used to lay off a day before the fight with just a little roadwork to break sweat and a shower and a rubdown—no boxing. Really wanted to break 200 because I didn't want the public saying—"Joe Louis, 202, and Conn, 170." This would make me feel like I was a bully taking advantage of a smaller man.

So, the last day I trained like I always did. Chappie was mad as hell. I dieted and drank as little water as possible. Anyway, I'd broken 200 and came in at 199½ pounds. Conn was at 174. But I made it to the weigh-in without any breakfast; I felt like shit. I had no pep, and as soon as I got to 555 Edgecombe Avenue, my chef, Bill Bottoms, had a good meal ready for me. Steak, black-eyed peas, and salad. He knew I needed pumping up.

When we arrived at the Polo Grounds—the night of June 18—there were 55,000 people on hand. Good house. We get to going right away. Bill Conn was like a mosquito. He'd sting and move. I kept after him though, but I couldn't catch him. Conn was just too fast, too much speed for me. First two rounds I gave it to him. Thought I had him and the fight would be over soon. But that tough Irishman stood up to my fists. By the time the third round started, I could feel the effect of his speed and left hands. I kept giving it to him, but he stayed in there. About the time of the fifth round, I knew I had him. I had staggered him with a left hook to the jaw and repeated rights and lefts—cut him over his right eye and gave him another cut over his nose. But Billy was surviving on speed.

By the time the eighth round came up, I was tired as hell, and I stayed that way until the twelfth. The twelfth round didn't help—I was completely exhausted, and he was really hurtin' me with left hooks. I was hoping that he'd lose his head and gamble because I could see myself saying, "bye-bye, title."

At the end of each round, when I'd hit my corner, me and Chappie would talk. We figured that my strategy would be based on him trying to slug it out with me. He knew I was getting tired and I was hoping for the toe-to-toe slug-out. I'd been studying him all night and I knew if he started to throw a long left hook, I had him.

At the end of the twelfth, Chappie said, "You're losing on points. You got to knock him out."

In the thirteenth round, Conn got too cocky. He knew, just like I did, he was winning. Conn don't come out boxing, now; he made his mistake. He wanted to try and slug it out. We got in a clinch, and he said, "Joseph, you're in for a tough fight tonight." I said, "We'll see." Son of a gun, he started that long left hook I'd been waiting for. I zapped a right to his head. He turned numb. I said to myself, "I gotcha now." Then I went into my routine rights and lefts, rights and lefts. He went down. I saw him trying to get up, but he couldn't. Referee Eddie Joseph counted him out in two minutes and fifty-eight seconds of the thirteenth round.

It was the eighteenth successful defense of my title. That was one hard win; Billy Conn had looked like the new "white hope." He had a big cheering crowd. I was no longer the underdog. People are fickle—they wanted to see somebody else up there, but I wasn't ready to give ground just yet.

I'd hurt my right wrist punching down on Conn's head in the seventh round. It nearly killed me for three rounds, but the pain went away. Conn sure knew what it was all about in a ring. He was one clever fighter. Only thing, if he'd kept his cool, he might have been the champion. But he didn't, and we'd meet again.

My showing with Billy Conn disturbed me. That sucker almost had it. So, for a tune up, I met with Jim Robinson in Minneapolis on July 11 in an exhibition fight. Hell, that was nothing at all. I K.O.'d him in the first round.

But September 29 I was to fight Lou Nova in New York at the Polo Grounds. Lou Nova was a strange guy. Maybe he wasn't so strange, though; he was always talking about Yoga and his own cosmic punch—nowadays people might understand him. I'd seen Nova fight Max Baer at the Yankee Stadium in April, 1941, and knock him out in eight rounds. I figured him to be a tough opponent. I didn't know if he was politicking this fight with all that Yoga and cosmic stuff or if he was sincere. Shit, I thought to myself, what the hell is a cosmic punch and what the hell is Yoga? When the press asked me, I told them I didn't care about his cosmic punch; I was just going to give him my regular right over a left hook and knock him out. I didn't like all that mysterious shit he was talking about.

Well, I guess it didn't matter, anyway, and he swelled the gate to over 56,000 people. We got in the ring and Nova gave me a hard time for about a minute. But as they say, sometimes a minute or a split second is all you need. This guy hurt me a little, and that always made me angry. When I saw my opening, I gave him a right, square to his chin. He went down and at the nine count managed to get to his knees and then wobble around on his feet. I knew I had him. Referee Donovan stopped the fight in a few seconds before the bell rang on the sixth round. Cosmic punch? Shit!

People still keep asking me how it feels to knock some-body out. At different times it feels like different things. I felt good knocking out Billy Conn, Max Schmeling, Max Baer and Carnera because there were so many people watching, and there was so much excitement. I mean, I was just coming up the ladder; all these guys had been champions or big shots. It made you feel good knowing you could beat them. Knocking out a Johnny Paycheck or Al McCoy didn't mean a thing to me.

Anyway, that night Marva and me went to a big party at the Theresa. Marva had a very good friend, Ivy Madden from Chicago, who was living in New York now. Ivy had rented the second floor of the Theresa for a big victory party. All the big-timers from Chicago and Detroit were there. Billy Daniels, who was singing at Small's Paradise, came over and gave us a few songs. It was fun. Marva and I seemed together, and the world was all right with me.

Around this time Ted Jones, my accountant, told me I owed $81,000 in taxes. I said, "OK. Pay it." He told me I didn't understand how to work big finance. So I asked him, what should I do? He said, "Don't pay them; let it build up some more, then we can make a deal and settle for less." What do I know? He's the tax guy. So I said, "OK." Lord to Jesus, I wish I hadn't listened to him. Each year after that, my taxes seemed to double.

After a nice Thanksgiving dinner with my family, I was feeling good about myself. Relaxing a little bit. Then on December 7, 1941, I heard on the radio that the Japanese attacked Pearl Harbor. Man, let me tell you, that rocked me. I couldn't even imagine anybody attacking the United States of America. I was mad, I was furious, you name it. Hell, this is my country. Don't come around sneaking up and attacking it. If a fighter had done that to me, I would have smashed him. I'm strictly for fair deals and open fighting. That night we heard that America had officially declared war on Japan. I knew I didn't have much time because I intended to get into this battle.

One day soon afterwards, I was at the Hillcrest Country Club in Los Angeles playing golf with Arthur Stebbins. While I was at the third or fourth hole, I got an urgent message that Mike Jacobs was on the phone waiting to talk to me. He told me that he could get a match for me to fight for the Navy Relief Fund. They needed money. I told him it's fine with me. Then Mike said he hoped I understood that I wasn't getting any money. I told Mike that I'd told him before, that was fine with me.

Mike went scrounging around to find the best opponent possible and zeroed in on Buddy Baer. He was a tough customer, and both of us had earned our money the night we fought. Buddy agreed and the deal was finalized—me and Mike donated all our winnings to the Navy, minus training expenses; Baer contributed one-sixth of his winnings.

The fight was scheduled for January 9, at Madison Square Garden, and I quickly got ready to train.

In the meantime, I got notice that I was to be awarded a memorial plaque given by the boxing writers' association of New York, the Edward J. Neil Trophy. Edward J. Neil was a sportswriter and a war correspondent who was killed in the Spanish Civil War in 1938. I didn't know the man, but he sure must have been thought real well of. So, it was a special honor. The trophy meant I was the person who had done the most for boxing the year before.

1942 started with all of us heading out to Pompton Lakes for my training. Only this time Chappie didn't look right, all of a sudden he's an old man. I said to him, "Come on, I'm the one who's supposed to shape up, not you." Chappie gave me a grin and said, "You just worry about yourself. I'll take care of me." But you know, I was concerned. Hell, Chappie's fifty-nine, but that ain't no old man.

On January 9, we went for the weigh-in. Buddy was 250 pounds, I was 205. Didn't bother me none, though. A little before the fight, while Chappie was bandaging my hands, he said: "Joe, I can't make it in the corner with you tonight." I look at him and say, "You got to." Then he went on about the terrible pains of rheumatism and arthritis he was having. He didn't even know if he could get up in the ring. Again, I promised him. "If you get up those stairs with me, I'll have Baer out before you can relax." Chappie said, "OK, and remember, that's a promise."

While I sat in my corner waiting for the bell to ring, I looked around Madison Square Garden. It looked like the Fourth of July. American flags were draped all around the place. Anywhere you could stick a flag, they had one.

I kept my promise. Buddy came out strong enough and gave me a couple of good left hooks. I punished him for that by blackening his left eye. Then I got in a good right to the chin, and he was down. He got up at the nine count, and I knocked him down and he went for another nine count. As soon as he got up again, I went to him. This time he was so wobbly that the referee stopped the fight. (Damn, it takes me longer to talk about it than it did to do it.) After two minutes and fifty-six seconds of the first round, it was over.

That night more than 19,000 people attended and brought in a sale of almost $200,000. My share that night would have been $65,200 and, after taking training expenses, I gave the American government $49,000.

One of the most thrilling things that night, though, was that my man, Wendell Willkie, was there. He'd made a great speech before the fight and I enjoyed it. I sure wished that he was my President. After the fight, he came around to the dressing room and we talked; I really liked that man.

Three days after the fight, I volunteered for the Army. It was no overnight decision on my part; I knew I'd have to go anyway and I really wanted to. It had all been discussed with Marva, Momma, my managers, and Mike.

I could easily have gotten an exemption by claiming that Momma and my wife were dependent on me, but I didn't go that road.

Hell, Momma was living fine, finer than she could ever have imagined. Marva was living like a queen. I mean, what could I say? "I have to be exempted so I can work so that my wife can pay the housekeeper."

This was an ugly war. I wanted to get in it, get it over with, and settle down. I was tired of boxing, now, sick and tired of the training and the traveling. When I went to sign up, the Army offered me a commission. No way I could be an officer. I'm not the type; I didn't have the education. Can you imagine me telling a bunch of soldiers, "Take that hill!"? I told you before, I'm no leader. I wanted to be just a plain, ordinary G.I.; I'd feel closer to people like me. If I had to spend time with all those men, give me somebody who I could talk with and laugh with. Well, they did that, all right. When I went to Camp Upton, Long Island, New York—I drove up in a chauffeured-limousine with Julian Black—they gave me my uniform and sent me over to the colored section.

THE ARMY YEARS

A T FIRST, BEING IN THE ARMY WAS NOTHING TOO much. That basic training program they put you through was like kindergarten stuff to me. I didn't feel any physical strain like some of the guys. I got some special privileges, of course, but I was still a soldier in the Army. Met a lot of nice guys, and living that way reminded me of my amateur fighting days when different athletic clubs would barnstorm together across the country. At first the guys would be in awe of me—like I was some kind of king, but I loosened them up. Nothing like a good card game with little side bets and some woman talk and some lies—you can get tired of always talking about fights and fighters.

But the fight game goes on. Mike called me and said the Army Relief Fund would like to set up a benefit fight between me and Abe Simon—no paycheck. Of course, I say OK. Those little push-up calisthenics I was doing in basic training were boring the hell out of me. But the title was at stake—and it had taken me thirteen rounds to knock Abe Simon out the first time we had fought, some time before. But this was late February, and the benefit fight was not scheduled until March 27 at the Garden, so I had plenty of time to get ready.

Before the fight, the Navy Relief Society wanted me to make a speech. I was nervous as hell. I think I'd rather have gone out and fought Schmeling again than make that speech. I didn't know what the hell to say, but while I was in training, Lucky Millander, a good friend of mine, came up to the camp, and I told him about my problem. You have to know who Lucky Millander was. He was a jazz band leader and a damn good one.

JOE LOUIS: MY LIFE

I was talking to Lucky, and some things he said to me stuck. When I got up on that stage, I said, "I'm only doing what any red blood American would do. We gonna do our part, and we will win, because we are on God's side." That became a very special message. Even got a letter from President Roosevelt congratulating me. Nowadays I heard you can even buy a record with this speech I made. Thank you, Lucky Millander.

The night of the fight was impressive. The Under-Secretary of War, Robert Patterson, was there as well as the Chairman of the War Production Board, Donald Nelson. They all made speeches saying how generous I was to contribute my purse and that the fight was being broadcast by short wave to the guys overseas.

Well, that was all well and good, but there was something wrong; Chappie wasn't there. Chappie had been ailing a long while now, and he was actually laid up at home, sick in bed. I had this terrible, deep-down empty feeling. Emptiness way down.

Anyhow, there's Big Abe standing up there with all his six feet, four inches and 255 pounds, ready to go. I had to get ready, too. There were about 19,000 people waiting to see this battle. Hell, I bought almost $3,000 worth of tickets myself and gave them to the poor black G.I.'s.

Abe started off the fight with a whole lot of pokes. It looked like a flurry, but I knocked off those little jabs. In the fourth round, I got tired of his buzzing around me. I let go with a couple of hard rights and left hooks and gave him a bad cut over his right eye. Near the end of the fifth, he was nearly out on his feet. When the bell rang for the sixth round, I gave him my right-left combination, and he was out for the count.

Well, I still had my title, and between me and Mike we gave the American government $75,000. Abe gave 15 percent of his purse.

JOE LOUIS: MY LIFE

It was a good fight. Abe didn't hurt me. Other than those little flurries, his hard head was more of a problem than his fists. The thing about the fight, though, was that I missed Chappie. I'm not taking nothing away from Mannie Seamon (he filled in for Chappie), but I just missed Chappie. He might have paced me better. In the first three rounds, I was too wild. Finally, when Mannie told me to slow down, I was able to take the fight. I needed the control from my corner.

In between all this, I was always calling Marva. We'd talk some, and I told her to keep in touch with Chappie and to see to anything he needed. She promised she would, and, knowing her, I know she did. But it was back to the barracks for a while, where a lot of guys were slapping me on the back and congratulating me. Fine. I really got a chance to look at a lot of those black G.I.'s. Some of them were just little kids who had lied about their ages. They needed to be home with their momma, if they had one. For some of those guys, this was the best they'd ever lived. Three square meals a day, a bed of their own—everything neat and clean. Then there was the common enemy—Nazi Germany. All those guys could relate to that. Wasn't a black man there who didn't understand what the Jews were going through. Somehow they could place their own lives into what was happening over there, and a lot of them, for real, wanted to get to Hitler.

Then you turn the coin over. Here are all these "niggers" ready and willing to go out and try to kill Hitler, and maybe get themselves killed, but they can't sleep in the same barracks with the white guys or go to the same movies or hardly get in officer's training. Made me start thinking.

When I got back to camp and had settled in, Roxy sent me a telegram saying that Chappie was in Chicago's Provident Hospital with pneumonia. I immediately asked for, and got, a five-day furlough. By the time I got to Chicago, Chappie seemed to be better. He was a lot thinner and looked older, but I was glad to see him well and alive. I'd go by the hospital every day, and we'd sit around jawing about the Abe Simon fight (he'd heard it on the radio) and practically every other fight I'd had. And in between times I got a chance to be with Marva some.

I remember asking her if she missed me now that I was in the Army. She said it seemed the same as when I was fighting; no difference. I didn't know whether to be glad or sad about that.

I went back to camp, where everything was back at the usual routine, when I got a call to come to the provost office—there was a telegram for me. I don't know about other people, but I know when I hear "telegram," that means emergency. I get to the office, tear the envelope open, and only see the words—"Chappie's dead." My God, my mind didn't register. I kept reading those two words until they blurred together. Chappie's dead, Chappie's dead, Chappie's dead. I broke down and cried. I don't know what I figured. I guess I thought I'd be heavyweight champion forever and Chappie would be always with me. Chappie had been another father, a teacher, and a friend, so when you really think about it, I lost three people, not one.

I called Freddie Guinyard, who'd sent the telegram, to find out the details. Seems like Chappie had been doing all right after he got out of the hospital, and then all of a sudden he had a heart attack that took him away.

The Army gave me a two-week furlough to attend the services at Pilgrim Baptist Church with Marva. There had to be at least 10,000 people there; the church couldn't hold them all—most of the people were standing outside. The pallbearers were me, Roxy, Black, Cab Calloway, Bill Robinson, and Carl Nelson. Chappie was buried at Lincoln Cemetery, and when the dirt went down on that coffin, I knew my life would never be the same again.

JOE LOUIS: MY LIFE

I have found that there's something in death that brings people so much closer; there's an urge that makes you say to yourself, "I got a lot to do, I can die too." During this furlough, Marva and me stayed pretty close together. I was so depressed. Marva was too. Chappie was her friend too; he was always looking out for her benefit as far as all those other women were concerned.

Well, there was a war on, and I returned to camp. The Army had set up an exhibition match on June 5 at Fort Hamilton in Brooklyn with one of my sparring partners, George Nicholson. This was a morale builder for the boys, a little free entertainment for them and some needed diversion for me.

My basic training was over, and the Army was trying to decide where to place me permanently, at least as permanently as you could get during those hectic years. Since I had Spring Hill and knew a lot about horses, they sent me to Fort Riley, Kansas, a Cavalry division. I couldn't have been happier.

Almost the first person I met at Fort Riley was a guy named Jackie Robinson. He was a helluva guy. He was just like he turned out to be on the baseball field; he wouldn't take shit from anybody or anything. I remember him saying he felt he was just as good as anybody else. Mind you, he would never say better than anyone else, but just as good—white, black, or green. If there would be anybody I'd have liked to be like in this world, I'd have to say it would be Jackie Robinson. And Jackie showed me a lot of respect; he told me I was his idol.

There was a lot of racism in the service—Jackie was complaining because he couldn't get on the camp baseball or football team. That made me real mad. I knew I had influence; I knew I was raising money for the Army and Navy, so I took myself and my influence over to Brigadier General Donald Robinson and I asked him about all this stuff about racial discrimination in ball playing. I told him, "Don't you know you've got one of the outstanding football players in the country in this camp, and he can't play on the team?" He asked, "Who are you talking about?" I told him—Jackie Robinson from UCLA. He apologized and said that he hadn't known about the situation and thanked me for bringing it to his attention. Then he said by all means he wanted Robinson and any other "qualified" Negro to play on the team.

I went back and told Jackie, "It's OK. You and any other 'qualified' Negro can join the football team." That stubborn cuss then said, "I'm not playing football unless they let me play baseball, too." I said, "Damn, Jackie, let's do this first." Well, after some back and forth talk between me and the Brigadier, Jackie wound up the champion baseball and football player for Fort Riley. Not only that, it opened the door over many parts of the country for integrated ball playing at other Army Camps, even in Georgia and Virginia, and they were tough customers.

Meanwhile, I heard from Marva; there's definitely a baby on the way. I was so happy I had to sit myself down and think, "Hey, I'm going to be a father. I'm going to have a baby." I know I said before that I'd never thought too much about having kids, but when you find out that there's one on the way, that's another story. I didn't miss a day calling Marva to see how she was doing. Momma was going crazy, saying she was really praying hard for this baby. Said it would make me settle down and retire.

I was promoted from Corporal to Sergeant. Pretty good, huh? The Army had figured that I could best serve them with morale building and refereeing exhibitions all over the country. I figured if the Army said that was best, it was. It did seem to cheer up the guys when I was there. Only thing, though, I told the Army I wouldn't appear anywhere to segregated Army audiences. I can be stubborn too. Hell, whites and blacks were all fighting the same war, why couldn't their morale be lifted at the same theater? I know a lot of people think I'm a quiet, shy guy, but when I make up my mind, that's it. The Army agreed with me and then I was only too happy to make everybody happy, white and black together.

When I got back to camp, I saw Jackie Robinson looking all sad. I asked him what was wrong this time. He told me they wouldn't accept his application for Officer's Candidate School. And seventeen other black enlisted men were in the same boat. Now, that really made me hot. I hightailed it back to the Brigadier's office, and we had a long talk. I told him that here was the Army offering me a commission, and I had no education, but the Army was turning down college educated men because they're black. It's bad enough having a segregated Army, but at least some blacks should be officers over their own people. We talked this through, but I wasn't satisfied with the answers I was getting, so I called Truman Gibson, Jr., a black serving in the War Department.

Truman Gibson, Jr., is a good and decent man—and he's still a good friend. He investigated, and as a result fifteen black guys, including of course Jackie, went to Officer's Candidate School. Yeah, and you know they did right well. Jackie came out a Lieutenant. Proud of myself, and him, about that.

You know, a lot of times those fellows at camp had problems. They didn't have money, and when they were in trouble they had no one to go to. It's bad enough if a relative dies, but when you don't have money to bury them, that's even worse. Hate to see a grown man cry. When they told me what was wrong, I'd tell them I'd call my friend Freddie Guinyard in New York and see what could be done. He'd send train tickets, or help pay for funerals, or make arrangements for hospital care and like that. Only thing is, he'd mess it up when the soldiers would call to thank him. Freddie would always say, "Don't thank me, thank Joe Louis. It's his money, not mine."

While I was busy helping a lot of those fellows out with

a little bit of money, I looked around and saw that I owed Mike Jacobs $59,000 and $41,000 to Roxy. It wouldn't be that bad if I were fighting. But nobody knew how long this war would last and I still needed extra money while I was in the service.

Meantime I heard from Mike Jacobs. He had made arrangements for me and Billy Conn to fight for the Army Relief. (Billy Conn had joined the Army shortly after I had.) Thing was, Billy also owed Mike money, more than $30,000. Put it all together, between the two of us, we owed Mike or the Twentieth Century Sporting Club about $90,000.

Mike sat down with the special Army committee in charge of the fight and told them our problems. After all, they were expecting a million-dollar gate on this fight. But there was a rule that nobody should get payments for private purposes while they were in the Armed Forces. Well, the special committee said that this law could be revised in this case in order to let me and Billy meet our bills. So I headed out to train at Greenwood Lake, New Jersey, and Billy went out to Mike's estate at Rumson, New Jersey.

We'd been in training for two weeks when we got special messages from Secretary of War Stimson saying the fight was canceled. Seems he was mad about all those money arrangements. Shoot, I was mad too. I didn't have to come into the Army; I could have gotten a deferment, or at least I didn't have to come as early as I did. I'd given the government over $100,000 and had raised I don't know how much helping to sell bonds. The Army knew I was good for a lot more money through fights and such. Well, then, I thought to myself, "This is the Army." So me and Billy volunteered to fight anyway without the money arrangement. Secretary Stimson still said no. Well, what the hell can you do? We were ordered back to our camps.

You know, the Army taught me lots of things. I didn't

have "shelter" provided by Roxy, Julian Black, and Chappie. Marva was in Chicago, Momma was in Detroit. I learned to make my own waves. Even though I didn't have these people around me, I found myself making all kinds of decisions, and I think they were mostly good ones. I was dependent on my own self. As I told you before, I'll follow anybody as long as I think they're right, but if I think you're wrong—forget it.

But I was missing Marva something terrible. Hell, it was the first time I'd be a father and the first time Marva'd be a mother. I set up what I thought was a nice place for her near the camp; we should be together during this time. Marva moved in and tried hard, but Kansas is too hot and sticky. She couldn't take it long and wanted to go home to be near her family and friends. I understood. Anybody having their first baby needs extra care and loving people around. I didn't have as much time as I thought I would and she went home.

It turned out just as well that she did. I ran into a guy who used to dance at the Cotton Club, who told me that he was dancing in a play called *This Is The Army* and traveling all over the country. He said that they were going to Hollywood to make the picture, so I thought, hey, that's a good gig for me. They were always telling me what a good morale builder I was, and besides, I loved Hollywood. I called the man who was in charge of the Second Command, and he arranged for me to go there. Well, I got all my orders ready and everything, and I was about to head out for Burbank, California, to play a role. Then I got the special message.

Marva had given birth to a baby girl. I was shocked, I was happy, I was foolish. Me—a father! Right away I phoned Marva and said, "Hey, Marva, heard you had a baby and it's a girl. Couldn't you do no better than that?" We were both so happy on that telephone, and Marva knew I was kidding. I got a week's furlough and headed straight for Marva and my baby girl.

What a beautiful baby. I looked at her eyes, her nose, her gums, toes, fingers. What God can do, with a little help from us people. We named the baby Jacqueline in honor of Chappie. (Remember his real name was Jack Blackburn.) We had talked this over and had made up our minds that whether a boy or a girl, the child would be named after Chappie—Jack or Jacqueline.

Oh, such a fussing over that child. Marva, of course, had a fairytale room for the child. All kinds of fancy kid's stuff and baby toys. From all the baby showers and stuff we could have opened a store. Momma was so proud and I just stood around with my big hands trying not to hurt the kid.

I headed off for California feeling good. Joe Louis— father; Joe Louis—Heavyweight Champion; Joe Louis— Sergeant, United States Army; Joe Louis—Hollywood actor. Hell, that's a lot, isn't it?

This picture took six months to make. Six long months. It's too long to be away from home. Lena Horne was there too, making another movie, and I was so carried away with her it wasn't proper. Lena would fuss with me about not coming to see her on the MGM lot to watch her making *Stormy Weather*. The trouble was there was another star there, Lana Turner, asking me why I didn't come out and see her on her set. I decided the best thing to do was not to go at all. By this time I really felt I was in love with Lena, but I was feeling like a dog. I wanted to marry Lena, didn't want to leave Marva, especially now with my new baby.

Fate decided everything. A friend of mine at the Hillcrest Country Club wanted to set up a golf foursome as part of a benefit for the U.S.O. Bing Crosby asked me to play golf with Arthur Stebbins, Lou Clayton, and Jimmy

Durante. They wanted some well-known women to keep our scores. I asked Lena and she said, "Good, fine." The day before the benefit, I called her to check about the time, but then Lena told me she wasn't coming because she was going to Fort Huachuca, Arizona, to entertain the soldiers. So I told her she already had made a commitment to me. Lena said she didn't give a damn; she wasn't coming.

Then she started giving it to me hot and heavy. Told me I'd been in town for a couple months and hadn't bothered to call her but a few times. She hinted about knowing that I'd been seeing other movie stars, too.

I figured the only way to settle this was to go by her house. When I got there, she was packing her bags to go to Fort Huachuca; I asked her again to come. Again she said no. I tried to explain to her that she might make more money in the U.S.O. benefit than the other thing. She kept packing.

One time Lena had given me a gold identification bracelet. "Joe Louis" was printed on the front, and on the other side it said "Lena." I'd had it for at least three years. I took off the bracelet and dropped it in her suitcase.

Well, then Lena started cursing me like nobody ever had. Before I knew it, I hit her with a left hook and knocked her on the bed. Then I jumped on her and started choking her. The thing, thank God, that saved her was that her aunt was in the apartment. Lena was screaming, and her aunt ran in and started trying to pull me off. When she said, "If you don't stop, I'll call the police," that brought me straight to. I stopped.

I left and went to my hotel. I was so scared I was shaking. I got chills because I realized I could have committed murder. I had never known such a feeling. What the hell made me do something like that? I'm not that kind of person. Passion can mess you up; next day, I couldn't show up for the tournament—my mind was ruined and my body felt too weak.

I called Lena to apologize and she hung up on me. End of romance.

Every now and then I get worried. I was hoping like hell the war wouldn't last too long. If it lasted for five years, I'd be thirty-four years old and out of the action. I wanted to return to the ring, but if I stayed idle too long, I'd be forced to retire, and I wasn't ready yet. There was too much money to be made. Believe me, I was used to the good life, and I couldn't make it any other way. Besides, I had a daughter; she had to have the best. And so I worried.

Well, now the movie was over, and I went on a long tour the War Department had set up, with Sergeant George Nicholson, my old sparring partner; Sugar Ray Robinson, a beautiful, promising welterweight; and Sergeant Jackie Wilson. For one hundred days we toured the country, setting up exhibition bouts. And when I was at Fort Riley, I helped set up and train a boxing team. Those guys were pretty good. Found myself doing a lot of talking to soldiers about physical fitness.

In between all this stuff the War Department called me to Washington. I sat down with some real big shots, and they told me they wanted to set up a series of tours overseas for the soldiers. OK with me, but I wouldn't head out till January, 1944.

In the meantime, Marva was flying all over the country. Whenever I found out I'd be someplace more than a couple of days, I called her and told her to be there. She always had that bag packed and was ready to come. Sometimes she'd say, "What about the baby?" I told her the baby wouldn't hurt any for a couple of days with our housekeeper there to take care of her.

Well, along around this time, I found myself and Sugar Ray at Camp Sibert, Alabama. We were waiting at the post bus station and sat down on the front bench. Along came an M.P. and said we had to move to the colored

OKeh

Licensed by Mfr. under U. S. Patent Nos. 1625755 and/or 1702564 (and other patents pending) only for non-commercial use on phonographs in homes. See detailed trade mark and patent notices on envelope. Made in U. S. A.

6475
(31374)

KING JOE PART II
(Joe Louis Blues) Blues Fox Trot
-Wright-Basie-
PAUL ROBESON with
COUNT BASIE and his ORCH.

Joe Louis at the start of his career, 1935. Under promotor Mike Jacob's early tutelage, Louis knocked out three former heavyweight champions: Carnera in six rounds; Baer in four; and Jack Sharkey in three. (Inset) Side 2 of Count Basie's paean to Joe Louis.

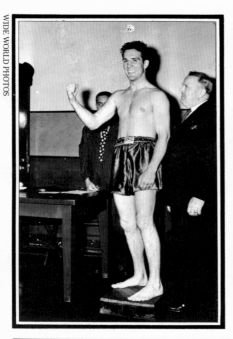

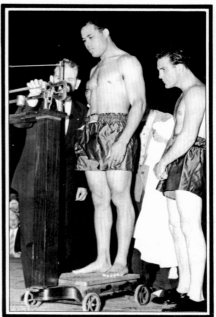

(Top, left) Overconfident and brash, ex–light-heavyweight champ Billy Conn weighed-in at 174 for the first Louis-Conn title fight, June 18, 1941, at the Polo Grounds. (Top, right) A more subdued Conn seemingly left the second fight on the scales as Joe's famous "He can run, but he can't hide" adage resulted in an eighth-round knockout. (Bottom) One-hundred-dollar ringside seats for the second Louis-Conn fight looked like a misunderstanding when it was all over.

(Top, left) Affable Abe Simon, although he outweighed Louis by 48 pounds, went only six rounds in their second fight in 1942 for Army Emergency relief. (Top, right) Known for his unorthodox, crouching style, Chilean Arturo Godoy went the full distance with Joe in 1940. (Bottom) Poker face meets Evil Eye. Lou Nova practiced Yoga for this 1941 fight but was an easy six-round knockout victim.

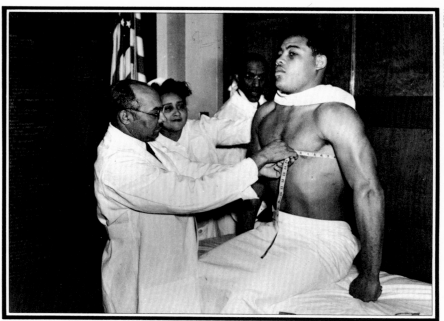

(Top) The world heavyweight champion breasts the tape for Uncle Sam in his preliminary draft physical, Chicago, October 14, 1941. (Bottom, left) Sergeant Joe Louis and Eddie "Rochester" Anderson in unfamiliar garb. (Bottom, right) Corporal Joe Louis on furlough from Fort Riley, Kansas, with his expectant wife, Marva.

(Top, left) Staff Sergeant Joe Louis working out in the gym at Camp Shanks, New York, prior to a bag-punching exhibition for his camp buddies and fans. (Top, right) Marva Trotter Louis at the start of her entertainment career, 1942. (Bottom) Joe Louis whispers advice but Bill "Bojangles" Robinson can only supply a rabbit's foot at the start of the "Paperweight" bout for the Colored Orphan Asylum in New York.

(Top) 11 West 125th Street, Harlem, USA. Crowds gather for the opening night of Joe Louis's restaurant, September 4, 1946. (Bottom) Dancer Bill "Bojangles" Robinson sampling the opening-night fare as the heavyweight champion looks on.

(Top, left) Four-year-old Jacqueline Barrow, daughter by Marva Trotter. (Top, right) Joe Louis, Jr., at two years of age. (Bottom) Joe and ex-wife Marva holding boogie-woogie piano prodigy, Frank "Sugar Chile" Robinson, 7, at the seventh annual American Negro Music Festival in Chicago.

(Top) Aged challenger Jersey Joe Walcott of Camden, New Jersey (left) and an aging champion (right) before their December 5, 1947 bout at Madison Square Garden. (Bottom) The second Conn win and an easy one-round knockout of Tami Mauriello were followed by a series of exhibitions such as the one pictured here at the Liberty A.C. in Washington, D.C.

Jersey Joe Walcott (left) grimaces with pain under a hard right by the champion. Not until the ninth round did Louis catch up with Walcott, but the rusty champion's blows lacked steam and Walcott eluded furious roundhouse attempts and backpedalled the rest of the fight. Walcott's sprinting tactics probably cost him the close, split decision.

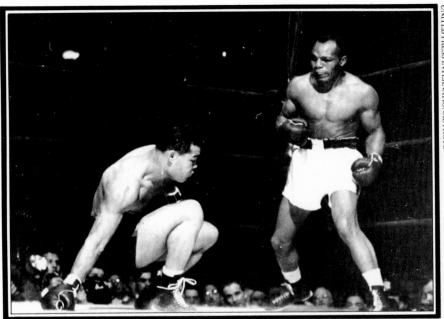

(Top) A surprised heavyweight champion is dropped for a count of two in the first round. Walcott also knocked Louis down for a count of seven in the fourth round. (Bottom) In a return bout, June 25, 1948, at Yankee Stadium, 42,657 persons saw Louis stalk Walcott and finally get to him for an eleventh-round knockout.

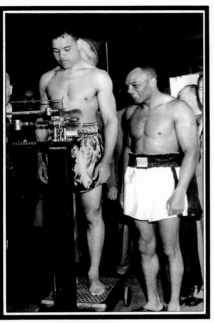

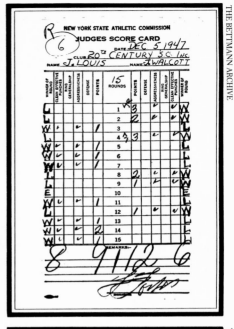

(Top, left) The weigh-in for the second Louis-Walcott championship fight. Walcott watches with a forced smile as Louis scaled his heaviest ever at 213½. (Top, right and bottom) Scorecards for the controversial first fight: Judge Frank Forbes called Louis the winner, eight to six and one even. Referee Ruby Goldstein saw Walcott the victor, seven rounds to six with two even; but Judge Marty Monroe gave the decision to Louis, nine to six, insuring victory for the Bomber.

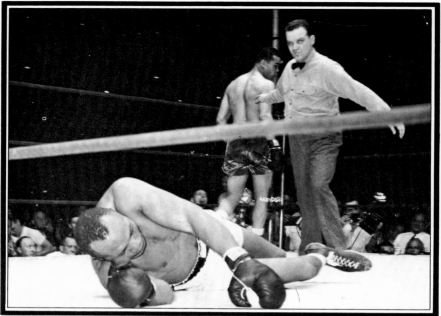

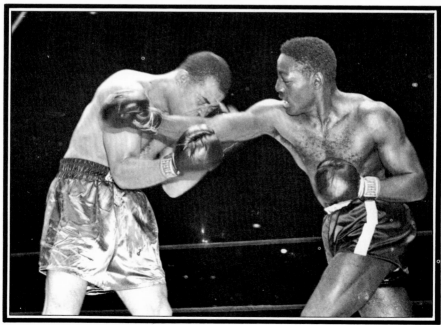

(Top) Walcott's finish in the second bout. Jersey Joe was ahead on points when Louis rallied in the eleventh round for a knockout victory. (Bottom) An undefeated but doomed champion came out of retirement to face Ezzard Charles, interim champion, but was badly beaten in his effort to regain the crown. Charles was too young and quick for the fading champ.

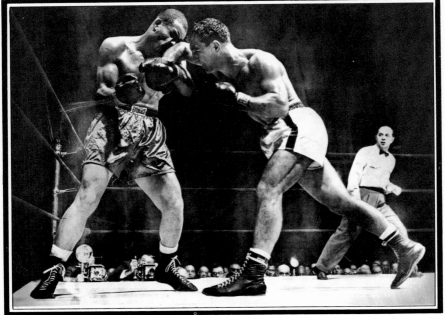

(Top) With ageless Jersey Joe Walcott champion after the upset of Charles, Louis again came out of retirement to try a comeback in 1951 against Rocky Marciano. Marciano's one disadvantage, a 67-inch reach, meant that he often had to leap and lunge to score. Louis (top and bottom) just eludes but is finally caught and begins to crumple under a Marciano forearm.

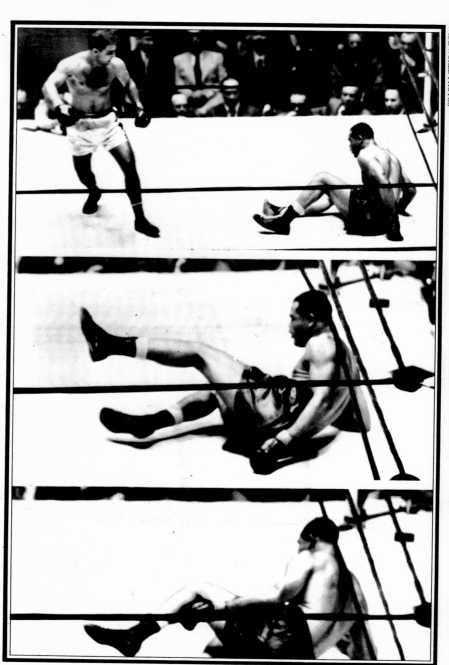

Beginning of the end. The first knockdown sequence in the fatal eighth round. Marciano lands a hard left hook (top) and stares at the fallen Brown Bomber. (Middle) Dazed, but still retaining some ring savvy, Louis bounces against the ropes and (bottom) starts to roll over, preparatory to taking an eight count on one knee.

(Top) The end. A Marciano haymaker has Louis helpless on the ropes and, with the fans and the press clamoring for the end, Referee Ruby Goldstein stopped the fight in the eighth round. (Bottom, left) The newlyweds: Mr. and Mrs. Joe Louis, the former Rose Morgan, Christmas Day, 1955. (Bottom, right) Joe, with his present wife Martha.

Louis and Schmeling meet a third time (bottom), thirty-seven years after their first fight (top) when Schmeling visited Louis at Pompton Lakes before the Jack Sharkey fight. Schmeling, heavyweight champ from 1930 to 1932, challenged Louis for the title in 1938 and lost.

section. I told him, "We ain't moving." He said, "Well, you're under arrest." OK, we went to the provost marshall's office and he gave me a lot of stuff like I'm a soldier and I have to do what the M.P. says. I told him, "Listen, I'm an American, I'm fighting in this war like anybody else, and I expect to be treated like anybody else." Told him that I'd go along with the Jim Crow laws in the towns, but I didn't see any reason that I had to sit in the back of an Army bus station. Well, the provost marshall started giving me a hard time. I just looked at him and said, "Let me call Washington." Well, of course they didn't, but news travels. Soon after, an order comes—no more Jim Crow busses in Army camps. That's fine. But you know, if I was just an average black G.I., I would have wound up in the stockades.

Just before I got ready to head for the European tour I really got zapped. Roxie was arrested for a charge of running the numbers racket in Detroit. Everybody was going down in this one; even Richard Reading, the former mayor, was being charged with conspiring to protect the numbers racket in Detroit. Man, let me tell you, this hurt. If it hadn't been for Roxie, I wouldn't have been World Champion. He took the chance on me and he could afford to. Only way he could afford it was to be in the numbers. Roxie didn't only help me, he helped I don't know how many other black people. There were kids who never would have gone to college if it hadn't been for Roxie; there were people who would have lost their homes if it hadn't been for Roxie; there wouldn't have been clothing and food for a lot of black people if it hadn't been for Roxie; there were churches that would have gone under if it hadn't been for Roxie. Hell! The numbers is only a game and some poor people keep themselves going on it, hoping to get rich. Damn, if you ain't got hope, what is there? Anyway, it turns out Roxie was sentenced to two-to-five, but he got out in about two and a half years.

JOE LOUIS: MY LIFE

But it's 1944, and I'm in the Army, and I gotta go overseas for my country. Fought all over the place; England, Italy, Africa. I remember the time I was in a bomber heading for London; Billy Conn was on this flight too. The landing gears were stuck, we circled for forty-five minutes. I prayed. I was scared to hell, but they finally landed it.

Well, anyway, while I was on this flight, Billy Conn said, "Joe, why couldn't you have let me hold the title for six months? I would have given it back to you." I said, "Billy, you had the title for twelve rounds and you couldn't hold it. How in the hell were you gonna hold it for six months?" That has been a joke with us over the years.

Another time me and some black soldiers were going to the theater in Salisbury, England. The ticket taker told us we'd have to sit in a special section. Shit! This wasn't America, this was England. I called for the theater manager and asked him what this was all about. He knew who I was and apologized all over the place. Said he had instructions from the Army. So I called my friend Lieutenant General John Lee and told them they had no business messing up another country's customs with American Jim Crow. He was real sorry; after that there was no more Jim Crow in the English theater.

The American and European tour took fourteen months. I covered England, Scotland, Ireland, Italy, and parts of Africa and came back to the U.S.A. in October, 1944. When they called me into the Special Services Headquarters and I told them about my experiences, they fell out laughing. Everybody was surprised I could make so many people laugh. Thing is they really didn't understand me; I could always make people laugh when I wanted to—but I got to know you.

My baby girl was growing up, and Marva and me had a real talking. I remember in 1943 that Marva met me one time in Philadelphia and we went to see a good friend of ours named Moms Robinson. I was as crazy about Moms as she was about me. Marva would go up to the little stage and clown around, singing. Moms listened to her and said, "You know, girl, you can sing. Why don't you do it?" When Marva asked me about it, I told her to forget it, or I'd break her neck. But she hightailed back and forth to New York to get voice training with, I think it was singer Dick Haymes's mother, on Fifty-seventh Street. I didn't know about it until I saw some signed checks. When I asked Marva what they were, she told me; she was working up a nightclub act. She said that since I seemed to like singers and chorus girls so much, she didn't see anything wrong about it. Maybe she was right.

Things were opening up for black people around this time, especially in New York. The war had brought lots of black people from the South looking for jobs in defense plants, and many of them making more money than they'd ever thought about. They needed someplace to spend it. That green money started opening a lot of doors. I remember when Barney Josephson opened Cafe Society Downtown in Greenwich Village. What was special about this club was that he not only hired black entertainers like Hazel Scott and Teddy Wilson, he let the black audiences in, too. I think it was one of the first big clubs in downtown New York to have integrated audiences. Not all those clubs did this, though. I remember Josephine Baker being kicked out of the Stork Club a few years later by Sherman Billingsly.

Then there was Fifty-second Street. They called it "Swing Street." Oh man, did they have great music there. There was the Onyx Club where Billie Holliday sang. At the Three Deuces you could catch Art Tatum playing the piano and Dizzy Gillespie tooting his horn; Kelly Stables had those great jazz musicians like Stuff Smith, Don Byas, and Hot Lips Paige; the last one I can remember was Tondelayo's—Eddie Haywood played a lot of piano there.

Black people were, for the first time, beginning to enjoy this country some. I thought about the war and all I'd seen. Most Americans hadn't seen those broken-up men and broken-up towns in Europe. I don't think a lot of American people could have understood the war unless they'd been there. Well, I guess wartime makes for crazy time. You see a lot of soldiers in these clubs trying to have the time of their life because any day they might be shipped out anywhere and never return. So I guess those places had their point.

Well, what I started out to say is that Marva made her grand opening at the Ebony Club on Broadway downtown. No bad place. Ethel Waters had just left there, and Marva was to open up with Duke Ellington's band and my friend Nat "King" Cole. Far as I could tell Marva did well, only trouble was everybody kept oh-ing and ah-ing about her costumes more than her voice. Marva had a special designer make up a batch of beautiful and fantastic looking gowns—she spent more on the gowns than she made in money.

She kept at it for a good while, but her manager told her she needed more experience to build up her voice and booked her on a bunch of one-night stands through the South. Marva got herself a chauffeur and set out to conquer the world. But after three months on the road, having to go to the backdoor of restaurants to get her food, eating and sleeping in the car, she gave up. I was glad about that. It's degrading for a woman who's had the best to be told "go 'round the back."

Anyway, seems like I was only in New York a short time when they wanted to send me to Alaska and the Northwest with Ruby Goldstein, one hell of a fighter during the twenties who later became a well-known referee. We were giving exhibition fights and general morale building sessions. Jesus Christ, if I ever thought Detroit or

Chicago were cold, I take it back. It was cold as hell, but me and Goldstein made it for two months.

But during the tour, while the world was having its war I had my own private war. Marva divorced me in March, 1945. I didn't want it, but I knew it was coming. Marva had wanted me to promise to stop fighting after the war was over. She was tired of my training in the camps all the time. She said my daughter hardly knew me; even if there hadn't been a war, the marriage conditions would have been the same. I told her I'd love to stop fighting but I couldn't. I was way over my head in debt to Roxy, Black, and Mike Jacobs. I couldn't live on those few pennies the Army issued me. I had to get back to making big money again.

I didn't feel too bad about Marva's money, though. Through the years she and Black and Roxy had made me buy up a lot of property and apartment buildings. As far as I was concerned, they belonged to Marva, so she wasn't hurting financially. Then too, my track record with other women was fairly well known. But, anyway, I kept on trying to make up with Marva. I'm a champion, and a champion sticks in there.

I sold Spring Hill and that hurt a lot. Marva and me had had some good times there, but it was costing me too much.

Well, thank God the war ended in August. We won it. I knew I'd soon be discharged, and I wanted to get back in that ring as soon as possible. Thirty-two years old, I had some good fighting and money-making years ahead of me. On October 1, 1945, I was discharged at Camp Shanks, New York. I tell you one thing, the Army was a great experience for me, but I wouldn't ever want to do it again. I'd been in for forty-six months and I'd traveled over 70,000 miles and was seen by close to 5,000,000 servicemen. I had been in ninety-six exhibition fights, and I had volunteered to do this. I don't know how many hospitals I visited, but I know a lot of guys seemed to feel better when I was there to cheer them up. When I was being discharged, they had a military review and I was given the Legion of Merit Medal "for exceptionally meritorious conduct." Major General Kells made a speech telling people how valuable I had been to the morale of the Armed Services; it made me feel great.

1946-1947
OUT OF THE ARMY

THE ARMY WAS NO EASY THING, BUT COMPARED with what I had to go through next, it was a song. I knew I had to make some money. Mike Jacobs knew it too; I owed him $100,000. As usual Mike was ahead of the game; he had Billy Conn all set up for a rematch with me. The fight was set up for June 19, 1946, at Yankee Stadium.

Mike had even put the ringside seats at one hundred dollars apiece. Funny how that came about. A newspaper man came up to Mike's office and asked him the price of the ringside tickets. Mike was just joking when he said one hundred dollars. Nobody ever heard of a price like that for a ticket in those days. You know something, that newspaperman went out and put that ridiculous price in the paper. The real knocker is that people started calling on the phone and buying those tickets. Mike said, what the hell, if they'll pay that amount to see the fight, leave it. And that's how one hundred-dollar tickets got started.

Just around this time I read in the newspapers that my old Army buddy, Jackie Robinson, had been hired by the Brooklyn Dodgers' Montreal Royals farm club in the International League. You know the expression "jump for joy"; well, it's true, because that's what I did. Jackie was the first Negro to play in modern organized baseball. Great God, I tell you it made me feel real good; I knew Jackie had the ability and, from Army days, I knew he had the guts to go through all he'd have to.

But in the meantime I needed some cash for Marva and some change for me. I was so far into debt, I had to borrow money promising to pay back on future fight purses, so when I went to Julian Black I didn't need to hear no kind of shit from him. He told me he didn't have any money. That really pissed me off because, knowing the type of man he was, I knew he had it. Must have thought I couldn't or wouldn't pay him back. Black knew the Conn fight was coming up. Couldn't go to Roxy, he'd just gotten out of jail. If anything, I needed to give him money.

I had a ten-year contract with Black where he got 25 percent of my earnings. Well, the ten years was just up. I told Black, he wouldn't have any 25 percent of me anymore. Instead I signed Marva on as my manager so she'd get that 25 percent. I'd rather do it this way than pay her the money in alimony. Then, along with Roxy, I took another manager, Marshall Miles from Buffalo. I'd known him a long time; I met him through Roxy and Black when I just turned pro.

I owed Uncle Sam $81,000 in back taxes, and he was waiting there in line, too. So I was frantic and knew I had to get something on the side to help me maintain some money. Then, like an angel out of heaven, an old friend, Billy Rowe, came up to me with a good proposition. He wanted to open up a public relations and advertising agency. I told him I never heard of a black public relations and advertising agency. Billy said that that was the point; he told me he'd researched the whole deal. Blacks, just in Harlem alone, were gambling away almost a quarter of a million dollars a day. Billy Rowe said if we had our own public relations office, we could convince big business that they should cater more to the black people. The money was there. The black people would buy more products if they saw black people as models; since I was a big name, maybe the money companies would buy all this.

Now, Billy Rowe was a smart guy; he had been Deputy Police Commissioner in New York and had worked as a columnist on the *Pittsburgh Courier* (a popular black newspaper). Dressed real sharp, and good-looking. Everybody in Harlem knew him, and he had all kinds of commendations from civic groups.

Billy Rowe felt he was sure to be a success. Black models, practically unheard of at that time (except Aunt Jemima and that man on the Farina box), could make money, the black newspapers could make money, and the white man would still get a bigger profit. He told me we could even get powerful enough to influence radio, newspapers, and magazines.

It sounded good to me, and I could still help my people do better. OK. We signed up together and opened the Louis-Rowe agency. He did the heavy work, I did the appearances. Our first job was to publicize the Louis-Conn fight—publicity and promoting ticket sales.

Hell, that was good, but I still knew I had to shape up for the fight with Conn. Conn was as hungry as I was, and in our last fight he could have been the champion. Those exhibition bouts in the Army were just fun and games. I needed some heavy training. As far as I was concerned, I hadn't fought in forty-six months.

The best way for me to get back in shape was to hit the road again, so Mike and my managers set up a bunch of exhibition fights for me. I headed out to the Northwest again, and between November and December of 1945, I fought ten exhibition bouts. Got a slight break and spent some time with my Momma. Then, hell, I spent some time with Marva. She'd been my wife for ten years, divorce or no divorce. I still wanted to come home. I must say Marva didn't get on a high horse and say no; we'd been through too much together. It settled into a sort of live-together and not-live-together thing; I had my freedom and she had hers. It worked. Marva always came through when I needed her.

Time to head out for Pompton Lakes and settle in for some heavy training. I wasn't twenty-seven this time, I was thirty-two, and Billy Conn was twenty-four. Mannie Seamon got the biggest, toughest guys around to be my sparring partners. Mannie was a jewel, but I still missed Chappie. To tell the truth, I looked like shit during the training. I was so out of shape reporters were giving me bad write-ups. But I wasn't worried, not one bit; I figured if the fight went fifteen rounds, I'd have to condition myself to withstand it. I moved slowly and tried to remember everything Chappie had taught me as well as listening to everything Mannie was telling me now.

I heard reports that Billy Conn was training up a storm. He was boxing all the time. I remember, when some reporter told me what he was doing, I said something like, "I hope he don't leave the fight in the gym." Roadwork was a steady-time thing with me, had to rebuild those muscles. Had to get my stamina back. I figured maybe I'd have to go the fifteen rounds; I didn't know what Billy would do. Behind all the money I owed out, the divorce and such, I had to win this fight.

Weigh-in time came and I looked real good at Billy. In four years he had gained somewhere around fifteen pounds. I was only up to 207. I knew he wasn't the same guy who almost took my title. I also knew that with all that extra weight he couldn't be the same fast guy he had been in the last fight. Knew he wouldn't be a prima ballerina this time around. The confidence I already had built up some more while I was looking at him.

There were a lot of things wrong with this fight. Mike had expected a $3,000,000 gate. He was disappointed— there was only about a $2,000,000 showing. But it looked fine to me; this was going to be the second-biggest money fight ever. The only one that had ever topped it was the second one between Tunney and Dempsey. I saw bills flying out the window, Marva making some money as well as my new manager, Marshall Miles, and thank God I could pay those back taxes and Mike Jacobs. Come on, Billy Conn; I knew I had him. I told the newspapers, "He can run, but he can't hide."

Well, the night of the fight we arrived in style—in

limousines, with motorcycle guards and all, and we could hardly get in the place. The attendants didn't want to let us in; those guys really took their jobs seriously. It took a while before we convinced the guards who we were and got to our dressing rooms.

The bell rang, round one. We came out and sparred a little, and Billy said to me, "Take it easy Joe, we've got fifteen rounds to go." That fool made me break out laughing. But I could see he wasn't fast at all for this fight; I was much faster. And it was a bad fight. Billy was jumping around dancing, and I was waiting for him to come to me. The crowd paid a lot of money for this fight and they didn't see much happening and they booed. I don't blame them.

By the third round I knew I'd have to go to him. The fight moved along the way I had planned for the first seven rounds—kept shuffling in, wasting no motion. I kept coming on to him like a heavy-duty truck and keeping up the pressure. Using what speed he had, he'd bob and move and try to stay out of my range, circling to my right and back-pedaling all the time.

I told Marshall Miles and Mannie Seamon before the eighth round started that I was going to go out and punch to see if Billy could take it. I got in there hard and opened up a cut under his left eye with a right-hand shot. His knees buckled with a right to the chin. Then I gave him a left hook and a right cross, and he was flat on his back. The referee counted him out 2:19 of round eight.

This second Conn fight was easier than the first; I felt good about that since I was four years older. But Conn and I didn't put on a good show. It wasn't my fault, but I'm a proud man and I wanted another quick fight so people would have no doubts about my abilities.

Now came the money time; I must have made close to $625,000 on that fight. Now, divide that in half, and Marva, Roxy, and Marshall got their share. I paid Uncle Sam the $81,000 I owed him for the first Conn fight, I paid Mike the $100,000 he had lent me, I gave Billy Rowe $25,000 to officially open the public relations firm; by the time I took care of some people I owed money to—you figure it out.

Anyway, I asked my managers and Mike Jacobs to find me somebody to fight. They told me to take a break and they'd look around for a September match. Mike said he was looking at Tami Mauriello, and he was going to see what he could do.

In the meantime, I was scrambling like a madman. I made half a million dollars, and I was broke. Again friends came through. Mike introduced me to two guys, Jack Roth and Lou Brooks; they had restaurants all over the Times Square area. They wanted to build a restaurant in Harlem on One hundred twenty-fifth Street; I didn't have to put a penny in it. All they wanted to do was use my name, and whenever I was in New York I was supposed to stop in. They promised a lot of money, but I don't remember the amount. Sounded good to me. It worked for a number of months and I got a little change, but I wasn't there because I was still fighting. Maybe it would have worked better if I'd been around. You know, black people aren't gonna patronize something just because your name's up there; black people around this time were beginning to get more aware of themselves. They were tired of taking a lot of shit—they got killed in that war, they helped build those ships and planes and bombs that bent Hitler and Hirohito. Don't put no jive restaurant on them just because the name says "The Joe Louis Restaurant."

Anyway, I was still in New York and I was tired of all this racism shit. Made me sick to my stomach when I heard that a black veteran, Isaac Woodard, had been attacked by some southern policemen who jugged both his eyes out with that billy stick policemen carried; they attacked him for no good reason. When the people heading the benefit committee for Woodard asked me if I'd appear, there was nothing else I could say except yes. It was a big thing held at Lewisohn Stadium inside of City College with Peter Lind Hayes and his wife Mary Healy, both white, helping to get it together. I remember when it came time for me to speak, I was all choked up, but I managed to say, better than I can say now, something like, "Nobody in America should have to go through Second Class Citizenship. Me and a whole lot of black guys went out fighting for the American cause, now we're gonna have to get America to give us our civil rights too. We earned them."

Well, just like old times, I had a little time to myself. Headed out to play golf. I was shooting in the 70s now. Played with the big boys, Ted Rhodes, Charles Sifford, Bill Spiller. God, those guys were great. If they had been white, or at least allowed to play in white tournaments, no telling where they'd have gone. They'd have had the big money and the time to develop themselves even more.

But the hell with the golf. I had more important things to do. I had to court me a lady. The lady's name was Marva. We sat, we talked. I told her we'd been through too much together; we'd had a child together. I asked her to marry me again, to try one more time, at least. She said yes. I was happy and I thought she was happy too—maybe this time it would work. I think Momma was as happy as the both of us put together.

Marva and I were just settling in good when Harry Mendel, a fight publicist, came to see me. He told me "some people" had a proposition concerning some fighter; they'd give a million dollars if I'd "do business." Harry said that they'd meet me on the Staten Island Ferry, top of the Empire State Building, in the middle of the Atlantic Ocean to make the deal. I laughed, "Ain't that some hot shit!" No, no. A million dollars tax-free is tempting and would be an easy way out of my problems, but no way for me, Joe Louis. I'm not built that way. I could see Chappie's ghost kicking me in my ass. I know I haven't been a saint about a lot of things, but one thing I know, my profession is boxing and my title is Champion. Got too much pride in myself and my people to mess that up for anything or anybody.

Mike set up a bout for September 18 at Yankee Stadium with Tami Mauriello from the Bronx. Mauriello was a big guy and he had proved that he could punch, although he wasn't any great hell as a boxer.

I didn't consider him any threat at all, so I was really surprised when in the first round he shot me a right on the chin that almost threw me. He hurt me and surprised me. But Mauriello was slow; he should have moved right in when he saw I was hurt. I went through a couple of combinations and had him down for a five count. Dropped him again and he still got up. Came back again, and I let it all go loose. Referee Donovan counted him out in the first round.

The fight was good, the last time I really felt like my old self. I had complete control, energy, power. I wonder sometimes if that wasn't my last great fight.

Shoot, it was over so quick, I didn't even have to take a shower. Freddie Wilson and me got in the car, and he drove me home to 555 Edgecombe. When I got to the entrance of my apartment building, I could still hear the roaring of the crowds watching the substitute fight. I thought to myself, someone landed a blow, and the roar was the crowd's applause. I looked at Freddie Wilson and said that if Tami hadn't hit me so hard to make me mad, I'd still be in there right now, fighting.

But after the money from the fight was divvied up and I paid some debts, there still wasn't enough money. I asked Mike to get me another match, and he said that there wasn't anybody else around. Well, back to the exhibition tours; I knew I could pick up some change doing this. But it was a problem with me and Marva, back to me traveling, traveling, traveling, but I had to have the money. So, in the fall I headed for Honolulu and Mexicali, Mexico. Must have picked up about maybe $90,000. Not bad.

Then Mike told me he had a great tour lined up for me in Central and South America starting in the winter of 1947. Fine with me.

Marva was doing well with her manager's share of the fight. She set up a trust fund for our daughter. I told her that it was a real good idea. Then she zapped me when she said she was setting money aside for our next child who'd be due in May. Great God! I was gonna be a father again. Figured Marva and me had got it made together now. But I knew I'd really need more money. Children need a lot of extra special stuff. So when a friend of mine named Jess Thornton offered me $20,000 for the use of my name for a milk company, I said all right. He changed the name to the Joe Louis Milk Company. I don't know, maybe they changed the name by now, but it sure lasted a long time.

All my other businesses had gone under—the Chicken Shack in Detroit and Swingland in Chicago. I was open game when my friend Truman Gibson, Jr., called me to see if I'd invest in his black-owned Superior Life Insurance Company. I figured this to be a good investment, and better than any restaurant or night club deal. So I went into this for a few big bucks.

Well, in February I started out for this grand tour. First stop Mexico, and I took Marva with me. Then of course there was the usual, Roxy, Marshall Miles, Mannie Seamon, Freddie Wilson, and Bill Bottoms. Let me tell you, Mexico City was a dream city—beautiful, clean, and nice people. No racial prejudice that I could see. But their prejudice ran along money lines. If you're dirt poor—too bad. If you got some good change—you're all right. I had money and I was a world celebrity, so I got the king treatment.

First exhibition fight was with my old friend Arturo

Godoy for a ten rounder. The people turned out like crazy and were enthusiastic; I got more cheers than Godoy.

Marva fell in love with Mexico City and she ran into a Mexican doctor who promised her a no-pain delivery. She decided that while I was on tour she'd stay in Mexico City, so she rented a real nice furnished apartment, sent for our daughter Jackie, Ethel, and a couple of her sisters, and stayed right there while I continued my tour.

I met Godoy again in Chile for a six rounder; we were practically getting to be tight buddies. Then we hit Colombia, staying at a hotel across the street from the Bogotá City Hall. Bogotá was a beautiful, wonderful city, with real warm people; only thing is they had armed troops all over the place. From there we went to my favorite spot, Havana, Cuba; that was a pure pleasure. But the tour was rough, with all the time traveling and the general wear and tear on your body.

March, and I had nothing scheduled until the beginning of June. Then Branch Rickey asked me to come to New York and talk with Jackie Robinson. Paul Robeson and Bill Robinson were there too. Rickey wanted us to tell Jackie what to expect because he was set to leave the Montreal Royals and join the big boys—the Brooklyn Dodgers.

We didn't need to say anything to Jackie. He'd been in the Army, he knew just what to look for. He knew he'd have to be strong and take the shit, or he'd close the door for black people in baseball for Lord knows how many more years.

I felt real good when Jackie said that if it wasn't for me and Jesse Owens, he wouldn't be where he was.

I headed back to Marva in Mexico City. She looked beautiful. Nothing prettier than your wife when she's expecting. Everything was OK. And so when, in the early part of May, I got a call from Billy Rowe asking me to meet with some clients in Oklahoma City, I left, telling Marva I'd be back soon.

JOE LOUIS: MY LIFE

Well, I did it again. While I was on the golf course in Oklahoma City, I got a message that Marva had delivered a baby boy. Rushed to the phone and said, "Well, Momma, you finally hit the jackpot." My son, Joe Louis Barrow, Jr. was born May 24, 1947. I was as proud as you can make 'em. Only thing is, I don't think till this day anybody who really knows Joe Louis Barrow, Jr., calls him anything but Punchie.

Anyway, the rest of the tour took place in the Northwest, San Diego, Spokane, and Los Angeles. All easy fights.

By now I was real tired of the exhibition matches. The money was good and guaranteed, but I asked Mike Jacobs to find me somebody for a championship bout; he said there was still nobody around. I told Mike to try for Joe Baksi, a quality heavyweight. Mike tried, Baksi said no. He was going to Stockholm to fight Olle Tandberg, a big-time Swedish heavyweight. Baksi said after he beat Tandberg, he'd meet with me. Only trouble was Tandberg beat the shit out of Baksi, and that left me nothing.

Then Mike got the bright idea to have another exhibition fight with a black guy named Arnold Cream, better known as Jersey Joe Walcott. I knew all about him and knew he was a damn good fighter, and I remembered him well. He had been one of my sparring partners when I was preparing for the first Schmeling fight in 1936. Jersey Joe looked good with me when we had our first workout, back then. Second workout, I must have hurt him some. Next thing I knew, he cut out of camp and never came back, and now here he is, fighting me for my title. One thing we had in common is that we both had fought Al Ettore and Abe Simon; only thing, though, he had been knocked out by both of them.

Mike wanted to set up a ten-round exhibition match. But there was a catch: the New York State Athletic Commission said no. Ten rounds has to be a championship fight. They said they'd only go for a six-round exhibition fight. I told Mike, OK, put the championship up for this one. Well, I knew Jersey Joe was a tricky fighter with a good right hand, but I didn't figure on any real trouble. It'd be a good gate, and the second time I'd defend my crown against a black man.

Well, it was June and there was a lot of negotiating to do. Mike was figuring on trying to get the fight on near the end of the year. As usual, I could use the break and I was grateful for it. I was tired and older. Headed back to Chicago, took care of some business deals, played a little golf, got to know my son, played with my beautiful daughter, and saw my momma. You know something, I was really feeling good; it could be, at times, a real nice life.

Before I knew it, it was November and time to train. But no more tingling feelings. I thought about those early pro days, when I'd get up before dawn and run and run for miles, and enjoy it. Used to look forward to getting in the ring with my sparring partners and get a kick out of tricking or faking them out. That was fun, but no more. I was over 218 pounds; that's too heavy. But taking off weight was harder to do now. I wanted to get down to about 210. It all made me seriously think about retiring, but Uncle Sam was really getting on my back, now.

Well, anyway, the day of the fight I weighed in at 211. To get to that weight, I hardly drank any water for a couple of days and barely ate any heavy food. I knew I didn't feel like myself, and this was my first championship bout since Tami Mauriello in September, 1946; that was over a year—a long time between fights. I felt it. So, when I climbed into the Madison Square Garden ring on December 5, 1947, I was hoping for a quick one.

In round one, Walcott hit me with a bunch of left jabs and hooks right away. When I pressed forward, Walcott stopped dancing long enough and hit me with a solid right to my jaw and floored me for a two count. I lost my head then, and I tried to take him out with lefts and rights, but Walcott ran away.

In the second and third rounds, I was still mad as a sonofabitch. I kept sticking jabs at his face and trying to bang right hands to his body. But he just danced away from me.

In the fourth, with the round less than a minute old, Walcott smacks a right to my jaw and down I go again. As I'm on my hands and knees taking a seven count, I say to myself, "Goddamn, am I really a twenty-to-one favorite?" When I got up, my head was ringing. I fell into a clinch to clear it up. Walcott shook me loose and started beating the shit out of me.

The next four rounds, I kept pressing him with jabs and body digs—he just kept back-pedaling.

I thought I had him in the ninth. I jabbed him into position for a right cross that landed just a little bit too high. As he fell up against the ropes, I poured lefts and rights to his body and his head, but he took them all—and fought back. When the bell rang ending the round, I knew my chance for a knockout was over.

For the rest of the night, Walcott got on a bicycle—like a black Bob Pastor. He was determined to stay the fifteen rounds, and he just fought in spurts.

When the fight was over, I just wanted to get out of that ring. I was so disgusted with myself and the way I had fought that I started climbing out before the decision was announced, but my corner pulled me back. I didn't care about the decision. I knew I won, since Walcott didn't come to me. After all, I was the champion, and he had to take the crown from me. The judges scored it like this:

9 to 6 in favor of Louis—Judge Marty Monroe,
8 to 6, one even, in favor of Louis—Judge Frank Forbes,
7 to 6, two even, in favor of Walcott—Referee Ruby Goldstein.

I won, but it wasn't good. The crowd booed the decision, and I felt like a piece of shit. All those thoughts about retiring disappeared. I knew I'd have to meet Jersey Joe Walcott again to erase the doubts.

On the way to the dressing room, I was thinking that all this would mess up my marriage. Marva was looking for me to quit; I didn't want to retire on a bad note like this; what the hell was I going to do about the government taxes?

After I got to my apartment at 555, I called Momma in Detroit. She told me how worried she'd been all during the fight. We talked some and she said, too, "I thought that would have been the last fight, but I know you got to go in there again and fight that boy."

As if everything wasn't bad enough, the next couple of days people were sending letters and telegrams and making phone calls to the New York State Athletic Commission, newspapers, the governor, and the mayor saying that the decision was wrong, that I had lost the fight. This was the first time in my fighting profession the fans weren't with me. Those boos went right down to my bones. I felt a depression I had never felt before. It was one hell of a way to end the year.

1948-1951
RETIREMENT AND RETURN

NINETEEN FORTY-EIGHT. THE YEAR STARTED OFF as badly as the last one had ended. Taxes. I was really getting in over my head. Seems like in 1946 I should have paid taxes to the tune of $196,000, but my tax guy, Ted Jones, figured that the $194,000 I'd lost in business should cancel out any debt I owed the government. The government didn't figure it that way. One tax guy went over my finances and found out I had been borrowing money from my own companies and hadn't paid taxes on the money I borrowed. I don't know, he might as well have been talking Greek to me. What I did know was I had no money. Had to borrow more money from Mike Jacobs, so I had to keep fighting. That dream of retiring with the championship seemed far off.

Right about here the only bright thing I saw was a trip that had been planned for Europe. It was called the Health and Holiday Show and some promoters in England were getting together an exhibition tour. I wanted to get away.

But I had two things to do first. I had to fight an exhibition match with Bob Foxworth in Chicago on January 29, and arrangements had to be made for a rematch with Jersey Joe Walcott. After talking through all the terms, Mike signed me and Jersey Joe for June.

Now all I wanted to do is to get on that boat. Pressure was getting too heavy on me. Marva, Roxy, Marshall Miles, Mannie Seamon, and a couple of friends got on the *Queen Mary,* and I left all those troubles behind. It was good being with Marva. And everything started out with a bang. Marva and me had a beautiful stateroom. All the people on the ship were always crowding round, talking to us. Must have been some kind of party every night.

When we got to London, the Health and Holiday people had rented a fabulous mansion for us. This was just after the war, but this place still had expensive oriental rugs, drapes, antique furniture and lamps, and a full staff of servants. The servants had a cottage of their own on the grounds.

We went all over London, did everything except meet the King. When I got tired, I'd hire a chauffeur and a guide to take Marva around. That's when I made a mistake. I had met some real outspoken English girls. One day when Marva had gone out to go shopping and sight-seeing, I invited these girls over. I figured in that big house, who'd find out anything? Anyway, me and the girls had a good time, but when they left and I was walking back through the living room, I saw Marva watching me. Oh man! I asked her how long she'd been there. She just looked at me and said, "Long enough," then she went upstairs and locked the door. Shit! Messed up again.

Well, in spite of all that, we managed to have a pretty good time, although Marva was calling Chicago every single day to check on the kids. I told her that for the money she was spending telephoning, she might just as well have brought the babies with her. But after what I'd put her through, there wasn't anything I could do. She bought silverware antiques, linen tablecloths, and such— what I was really afraid of was going to Paris and her seeing all those clothes.

Some people in Sweden wanted me to put on an exhibition tour there. I would have loved to, but they didn't have any money to pay. Right through here, I needed the money bad. They promised me a lot of ice skates, I mean, but what the hell can you do with ice skates?

Paris was as beautiful as they say, and the people were

real nice. Saw everything, went to the museum, went up in the Eiffel Tower, sat at the sidewalk cafes. It was a real ball. Marva must have spent half of what I earned buying clothes by that French designer Jacques Fath. Then she did what I'd asked her not to do: she cut her hair. At first I didn't like it, but then when I got used to it, she looked real cute.

Then we went on over to Rome, for a few days and the people really went wild over me. I'm glad they did, and I really needed it to get my morale up again.

Before you know it, it was time to go home again. We came back on the *Queen Elizabeth* with two white poodles, named Peter and Paul. Marva and me had really fallen in love with them, although we really bought the dogs for the kids.

It was a nice trip back. Didn't have any problem till we got to Customs. First off we had to pay $1,000 in customs duty tax. That wasn't so bad. But when they opened a German-designed foot trunk I had bought, they found it full of expensive French perfume. Marva's stuff had already been cleared, and when she saw that trunk full of perfume, she told the customs guys to put it with her things. When I tried to tell her that it was Marshall's and Roxy's stuff, she wouldn't buy it. She said they could ask her for the stuff whenever they wanted. Well, to this day, Marva's still got the trunk and all those beautiful glass perfume bottles.

I'd escaped for a while and it was good for me. Yet I knew what I had to do—I had to beat Jersey Joe. But my heart wasn't in this fight coming up. Seems like I had planned everything right, so how come it was all going wrong? I didn't want this fight, but I had to go through all the aches and pains again and you know what for?— money. Tax people sniffing around me again. People, fans, losing faith in me. I thought to myself, maybe I should have stayed at the Ford plant. Then I think, hell no, I've had too good a time, I've had too much money to go for that. I decided it was all worth it—off to Pompton Lakes to train again.

June 25 at Yankee Stadium—good crowd, good money. The bell rang and me and Jersey Joe got it on. I was 214 pounds and Jersey Joe was 194. This time I fought for me. I had no intention of running all over that ring, Jersey Joe had to come to me. But Jersey Joe figured this out, too. He knew if I caught him, I had him. The result of this was that nothing much did happen—the crowd booed for nine rounds. In the tenth round, the referee, Frank Fullam, said, "Hey, one of you get the lead out of your ass, and let's have a fight." Jersey Joe was starting to look a little tired, and I went after him in the eleventh round. I let go with everything I had. Jersey Joe made the same mistake Billy Conn had, he got overconfident and careless. When I saw the opening, I gave him a right to the chin and three lefts to the head. I knew I had him. His legs gave out and he dropped his hands. At the end of two minutes and fifty-six seconds of the eleventh round, he was counted out.

Before the fight, I figured the crowd was all for Jersey Joe, but after the fight it sounded like old times again. The cheers were for me and I loved every minute of it.

I was feeling a little bit better about myself, but things weren't quite going so well at home. I had told Marva that starting the end of September and through December, I was going on an exhibition tour, and I told her to get her traveling bags packed. That's when Marva told me to sit down. As nice as she could, she said she couldn't make it with me anymore. When she was younger, she said, it was exciting dashing all over the country, but now she couldn't and wouldn't do it. She told me the kids were always running to Ethel instead of her when they hurt themselves or were proud of themselves. Told me it was bad enough they didn't have a father around, but not to have a mother around was too much. She said she wanted a divorce. Deep down, I knew this was it.

She told me about myself. How when the kids had a birthday, I was always out of town and never remembered. Then she told me how she'd buy the kids presents in Chicago and have them shipped to wherever I was and have Roxy ship them back home in time for the kid's birthday so they'd think the present was from me. I felt real bad. I told her I always brought the kids presents when I came home. That's when she said my timing was off, and my timing for marriage was off too.

I didn't know what to answer. One kind of way, I felt a relief. Even giving her everything I thought she wanted, I wasn't really giving enough. I wasn't the kind of husband you read about in books. I had no intention of being faithful—too many pretty girls out there. Only thing, I personally didn't feel this should mess up my marriage. But then you know it takes two people to make a marriage. I sighed inside and said to myself, "What the hell, if we break up, I don't have to feel guilty about nothing. We both married too young, anyway. Maybe we both need to grow up some more without each other."

I asked her what she was going to do, and she told me she wanted to buy a home she'd seen recently. Then she was going to see if she could pick up where she left off thirteen years ago with her designing. Said she never wanted to get married again, and, of course, I could see the children anytime I wanted.

Well, that did it to me. I begged, I pleaded, but this time I knew it was final.

Time was heavy on me right through here. I was real grateful to my friend Truman Gibson, Jr. He knew I always was trying to help black kids. So we set up some Joe Louis Youth Clubs under the direction of the Superior Life Insurance Company. We'd arrange picnics for the kids, set up boxing rings outdoors, get track meets together. Summertime, black kids need something to get their minds from getting idle, and I needed it as much as they did.

Then Truman Gibson helped me set up the Chicago School of Automotive Trades. A lot of black kids couldn't get a good break in school; nothing for them to do out there if they couldn't get a job. So if they could be taught to use their hands, maybe they wouldn't wind up snatching somebody's pocketbook and landing in jail. This school was for young and old; my stepbrother, Pat Brooks, started there and graduated, too. My career was grinding down, and we both knew that he should have some kind of trade to fall back on.

I was really feeling worthwhile now, and for a little pleasure, I went back to golf. Sugar Ray Robinson was having a golf tournament in July, and I had to be there. I headed out to West Baden Springs, Indiana, for some practice before I left for New York, then I got a date to play in the United Golf Association in Indianapolis in August. The UGA was the same as the Professional Golf Association (PGA), only difference is the stakes weren't as high, and the UGA was all black. Well, like they say, if they won't let you join the party, have a party of your own.

While I was keeping myself as busy as I could, in the back of my head I was telling myself that after some more exhibition fights I would hang it up. I had to retire. I talked to a lot of my friends about it. Hell, I was thirty-four years old, but as far as boxing goes, I was an old man. The thought of retirement felt good; now I could really play golf.

September 30—and I started out on the tour. Headed through Washington, D.C., Atlanta, Georgia, Norfolk, Virginia, and then I ran into a problem in New Orleans. I had to get a plane out fast to meet for an exhibition bout in Nashville, Tennessee. I called Eastern Airlines to have their limousine pick me up at my hotel. Those rotten people told me they weren't going to do it. I managed, by luck, to get to the airport just on time, but swore I'd never fly Eastern and told all my friends to do the same. After a while the story must have gotten back to Eddie Rickenbacker, the President; he sent me a letter of apology.

From Nashville I went on to Boston, Cleveland, Detroit, St. Louis, Oklahoma City, Kansas City, Cincinnati, Chicago, Philadelphia, and finally Lewiston, Maine. Must have had close to twenty bouts including another decision over Billy Conn. Finished up before Christmas, just in time to pick up some nice presents for my family and rest up a bit before I went on my next series of exhibitions starting January 10, 1949.

1949. Divorce proceedings were going ahead, and Marva was bargaining for the same deal as she had with our last divorce, but we still stayed friends. She understood I wasn't going to change, and I understood I wasn't the kind of man she needed for a husband. I had to rake in all the money I could now; I had to get my life settled.

So the tour started January 10 in Omaha, then on to Topeka and Wichita, Kansas; Toledo, Ohio; Moline, Illinois; and Rochester, Minnesota. When I got to Miami to meet with Elmer Ray on January 25, I went to see Mike Jacobs.

Mike was still sick as hell. I tried to cheer him up and he tried to cheer me up, but when I went back to my hotel on the South Side of Miami, where the colored folks were allowed to live, I sat around in my room for a while and said to myself, "No shit, Joe, you got to quit." I was real depressed over Mike. I knew he'd never be back. I knew he didn't have it anymore. I didn't either—I knew that. I was tired and needed a new way to make money.

I thought and I thought. I figured if I was to retire, and I knew Mike would never come back, maybe I could form a boxing club of my own. Then I thought about the Chicago Stadium owned by Jim Norris. Norris seemed to own a piece of just about everything in sports in this country. He had the Detroit Red Wings and the Chicago Black Hawks hockey clubs, the Chicago Stadium, and I hear he was ready to move into Madison Square Garden now that Mike was sick.

What was to lose? I called him in Chicago and told him I wanted to retire and I thought I could get the heavyweight championship for us. If I retired, I could name the two guys that would fight for the title.

I hardly had any time between the exhibition bouts, but Norris wanted to talk about it. He was interested. I told him I'd be up in March and we'd see what we could work out. So after going through a lot of cities in Florida and a stop-off in Savannah, I headed for Kingston, Jamaica, for a three-round bout with Edgar Edward.

Had a few days in the sun and then went straight to Chicago. On March 1 I called a press conference and announced that I was retiring as the undefeated Heavyweight Champion of the World. How could I explain? I felt good that I was retiring with the title, I felt bad leaving the ring. I don't know, I still don't.

But, down to business. Me and Jim Norris and Arthur Wirtz got our heads together. I told him I'd name Joe Walcott and Ezzard Charles as the two leading contenders for my title.

Let me tell you a little bit about Ezzard Charles. He was born in 1921 and was from Cincinnati, Ohio, by way of Lawrenceville, Georgia. Charles was a great boxer with speed and stamina. He had just turned pro in 1940, and his record was excellent even if he did run a little light on weight—he'd been an outstanding middleweight and his best weight now was 180 pounds. Well, anyway, me and Norris talked it over with Abe Greene of the National Boxing Association (N.B.A.), who agreed that Walcott and Charles were the most likely contenders and that he'd recognize the match for the championship. Then Norris asked me how much money I wanted for getting the match together. I told him $250,000. Norris told me he'd give me $300,000 to get the match going, a salary of $20,000 a year, and he'd make me vice-president of our new corporation—the International Boxing Club.

I knew we'd be competing with Mike Jacobs's Twentieth Century Sporting Club, but with Mike no longer there it didn't seem to matter. Besides, I'd paid my dues to Twentieth Century; I'd made I don't know how many millions for them. I hired Truman Gibson to work with me because I still was signed up for a batch of exhibition bouts for the month of March, and we got Walcott-Charles fight set for June 22.

I liked the next tour I went on; it took me through Cuba and Texas and wound up in Washington, D.C. I had no fights scheduled until October, so I checked into New York. There I saw my partner Billy Rowe and did public appearances for him.

Got to admit, I missed going home to Marva and the kids, but that was over now. A good friend of mine name of Kiah Sayles, a liquor salesman, went around with me a lot now; he took me to an after-hours brownstone right off St. Nicholas Avenue and One Hundred Forty-eighth Street. They didn't have a sign hanging up there, but anybody who was anybody knew it was Johnny Walker's. Walker and his partner Chink Cunningham ran the numbers and bookmaking on St. Nicholas Avenue. So they set up this real high-class drinking place. Well, you know, I was only drinking Coke, but I enjoyed being there. Everybody came in there—Billy Daniels, Lana Turner, Billy Eckstine. I loved it when Tallulah Bankhead came in; she was one tough woman. Liked to watch her drink down a whole goblet of bourbon in what seemed like one swallow. One night the whole chorus line at the Copacabana would be there, the next night the Zanzi-

beauts—the black chorus girls working at the Club Zanzi-
bar. They were cute as hell. They'd come up to me with
some sad story asking to borrow twenty dollars and, hell,
I'd give it to them. They really didn't jive me out any
money, I knew what they were doing. My pockets were
full and if it made those pretty little faces light up—what
the hell.

But I had to get back to Chicago Stadium to take care of
business. Had to see who's going to be the next heavyweight champion. So on June 25 Charles and Walcott
went at it. I can tell you this, it wasn't anyone's idea of an
exciting fight, but Ezzard Charles won the fifteen-round
decision. He looked dull, but he worked like a scientist
and became the new heavyweight champion of the world.
I felt the title had gone into good hands. The N.B.A.
thought so too, but the New York Boxing Commission
didn't think Charles should be champion. New York felt
there should have been more elimination fights with some
foreign boxers involved also.

I got pissed off. Other champions had done what I had
done; way back when, Jim Jeffries did it too. No other
former champion went through this shit. Why me? Was it
because I'm black they don't figure I should call the shots,
or was boxing becoming more organized, or was it that
they just didn't want another black heavyweight champion? Ezzard Charles would have to prove himself.

You know, though, I felt strange watching those guys
up there going at it. I almost felt dead, like some kind of
ghost looking on. I kept telling myself, what the hell, I'm
tired, but I did my job and I did it better than anyone else
had in Lord knows how many years.

But out of this some real good things happened. We
signed Ezzard Charles up to meet with Gus Lesnevich in
New York in August. Well, this was the first time a black
heavyweight champion was being brought forward into
the big time by a black promoter—me. Mike Jacobs
taught me well. I knew the pitfalls, I knew the bullshit. I

knew what I was doing in promoting Charles. Only trouble was, Charles was catching hell because people were saying the only way he could really be recognized as the titleholder was to fight me, but I pushed that out of my head. I don't want to fight with Charles; I just want to manage my business and play golf. I knew, for the moment, that I was finished with boxing—too old, too many other things to do.

Ezzard stopped Gus Lesnevich in seven, and I set him up to meet with Pat Valentino in San Francisco on October 14. And while I was looking at the calendar, I saw that I had to go on another exhibition tour from October through December. I swear to God I hated the thought of it, but I needed the money. Those taxes were still sitting there mounting up.

Hell, I even agreed to endorse some cigarettes to make the money. I can laugh when I think way back, when I was coming up, how I'd be insulted if somebody asked me to do that. I still didn't smoke then, but now Uncle Sam was breathing down my back.

I was supposed to meet Curtis Sheppard in Baltimore October 10. Good! Gave me a little break and a chance to see the Dodger-Yankee World Series in New York. Things were looking up; not only could I see my man Jackie Robinson play with the Dodgers, but Don Newcombe and Roy Campanella too. The Dodgers had three black men— that's baseball history—but my heart broke when Yankee Tommy Henrich hit a home run off Don Newcombe in the bottom of the ninth to defeat the Dodgers 1 to 0. The Dodgers lost the Series to the Yankees in five games. But none of that mattered to me when I later learned that Jackie Robinson got the most valuable player award in the National League in 1949.

So, I finished out the year doing exhibitions, and I was happy to hear that Ezzard Charles knocked out Pat Valentino in eight rounds. Hey, I was getting to be a real promoter.

I'd made about $300,000 in exhibition tours in 1949. Then I made a damn good dollar with my investments and companies. Seemed to me I should have been all right, but I wasn't. More money I made, the more the government took. And when my lawyers and the tax people got together, I was really in the dark. I knew I owed the government $50,000 a year just in interest and penalties, and that wasn't even touching the main tax, which was well over a quarter of a million dollars. Had to keep working to pay taxes, but the more I worked, the less I had. I couldn't afford to sit on my ass, either.

Marshall Miles was bitching that Mike Jacobs hadn't done me any favors by lending me all that money; he felt it had made me fight too long to pay him off. I don't agree. Hell, Mike gave me money when I needed it. I'm no child, I knew I'd have to pay it back one way or the other. I got what I wanted when I needed it, and let the devil take the hind parts.

Early in 1950 a friend of mine named Al Lockhart, a black public relations man, came up with the idea of a soda drink called the Joe Louis Punch. Sounded good to me. Al figured while I was out on exhibition, I could promote the punch.

So I headed out again on the exhibition trail and I must have hit everywhere from Hollywood all the way down to Rio de Janeiro. From the beginning of January till the end of April, I had at least twenty-three matches. I was damn tired.

The Joe Louis Punch didn't go over the way we expected. It was a good idea, but we didn't have enough money to push it right, and besides, Coca-Cola was king. Next thing I know the government had filed a $59,000 tax lien against me. They froze any money I could get from my properties; they also let me know I couldn't even sell my properties unless the government received the money. They wouldn't allow me the expense money for training camp and they wouldn't allow me the cash settle-

ments I gave Marva after each fight, telling me something
about the remarriage complicating things. Tell you the
truth, it was nothing but confusion.

I had no idea what to do about all these problems; I
figured I'd try and ignore them. But I couldn't forget this
tax thing gnawing at my brain. Jesus Christ, these tax
guys hang onto you. Always calling you up. Showing up
where they don't belong. Getting on your nerves.

If you think that's bad, listen to this: I was out in Los
Angeles on the golf course when some guy came running
up to me to show the papers. I couldn't believe what I
read. Marva had married a Dr. Albert Spaulding on May
21, 1950. At first I didn't feel anything at all because I
was too numb. Last time Marva and me had talked seriously, she said she never wanted married life again.
Whatever happened must have happened fast. I got to the
phone as quick as I could and talked to Marva for a couple
of hours. I couldn't believe she'd do that to me. I guess I
just thought she'd be mine forever. Then I started raising
hell about my children. What's gonna happen to them?
What's this Spaulding like anyway? Marva calmed me
down and said there was no way she would change her
mind. She had met and fallen in love with a good decent
man who loved the kids and would do anything he could
for them. Of course, I'd always be able to see the children
anytime I wanted.

I called Roxy and he said he had talked to Marva too;
he told me there was nothing I could do. Then he reminded me that I had stayed at a Dr. Spaulding's house in
West Virginia, and he was the father of the man Marva
had married. I remembered that I had liked the older Dr.
Spaulding very much, and I hoped that the younger one
was like his father for Marva's and the kids' sakes.

My crazy little world was crumbling all around me
now. Nothing left for me to do, so in the middle of the
summer, I announced that I'd decided to come out of

retirement and challenge Ezzard Charles for the championship. The reason—taxes. On the other hand, I tried to make myself feel better by saying that I knew I could take Charles, and besides, I'd be the first retired champion to regain his title.

The only thing was that I had just six or seven weeks to get ready. Ordinarily that would have been enough, but this was my first real fight after a two-year layoff. In the back of my head, I knew I didn't have enough time. The IBC wanted the fight in September at Yankee Stadium, but I figured I'd rather have it at the Garden in December so I could condition myself more. But Jim Norris insisted; he felt I could do it. The thing is, I always like to show my best. Besides, too, I'd been watching Charles. Sure, he was one hell of a boxer, but I didn't think his punches could hurt me.

But Charles knew that everyone didn't recognize him as champion, so he really wanted to get in there and mix it up with me. If he won, there'd be no question about his crown. We both had a lot at stake.

But, you know something, while I was sitting in the dressing room on September 27, it was all I could do not to tell Mannie Seamon to call it off. I wasn't ready for Charles, but what the hell—the government needed their money, and I had to live, too. It wasn't like the old days.

I was thirty-six years old, weighing 218 pounds; Charles was twenty-nine and 183½ pounds. I figured the extra pounds would give me an advantage, but I was wrong.

The fight started out with Charles jabbing me and punching me around the ring. He was younger, he was faster, he was lighter. Charles never really hurt me, he just wore me out and really cut me up. He hooked, jabbed, and got some good lefts to my stomach. When he started the crosses to my face, I dazed some. When I saw an opening, I couldn't get to it fast enough—my reflexes were rusted and my coordination was messed up. I tried to get off, but when I got him in trouble, I couldn't react fast enough.

After the fifth round, Sugar Ray Robinson, who was at ringside with Acting Mayor Vincent Impellitteri, came up the aisle and told my handlers, "Joe's got to keep sticking with that left hand. He's got to take the play away from Charles and keep him off balance."

From the seventh round, I knew I just didn't have it. I was washed up. It wasn't about reflexes or something like that. I simply didn't have it. I said to myself, "Oh, if I just could have gotten to you five years ago." But it wasn't five years before, and it was the fourteenth round and I was bleeding like a stuck pig. When the bell sounded for the fifteenth round, I was so exhausted, Mannie Seamon and Marshall Miles practically had to lift me off the stool.

Well, Charles retained his title and I looked like a shithead. It hurt real bad—not Charles's punches, but my pride. I underestimated Charles; he was a careful, smooth and easy fighter. He took no unnecessary changes. Hell, after the fight, Charles felt bad, too. After all, we were friends, and I had had quite a record in the ring. But then, business is business.

I was so exhausted I didn't have the strength to put my clothes on. Every part of my body ached and I could hardly see from the blood cuts over my eyes. I have to say, though, Charles successfully defended his title, but the people were on my side. I heard about all the crying and the telegrams and the letters from people telling me how sorry they were and how much they respected me. All that made the defeat a little softer. When I called Momma, she begged me to stop now, but she couldn't understand how much money I owed out. I was an old man now, but still dangerous with somebody who wasn't as good as Charles. The government wanted their money and I had to try and get it to them. Whether I was some kind of symbol or not didn't matter to them—Jim Norris booked me to fight Cesar Brion in Chicago on November 29.

With a little time off, I headed out to Chicago to see my kids. I took Punchie out to the golf course with me; he was about three years old then. That's where I met Al Spaulding, who turned out to be a golf nut too, and he was damned good. So there was Punchie running between me and Al Spaulding, calling him Daddy Al and me Daddy Joe. Finally we got to talking and I found out I really liked this guy; Marva made a wise decision. Al and I are still good friends.

In the meantime, though, all through this period, I was trying my damndest to get myself set up and straightened out. I went along with Sugar Ray Robinson when he suggested we go into a distributorship of Canadian Ace Beer. Then it turned out that one of the members of the distributorship had a shady background and we ran into some trouble with the liquor authorities—as if I didn't already have enough trouble.

Then Truman Gibson and me headed for Detroit to talk with Henry Ford about getting a Ford franchise for a dealership. Well, I guess Henry Ford didn't mind all those black people buying his cars, but he wasn't ready to let blacks in on the business end at that time.

So it was back to the ring—I fought Cesar Brion in November, won the ten-round decision, and lined up a series of fights for 1951.

1951. I still wanted that heavyweight crown again; I convinced myself I could still get it. I wanted the money it would bring, and I don't mind saying now that I wanted the cheers, too. Well, OK. I had to go the regular fight route, no exhibitions. Had to knock out or beat decisively all opponents leading up to Charles.

JOE LOUIS: MY LIFE

First I started off with Freddie Beshore in Detroit on January 3. No sweat here—K.O. in four rounds. Then I met Cuban heavyweight Omelio Agramonte in Miami and won in ten rounds. On February 23 in San Francisco, I K.O.'d Andy Walker in ten. A rematch with Omelio Agramonte ended the same way it had before, a decisive win in ten rounds. Then I got a match with Lee Savold, who held the British Empire heavyweight title. If I could beat him, I'd have climbed up to the top of the ladder. Met with Savold in New York, and it was an easy K.O. in six.

After that fight, the people started coming back around me. Walter Winchell and Jimmy Cannon gave me some good writeups in the papers. Met and clowned around with Milton Berle. Even Mayor Impellitteri came to my dressing room to congratulate me. I was feeling good again and told Jim Norris to start getting ready for me to meet with Charles again so I could get my title back that fall and make some decent money.

But in the meantime I headed back to the golf course again, because I didn't have another fight until August. I hadn't planned on anything special around this time, just some easy golfing and relaxing. All that was alright until I heard from my friends Ted Rhodes, my pro, Bill Spiller, and Charles Sifford. They said that the all-white PGA decided they couldn't play in the San Diego Open. Then they gave me a message from Horton Smith, President of the PGA, telling me not to show up either. Well, the funny thing is I hadn't thought about playing till then. But all this made me mad as hell.

I called Walter Winchell and gave him the story. He said, "Who the hell is Horton Smith? He must be another Hitler." Winchell put the story on the air that night. And Rhodes, Spiller, Sifford, and I headed out to play in the San Diego Open.

Well, let me tell you, it was something else. As soon as

we arrived, they held up the match. Horton Smith called a quick meeting with Jimmie Demaret, Jackie Burke, and Sam Snead; they were all on the committee. Burke and Demaret were raising hell with Horton Smith for holding up the match. They must have argued for two hours and everybody was getting itchy. Finally, Horton said, not too nicely, we could play this tournament but for us definitely not to expect to play in the Arizona Open. We won that battle. We started playing and before we finished one round of golf, we received over a hundred telegrams congratulating us on getting a chance to compete with white golfers.

With that and Walter Winchell's broadcasts behind us, we went to Arizona and, with no problems from a nervous Horton Smith, signed up. This was a breakthrough I was proud to be a part of.

Everything was going along OK and I was looking forward to meeting Ezzard Charles. Now, damn if this wasn't my bad luck poking out again. Charles gave Joe Walcott another go at the title, and damned if Walcott didn't knock him out in the seventh round. Well, now, Walcott definitely didn't want to meet with me again. I didn't blame him. He wanted to hold onto that title as long as he could. So I had a rematch on August 1 with Cesar Brion in San Francisco and decisioned him in ten. Then it was Jimmy Bivins in Baltimore on August 15 with a win in ten; only thing was, I hurt my right hand in this one.

Well, Joe Walcott was still not gonna come to me, that's for sure. And then along came the new "great white hope"—Rocco Marchegiano, better known as Rocky Marciano. Rocky had a tough reputation. He was out of Brockton, Massachusetts, twenty-seven years old, and in thirty-seven fights he had thirty-two K.O.'s. Tell you the truth, I didn't think too well of Marciano and I wasn't anxious to fight him. I kept looking at the throne; that's what I wanted. But Marciano was getting very popular, and Jim Norris smelled money. He knew a money maker when he saw it. And I still owed the government one million dollars and maybe $100,000 a year in interest on unpaid taxes. I don't think I had made over $180,000 in any fight since Ezzard Charles. I needed money. So, although I didn't want to fight Marciano, I couldn't turn down the guaranteed $300,000 for one fight. Marciano got only 15 percent of the gate, but he didn't care. He was on his way up just like I was in 1937 when Mike and I made that deal with Braddock.

I didn't figure on any problems with Marciano. He was strong, sure, but he fought like a street brawler. Figured I could outbox him anytime, and I needed the money too much to turn it down.

On October 26, 1951, when I climbed into the ring at Madison Square Garden, I felt confident. I felt even more confident when I knew I had won three rounds out of the first five. Yeah! I was right, he was a street brawler. He couldn't touch me when it came to boxing. Marciano was strong, though. I figured with a little more training he could do it all. But right then in the ring I knew I was busting him up with my jabs.

Everything was fine until the seventh round. My age gave me away; all of a sudden like my legs gave out. They had to lift me off the stool for the bell in the eighth. Marciano knocked me down once with a left hook. I managed to get up, after taking an eight count. Then he caught me with another left that put me up against the ropes and followed with a looping right hand. But I just couldn't get out of the way. It hit me on the neck, and I fell through the ropes. There I was, with my head against the ring apron and just my legs still in the ring. That's the last time I got hit in the ring. Made up my mind it would be.

I'm glad I wasn't fully conscious when Referee Ruby Goldstein stopped the fight. There was no doubt Marciano had beaten the shit out of me.

The better fighter won, but I wasn't really hurt until the

knockout. He was a good puncher and very strong. He hit harder than Max Schmeling. I wasn't disappointed. I did the best I could. I wanted no sympathy. In my mind I had only taken the fight because there was a big money deal in it. On the other hand, I felt sorry about all those people around me who were crying. Sugar Ray was there in the dressing room sobbing like a baby. Marciano came into the dressing room crying and saying, "Joe, I'm sorry." I understood him, but my needs and interests had changed. I was just as sorry to see him standing there crying as I was sorry about myself. Times had changed, and all I thought about was that $300,000 and trying to work out some deal with the government. When I was on the rubbing table, the doctor of the State Athletic Commission said to me, "Joe, you can't fight for at least three months." I turned my head and looked at the doc and said, "Do you mind if I don't fight no more at all?" I remember him looking at me, smiling and saying, "That's good." Right then I knew I wasn't going to make another professional fight. I was thirty-seven years old. I thought, like many fighters before me and after me, that I'd always be some kind of superman. That's the dream. Not the reality. I just didn't have it anymore.

I had to be practical. I wasn't any threat to any young upcoming challenger, but I had the Joe Louis name. I decided to try and be smart and market that name. The Korean War had started; the American Armed Services asked me to go to the Far East and do a few exhibition bouts for the boys in the service. More morale building while those American tax men are demoralizing me. But they did promise me some tax-free money, to help pay off those back taxes. I know it sounds like some kind of a joke, but what the hell else can you do?

So I headed out for my last exhibition tour. In November I go to Tokyo and Sanda, Japan, and Taipei, Formosa. I got a few private exhibition tours while I was at it. One thing I learned from the Far East was a love of beauty and cleanliness. In spite of the war, these people were clean, neat, and they made everything look artistic. First time in my life I looked at a wrestling match and said to myself, "Man, this is an art." But I only netted about $20,000 and it was getting near the end of December.

I looked at myself and wondered what the hell I was going to do now?

1951-1960
AFTER THE RING

WELL, ONE THING, I DIDN'T HAVE TO LIVE AS furiously. Didn't have to jam all my pleasure into a few free weeks or months. Didn't have all those aches and pains. And, you see, I didn't feel bad about anything. I had seventy-one fights as a professional —fifty-four knockouts, sixty-eight wins, and three defeats. I successfully defended my title twenty-five times. I was the world heavyweight champion for twelve years. I earned five million dollars. I owed the government one million. Not a bad record. There was never a time I was ashamed of my ring record. There was never a time I felt unfaithful to my profession, and in boxing that's saying a lot.

On the other hand, I'd be lying if I didn't say I missed the applause. I did. Applause is like a kind of love, and when 40,000 or more people are applauding you, that's a lot of love. Oh, I got all the recognition I wanted and that made me real happy. I couldn't go anywhere without people calling "Hey, Champ," and "About thus-and-so fight. . . ." Always tried to be courteous and polite, but there's nothing like the referee holding up your right arm after a fight and the announcer saying, "And still the World's Heavyweight Champion." And there you are, just one man. Yeah, I missed the ring. Yeah, and I missed the big money, too. Didn't have any of the things I should have had. I guess I tricked myself into thinking I'd be The Champ forever and I'd be able to catch up financially. Didn't work that way, though.

Had some time to spend with my kids, had some time for Momma and some time for golf. Worked a lot with Billy Rowe, taking clients out to lunch and dinner. I was,

JOE LOUIS: MY LIFE

I'd say, having a good time with no worries except taxes.

Around about here, Sterling Silliphant, a big-time producer at Twentieth Century-Fox, thought someone should make a movie about me. I was excited by the idea. Coley Wallace, a Golden Gloves Heavyweight Champion, was cast as Joe Louis—Coley looked a lot like me when I was younger. It wasn't a bad movie, but it wasn't too good either—they said they ran out of money part way through. Still it was fun hanging around Hollywood again, being a consultant and meeting new friends. Plus, of course, seeing my old ones, men and women.

Only thing was that around the end of the year, Momma took sick with a heart condition. First she seemed real bad and I was scared as hell, but Momma's a real tough lady. She even surprised the doctors, and before you could bat an eye she was out of the hospital and staying with my sisters while she recuperated.

But as soon as I got over that shock Mike Jacobs died in January, 1953. He was seventy-two. Mike was game up to the end, though. The day before he died he had gone to the races at Hialeah Park. They had to rush him to the hospital and put him in an oxygen tent because he'd had a bad heart attack. Mike didn't make it through. I don't know how to tell you how I felt. If it weren't for Mike, willing to take a chance on a black boxer, I would never have gotten to be champion. Mike opened the door so other black fighters could get a better chance. He helped break down a lot of prejudice in the fight game, and he's the one who helped get rid of the crookedness in the heavyweight division.

Mike treated me like a spoiled son but gave me a way of life I never would have dreamed of. Through Mike I was able to help a lot of people. I loved Mike Jacobs. I still miss him.

Seems to me when a year starts out bad, there's no way it'll straighten up. The government told me I'd have to pay gift taxes on the money I'd given Marva in 1947 and 1948. The government wouldn't allow the money as a divorce settlement. What could I tell them, except to add it to the bill?

Then around the end of 1953, my sisters called me and told me Momma was not doing well. I dropped everything and rushed to Detroit. I was scared when I saw Marva there with Punchie and Jackie. Momma had called Marva and told her she didn't feel she'd be around too long and wanted to spend some time with her grandchildren. Well, after a while everything seemed to be going along all right, and Marva stayed two weeks. The family seemed to ease up some, and everything settled in its place.

I'll never forget December 13, 1953, as long as I live. I visited with Momma that day and we talked about what we were going to do during the Christmas holidays. Momma was staying with my sister Emmarell and said she wanted a big Christmas feast with all the family around. I left her feeling good and went to dinner with a friend of mine, Dr. Robert Bennett. We had just finished eating and were setting around talking when the phone rang. Dr. Bennett answered it, looked at me, and said, "Joe, let's get over to your sister's house. Your Momma's not doing too well."

Yeah, you guessed it; Momma died. There was nothing I could do but cry. Who ever believes their mother can die? My sisters and Marva took care of all the arrangements; I was too down to do anything. But people were real good to me, and telegrams came from all over the world. I don't think I ever got over her death, though. My number one fan, my number one advisor, my momma.

Momma left a little estate to be divided with the family. My share was about $660. The tax people took it.

It took me a long, long time to get myself together. All my old friends, new friends saw me through this saddest period of my life. But then, you know, I had to move on. I know Momma would have expected it of me.

JOE LOUIS: MY LIFE

Thank God I had the Louis-Rowe agency. It kept me busy and made me some money. You know, I never liked real big fancy parties, but as part of my job I had to go. Now, I'm not putting these parties down. Lord knows I met all the big important people, and you know something, they were glad to meet me, too.

I remember when I used to run into Rose Morgan at a lot of affairs. Liked her right away. She was a real lady, tall, brown, good-looking. Always dressed just right, always had the right makeup on, and the right jewelry. She is a sweet, open, sensible woman. And she's damn smart. She came out of Chicago a few years before and was the most important woman in black beauty culture since Madame Walker invented the straightening comb and curling iron.

I used to like to talk to her. With just a little help from her family, she set up the first all-around grooming parlor for black women. They could get their hair done, their nails done, massages, makeup. Rose had a big staff working for her out of a three-story brownstone on One hundred forty-eighth right off St. Nicholas Avenue. I don't think there was a white operation downtown that could top Rose Morgan's.

So when I'd meet people like Rose, I'd feel better because I knew black people were moving along on up. But all that didn't help me too much. About this time I got hauled into traffic court and had to pay $300 in back fines. That wouldn't have been so bad, but I never had a violation. My problem was lending my car to people who kept thinking, "Joe Louis can't get a ticket." Now where the hell were these people when I had to lay out that $300?

On top of all this comes the big scooper. Those tax people went out and snatched my kids' annuities that Marva had so carefully put aside. Losing my kids' money hurt me a lot.

Well, in between all this shit, I was trying to earn as

much as I could. I wished I had as much money as I had women; I'd have been a rich man. I'm talking about making money any way I could. I even refereed some boxing matches, wrestling matches. Got to make that buck.

There were some bright spots too. *Ring Magazine* inducted me along with Jack Dempsey, Henry Armstrong, and others into the Boxing Hall of Fame in October, 1954. That felt real good. That meant that I'd be just what my friend, Billy Rowe, said I'd be: "the Immortal Heavyweight." I wouldn't be forgotten. Made me think that maybe a hundred years from now some little black boy would be thumbing some book or magazine and be glad that I had been born.

Then in 1955, I get a real nice offer to host at the opening of the Moulin Rouge Hotel in Las Vegas. This was a white-owned hotel, but they planned to cater to all the blacks who were starting to pour into Las Vegas. At one time in Vegas, blacks just couldn't go to those fancy hotels. All the black hotels and gambling were on the other side of town. Black people coming to Vegas mostly stayed in some little colored boarding houses. Even the big black stars who came to Las Vegas to entertain in the big white hotels wound up crosstown when it came time to go to sleep.

So, somewhere along the way, somebody white figured out that a lot of black people are big gamblers. Why not? They don't have a thing to lose except the few dollars they make. Some blacks got lots of money and they want a good place to stay—so you get the powers that be opening up some decent places in Vegas proper.

Well, I have to say the Moulin Rouge did it up proper. They asked me to be host at their opening. They invited every important, influential black person they ever heard of to a press junket and flew them there. It was a big to-do. John Johnson of Johnson Publications (*Ebony* and *Jet,* at that time), Geri Major of the *Amsterdam News,* Evelyn Cunningham of the *Pittsburgh Courier,* and more people whose names I can't remember from *Time*, *Life*, etc. Anyway while I was going down this list, I saw Rose Morgan's name. I said to myself, "Aha." I remembered Rose very well from New York and made arrangements for her to sit at my table. I really wanted to get to know Rose better. In the back of my mind, I had some idea about putting out a cologne called "My Man," and I wanted to talk with Rose about it. Rose was a little confused because she thought she'd be sitting with the people she came with. When I came and sat down beside her she asked me about it. I just told her I wanted her as my personal guest. Then she turned and looked at me a little different.

After dinner and the show we played a little black jack. And then Evelyn Cunningham came by asking me to take her and Rose around the city. All they had seen was the hotel. I drove them around and then I dropped Evelyn at the hotel and I said to Rose, "How about you come with me to put up the car?" Well, I put the car up and I figured Rose and me could spend some time together. I was doing some sweet talking but Rose suddenly said, "Sorry, I have to go in and rest myself. I've got to get back to New York tomorrow." I look at her like she was crazy. "Going tomorrow!" Maybe I had lost my touch.

Well, damned if she didn't go. As soon as she got back to New York, I was on the phone asking her when she was coming back. She politely told me "No"; she wasn't coming back anytime soon. She opened a bigger salon on One hundred forty-fifth Street off Amsterdam Avenue and she let me know she was a serious businesswoman. Well, it looked like I'd have to bide my time till I could get to New York, but I stayed in touch with Rose.

Then I got invited to the *Ed Sullivan Show*. I called Rose and asked her to pick me up at the airport and she did. I was in New York for a couple of days, and I really enjoyed being around her. I liked watching her run her business. I was impressed.

Then I had to go to Buffalo to referee a wrestling match. I called Rose on Saturday and told her to catch the next plane up. She politely (always polite, this lady) said, "I can't come now, I have a business to take care of and I've got a payroll to make out for sixty-five people," but she said that after she closed shop she'd be up. My friend, Kiah Sayles, and me met her at the airport in Buffalo.

I told her, "Look, baby, don't you know when I say come, you must come." Well, she went into that business thing again and after two days, I said to her, "Look, let's get married." At first she said, "No, we don't know each other well enough." I ask her, how long does it take? Give me a schedule. I could see she was starting to think about it.

Well, she thought for awhile and we wound up getting married Christmas Day, 1955.

It was a real nice wedding. We were married in Rose's beautiful home in St. Albans, Long Island. Billy Rowe was my best man. Rose's family and personal friends were there. Count Basie, Roy Campanella, my sister Vunice, Freddie Guinyard; altogether there were about a hundred and fifty people including the press. Next morning, I think every paper in America ran the story. I was back in the headlines again.

The top of 1956. I'm married. I'm broke. I'm still catching hell from the tax people. I guess when they saw I'd gotten married, they figured to check on me some more. Rose had nothing to do with my tax problems, and it annoyed me that her name should be brought up for anything. The thing that bothered me so much is that it never crossed my mind to try and gyp the government out of the money. I had every intention of trying to pay the money I owed—even if it was close to a million dollars. The problem was where the hell could I get that big money again? The papers and magazines had all kinds of articles about my tax problems. Fans were sending me money in the mail. Even kids were sending me dollars out of the little money they saved. One little kid even mailed me a dime. It was times like this I almost cried. I never appreciated anything so much, but I sent it all back. I had gotten myself into this mess and I had to try to find a way to get out myself.

So when Ray Tabani, a professional wrestling promoter, came along with a $100,000 guarantee for me to wrestle, shoot, I didn't think twice about it. Rose was real upset. She said to me that it was like seeing President Eisenhower wash dishes. I told her that it damn sure beat stealing. I honestly didn't feel there was anything dishonorable about it, but then when you're broke who can see straight?

Had my first match in March, and I won. It felt good having some money in my pockets again. I took care of as much as I could with the taxes and I had a little left over. I took Rose out on the town. By the time Rose and me wound up at Red Randolph's bar on One hundred twenty-fourth and Seventh, I had about $150 left. Rose got mad with me because, when an old friend asked me if he could borrow $100, I lent it to him. She told me I didn't value money. I let her know that it made me happy to be able to give it away; she told me I must be insane with joy, then.

I was happy again. I invited my kids Punchie and Jackie and their little half sister Alvita (she was Marva's daughter by Dr. Spaulding) to spend a month with me and Rose that summer. All the kids called me Daddy Joe and Rose, Momma Rose. It felt good having them all with me. Only thing is I had some more wrestling bouts coming up and didn't have the time to spend with the kids. Rose came through like a champ. She took them all over New York and on picnics at Coney Island and stuff like that. The main thing is that they had a good time.

Things were looking up. Buddy Rogers, the wrestler,

asked me to come and referee one of his matches in Washington, D.C. From there I started getting offers from all over the country at $1,500 per assignment. So, you know, I was doing two and three matches a week. It was such a big thing in Washington, Rogers said, "How about you boxing and me wrestling?"

Between the boxing, wrestling, and refereeing, I started making a good buck, but it was work. I was doing fine until along came a 340-pound wrestler named Cowboy Rocky Lee. I was down on the canvas when he accidentally stepped on my chest. I felt a sharp pain. When they examined me they found that Rocky had cracked one of my ribs and the rib had damaged some of my heart muscles. I said to myself, "Oh shit. There goes that good dollar." No way the commissioner would let me in the ring to wrestle anymore.

If that wasn't bad enough, the government was saying that the IBC was a monopoly. Jim Norris went to court about it, but the judge ordered the corporation closed. There went my $20,000 a year pay.

Now I had nothing to depend on except refereeing. Rose was glad in a way; she didn't want me wrestling anyway.

Looking back on everything now, I got to admit I was feeling low. Lower than I'd felt since I couldn't remember when. But you know sometime when you're feeling that bad, something or somebody comes along that can lift up those heavy spirits. Well, Representative Alfred D. Sieminsky (New Jersey Democrat) really made me feel encouraged. You know what that man did? He introduced legislation to ask the United States government to forget about those back taxes I owed. He said that I'd done a lot for the country, and that whenever the government called on me, I was ready, willing, and able.

It didn't work, but I thought that was a real beautiful gesture. I felt real good that Mr. Sieminsky and the state of New Jersey thought that much about me and that the notion was considered.

I was home a little more often now, and really got hooked on TV. One night when Rose and me were looking at some quiz show, I said, "Shoot, I can answer those questions." Damned if Rose didn't write Dennis James, host of the *High Finance* show. Dennis James said that he'd be glad to have me and Rose on the show and they agreed that if we won any prizes, Rose would like the prizes converted to cash so I could pay off some of my taxes.

Rose and I did alright. We lasted about six weeks. A lot of people were surprised when I answered some of those questions. I mean, the show was built around being able to answer questions about what was in the Sunday papers. I'm no big-time reader, but I can read. You better believe I read those papers like I never had, and what I couldn't answer, Rose could.

The show was a lot of fun, and we won about $60,000. Later on in the office, when the man is ready to hand us the check, the tax people came to snatch it out of Rose's hand. Rose said, "Oh, no. Half of this is mine. I'll give you Joe's half after I deposit this check." She told them I needed a $5,000 allowance for clothes. I mean, I had to get some new clothes for the show, because I had gained so much weight. They dickered back and forth and Rose basically won. They allowed me $4,000 for clothes. At least that $25,000 kept them quiet for a little while.

Around about this time a lot of people all over knew I was having big financial and tax problems. Way out in Norfolk, Nebraska, George Reeves, President of a pipeline company and a mortician, as well as John Youngheim, a commercial pilot, got together with some other business-men and set up a charter fund to help me out of my problems. Jack Dempsey was the Honorary Chairman. They helped me the best they could. They even tried to talk to the government about some kind of reasonable settlement, but I was in so far that the dent they made was very small.

Then the Harlem Globetrotters tried to raise money through a benefit game for my taxes. Again, the dent was small. But the most important thing was that these people cared about me.

I tried my best with Rose, and Lord knows, she tried her best with me. I tried to get domesticated, but old habits are hard to get rid of. One time there, I think we were doing alright when we tried to get the "My Man" men's cologne product together, but that didn't work out. There wasn't a depression then but the backtail of a recession. I guess the last thing a man, especially a black man, was thinking about was some cologne.

By 1957 the marriage was getting shaky. Rose couldn't get used to my hours. I liked to go out and be with my friends all night. She couldn't go out every night because she had her business and had to be up early.

Finally, Rose and me had a long talk. She let me know what she wanted out of marriage. She wanted a husband who was around; she wanted children. She felt that we should get an annulment. I guess it was OK with me. I had to agree with what she said, because she was right. I think both Rose and I expected different things out of the marriage, and I guess neither one of us was satisfied with it the way it was. One thing, though, I have the greatest respect a man could have for Rose. She tried, I tried. It didn't work; we separated that summer of 1957, and the marriage was annulled the next year.

I won't say I was depressed, but I sure didn't feel like tap dancing. So when Sarah Vaughan invited me to a party she was having at her apartment on Eighty-fifth Street, I went. I was talking to a girl I knew, name of Opel Jackson. She said to me, "Joe, you should see my lawyer, Martha Malone Jefferson. She's the finest thing in California, and she is real smart. She's the first black woman attorney admitted to the bar in California." I said to myself, "That sounds like my kind of woman." Got Opel to call her on the phone right there at the party. I liked the way Martha talked. She was cool and nice. Told me she'd be glad to meet me when I got to California—if she had the time. Now, that "if she had the time" really got me interested.

Well, I went to Los Angeles and she found the time. Martha was easy to be around. She had a real busy law practice and she didn't care about running from this party to the next, or entertaining all the time. Made no difference to her if she was meeting the President of the United States or the janitor down the street. She had her own ideas about what she would do and what she wouldn't, and she'd tell you so. I used to call her "Sergeant." You could be real comfortable with somebody like Martha.

But I had to travel where my work was, and that mainly was refereeing wrestling matches.

In early 1958, I was talking to my friend Kiah Sayles in New York and told him I was going to Beaumont, Texas, for a job. He told me there was a girl down there who was something else, and I should meet her. Her name was, let's say, Annie Mitchell, and she and her husband owned a funeral parlor. I told Kiah I'd look her up. It was the biggest mistake I ever made.

I should have known nothing good was going to come out of this. When I got there, I found out her husband was dead. He'd been killed by one of their employees. When I asked what happened, Annie said her husband had fired this guy who worked for him when he found out they were seeing each other. The guy got mad and shot and killed the husband.

Can't explain why I took up with her. She wasn't the kind of woman I usually went around with. But she did a lot of traveling to different cities with me. I remember one time we went to Roanoke, Virginia. I was to referee a wrestling match there. When I came back to the hotel, she had two glasses of orange juice on the table. I drank one glass and we went to bed to make love, and that's all I remember till I woke up the next day. She had drugged me. I know, I know, I should have split right then with her. Why did she drug me? I don't know. Maybe she had someplace to go or something to do and didn't want me knowing about it.

Got to admit, though, she was some kind of fine-looking woman. Chinese-looking with real long hair and what seemed like an easygoing manner, and she was smart. Always get suckered by a good-looking, smart, business-type woman. Of course, at the time, I didn't realize what kinds of business she was into.

Then I had to go to Milwaukee for a speaking engagement at a church. Afterwards Annie and me went to the hotel there. I was all tensed up and tired of running all over the country; I was feeling mighty sorry for myself, especially since I'd heard from the tax people again. As I was getting into bed I told Annie, "I think I've had it." I turned my back to her when all of a sudden I felt a sharp pain in my ass. I jumped up and saw her throwing a needle in the corner. She said she was just trying to give me something to "relax" me. Yeah, I did it again. I let that pass because I didn't want to start a hassle with her, and I felt good right then.

After that she had me good. She was always finding ways to "relax" me. A little bit of a needle prick and I was feeling good. I felt like a millionaire and a world heavyweight champion again, and I guess that's why I didn't pay enough attention to all the shit she was putting down. She wore all kinds of wigs and she wasn't wearing that stuff to be glamorous. She was disguising herself. But I was in funny land and let it slide.

I remember one time we went to New York and I was hanging out with my old buddy, Freddie Guinyard. It was just like the old time. We went to the Hotel Theresa and Small's Paradise. Dinah Washington, Brook Benton, Cab Calloway. It was great. I wanted to be with those people and they wanted to be with me. Me and Freddie went over to the Apollo and laughed at Pigmeat and Butter Beans and Susie and went backstage and really enjoyed ourselves. But Freddie kept staring at me; finally I asked what the hell he was looking at. He said, "Nothing, Joe, but you act like you're out in space or something." That made me nervous. I didn't want anybody to know what my problem was. I just told Freddie that I had a lot on my mind. Maybe he bought it.

Then the government tax people and me had another little talk. I signed an agreement with them to pay them $20,000 yearly on back taxes. I must have been earning about $33,000 and when I paid $12,000 tax on the $33,000, plus the $20,000, I'd only have $1,000 left. You know, something like that can depress a man. Well, there would be no way I could honor that $20,000 a year and still be Joe Louis so I just tried my best to give them what I could.

Nothing got better. Went on a trip once to a Holiday Inn. Annie kept disappearing for long periods. I found out later that they were making a pornographic movie in the next room, and Annie was the star. Maybe that's what she'd been doing all along, and maybe that's why she was always "relaxing" me.

Then I'd notice something else. Sometimes she had tons of big money and then it would seem to disappear. It was around this time I started hearing that she had Mafia connections and was delivering drugs for them. Some people said she was using me for a shield because nobody would suspect that anybody with Joe Louis was doing anything wrong.

I knew I was rolling in shit, but I couldn't seem to move out of it. Then in early 1959 a friend of mine wanted to open a Brown Bomber hamburger joint. He gave me

$10,000 to start getting it set up. I gave Annie $2,500. Later on, I discovered she gave it to her Mafia pimp.

Tell you the truth, I didn't know what to do. I wanted out. These drugs were getting to me. I don't want anyone to know. Hell, little kids and young fighters were still looking up to me. I couldn't let them down, but I couldn't move, either.

This is one time that the American government helped me out. The F.B.I. came around to talk to me and said that they didn't think I knew what I was into. They told me Annie and the people around her were being watched. These guys were about my age and also talked a lot about my career and boxing. They were real nice.

After they left, I knew I'd have to get out of this mess. I remembered a long time ago, when I was leaving Alabama on the train and seeing all those prisoners lined up with a ball and chain. Yeah! And I remembered making myself a promise when I was twelve years old that I wasn't ever going to get myself into anything that would chew me up like that.

I quit that whole scene and headed back to Los Angeles. What I needed was some kind of order, love, and intelligence in my life, and I knew just where to find it.

Martha Malone Jefferson and me took up where we left off, and to this day I wish I had never gotten myself mixed up like I did.

After a while, being around Martha, I started feeling better. My body felt better. I didn't have those big highs that made me feel good, but I didn't have those extra big lows that make you think nothing's ever going to be alright again.

I started healing up and I asked Martha to marry me— and she did, in Winterhaven, California. Just a plain civil ceremony without a lot of fuss.

1960. Life was good to me again. I was grateful to God; I'd even started going to church with Martha. She had a beautiful Spanishtype house with about ten rooms filled with fancy expensive antiques. When we got married, I think Martha had about three television sets. After I settled in she got about five more. She even had one set in the bathroom.

Martha never hassled me. She had her law practice and was busy all day. As for me, if I didn't have a job refereeing, I was over at the Hillcrest Country Club or the Fox Hills Country Club. If it was raining too hard, you'd find me in front of one of those eight television sets.

When the money got low and I got tired of looking at those TV sets, I'd get my ass up and try something else. Ran into my old friend, Leonard Reed, a dancer and comedian, who suggested we get up a nightclub act. We did a ring scene, which I thought was funny. I mean, with Lenny being skinny and short, and me so big and tall. When we'd do a comedy skit, I'd try to play the straight man. The act didn't do well. I think a lot of people didn't want to see me in this role either.

Then sometimes, I'd pick up a little change going to training camps at the invitation of some big promoters. My name was still a big draw, and I liked being around the camps watching the new fellows work out.

Well, hell, I was doing fine, but damned if the whole world didn't come into my life again. Cuba had a revolution; the guy in charge was Fidel Castro. He threw President Battista out. And with him throwing out Battista, the American gangsters went out too. That meant no more big-time prostitution, no more big-time gambling, and no more United Fruit Company of America ripping off the Cubans.

Fidel Castro said he would see to it that there would be no more corruption on his island. That was fine; the Americans first hailed Castro as a savior. Everybody loved him because he threw out all the bad guys, and now the good guys were in and everything looked alright. Right about here, Billy Rowe called me. He said we had to get together because Castro's people were interested in having black American tourists come down to see how he was making Cuba a better country. Well, that was alright with me. I loved Cuba—been there many a time. I knew Cuba was the only place a black man could go in the winter for a vacation and not be discriminated against. The Castro government signed a contract with our agency for $287,000 per year for encouraging tourists to visit.

Everything looked good. We weren't getting bad vibes from anybody. I set out and got over a hundred important black people to travel to Cuba and enjoy. But in the meantime the U.S. government was beginning to have a fit; seemed like Castro don't want to do what the U.S. said. So when I got to Cuba I met Castro, who told me that he was being accused of being a Communist. He said he had gone to America, France, and England to get arms to defend his country, and they'd refused him. He was always afraid that the group that had hung around Battista would try to take the country over again. So, since everybody else had turned him down, he went to Russia. Castro said he had no choice. Personally, I liked Castro very much. I thought he was a fine man.

Well, me thinking he's a fine man and what the American government thought were two different things. Next thing I knew, America cut off diplomatic relations with Cuba and there I was with my ass out bare again. Since I had endorsed Cuba, everybody began to call me a Communist. Can you think of anything stranger? Me, the lover of money and the best that money can buy, a Communist!

Shit! The thing that pissed me off is that we had the tourist contract with Castro before the United States got upset with Cuba because he'd lined up with the Russians. Well, it was all fate again. I get another chance and I have to give it up. America. I got rich and I got poor here. This is where I belong. I told Billy Rowe, we had to cut the Cuban tourist contract or we'd lose everything. Billy's a sensible man, and we did it.

Then, like I'm a criminal, the tax people gave me a rundown after this Cuba thing. Well, Martha got real mad and when Martha gets mad, things happen. She told the tax people that if they kept on bothering me, I wouldn't be able to get or hold a job. Martha told them that they had to realize that an athlete's career is only a few years, and because he makes all that money at one time, it has to last him the rest of his life. Then she went ahead and said there was no way I could pay off the $1,300,000 I owed them. Well, Martha's a good lawyer and they listened to her. Commissioner Dana Latham of the Internal Revenue Service made an appeal to Congress. He told them that they had gotten all they could from me and that an American should be permitted to have enough money to live on. Well, he let them know that I couldn't make a lot of money again and that they should leave me alone and not make me miserable.

The government never canceled that debt, but they agreed to just tax me on what I make now. Lord help me, if I make a great big dollar again, I guess they'll take it. But then, where the hell will I make a big dollar again?

1960s
TAXES, WOMEN, AND MARRIAGE

M Y OLDEST BROTHER, LONNIE, DIED IN 1960. HIS
death made me feel real low. I thought about
the many times me and Lonnie had fussed and
argued. I thought about the good times we had had together. I thought about all the pretty girls we had picked
up. Then, too, I was a little jealous of Lonnie. Momma
loved him so much. The thing though that hurt me most
of all is that Lonnie's death was caused by fumes from
a gas heater. See, Lonnie lived alone in a small apartment above the shoeshine parlor he owned. Now, I don't
know what it means, but the police investigators say that
the heater was lit but a piece of the exhaust pipe was
missing.

There are only two conclusions you can draw from that,
that a piece of exhaust pipe fell off or that Lonnie had
taken it off. I'd hate to think my brother committed suicide. You see, if he committed suicide, I should have
known he was in trouble and done something about it.

With the Cuba deal off, Billy Rowe and me had to scout
around to see what we could do to make some money.
Billy tried talking to all the big white people who owned
everything. He tried telling them how to reach black
people by employing more blacks, making movies about
blacks, putting blacks on television. He said the Louis-
Rowe agency could work it all out for them. Billy's a great
talker, and he started getting bigger accounts, but he had
help from all those riots in the black ghettoes. Add all the
white people who were starting to demonstrate with
black people, and all of a sudden there were a lot of black

people getting decent jobs. Getting jobs they never would have got if those big white guys hadn't been upset with white college kids getting jailed and sometimes killed along with black people. After all, American black people were just asking for what they deserved.

I tried in my way to help out, too. I spoke to white groups who were starting to ask, "What do these people want?" I spoke to black groups and tried to keep them encouraged. I told them the things I had gone through and still was going through. I hope it helped some.

Times were so different now. I guess everything really caught fire back in 1955 when Rosa Parks refused to move to the back of the bus in Montgomery, Alabama. When they arrested Rosa Parks, I don't think there was a black woman alive who didn't cheer her or cry for her. The most important part of her arrest and all was the appearance of Dr. Martin Luther King.

Dr. King zapped it to the white people. He was the one who let the world know that black people count for something, told white people we could shut down the whole bus company of Montgomery because blacks wouldn't ride unless they could sit where they wanted to. The next step was easy. Dr. King showed black people they could make things change by working together.

Well, I listened and watched Dr. King. He was more exciting than watching a new fighter come up through the ranks. Win a few, lose one, start again, only stronger. From the beginning, he had the makings of a champion. When I found out he wanted to talk to me, I laughed. Shoot, I think I wanted to meet him even more. He was the new champion. I had tried in my way to ease the load up some as far as race relations go, but I was out there just by myself. Now, Dr. King, he had organized the people. He had more strength than I'd ever have.

I think about America often. I know how beautiful it is, how rich it is. I know because I've been through practically all of it. I even know better because I've been all over the world. Don't like to take unnecessary pride in myself, but I've seen it all. And because I've seen it all, I get sick sometimes way deep down inside myself. There is so much here. Can't there be a way we can share it? It makes me sick inside to see people, because they're black, catching so much hell. Something is wrong with that.

I know I caught hell all during my career because I was black. Oh, so many special things had to be done to make room for me. Why? So many times I had to speak out when I saw some terrible injustice going on, and I don't consider myself a speaker—just a damn good fighter. Some of the white people listened to me, and some changes were made. But Dr. Martin Luther King—he's educated, he's smart, he's got the black people behind him, and the whites are listening. I loved that man, but then I always love a champion.

I remember the time he asked me to come to Birmingham, Alabama, to a demonstration meeting. Of course, you know I went. There was a whole plane of people going down there. Nat King Cole, Mavis Logan, now the Commissioner for Human Rights in New York City, and a whole bunch of other people. My friend, Billy Rowe, was with me, too. I think it was at a college campus or something, and all of us were sitting on this stage platform. All of a sudden, there was a loud noise and the stage started collapsing. Everybody was screaming that a bomb had gone off. As the stage was falling apart, I looked at Billy Rowe and said, "You think we made a mistake?" Well, Billy and me started laughing like two fools. But the affair worked out real well. I was always happy to help Dr. King.

Then there was the time me and Dick Gregory, the comedian, got together with Jesse Gray, who was always fighting the slum landlords. We were protesting the rats and the rat bites that the babies got because the houses were so run-down and the landlords wouldn't make repairs. You know, I was a grown man, but I'd get tears in my eyes when I'd see those babies with rat bites all over them. I'd cry even more about the babies I didn't see because they were dead.

The people would all be there looking at me, expecting much of me, I felt weak and disappointed in myself because I couldn't do more. It gave me a bad feeling. I don't know how to get rid of rats, or get proper seats on a bus, or help you from busting your bladder because they won't let you use a "white" restroom. It frustrated me, but I tried talking to people I knew in the government, and I hoped it would have some influence on the laws that would be passed.

All kinds of things were happening to black people during these years. On February 25, 1964, Cassius Clay won the heavyweight title from my friend, Sonny Liston. Then he told everybody he was no longer Cassius Clay but Muhammad Ali and a member of the Black Muslim religion. Now, I don't know what the hell any of that means. At that time, didn't know nothing about no Muslims at all. Of course, I have to admit, I knew about Malcolm X and I admired him. I admired him because he was talking about the problems of all the blacks, not just Black Muslims.

I didn't believe in changing your name or your God at that time. I still don't, but now I understand better. Nowadays you see people with all kinds of X's after their name. If they feel it makes them a better person, or a person who can do more for themselves and other people, then that's fine with me.

Billy got me some good bucks advertising for Ehlers Coffee. I can see it now. There's me smiling and the quote under all the pictures saying, "My house is never without Ehlers Coffee." Then, too, we got the Chesterfield Cigarettes endorsement. At that time, I still wasn't smoking, but I said that Chesterfield was the most popular cigarette in restaurants. I did a little TV stuff, got paid for magazine articles. I just kept searching for ways to successfully support myself.

Then I still had a few things I was trying to do on my own. For a while I had a boxing-promotion franchise in California. I promoted a fight for Cassius Clay against Jerry Quarry on closed-circuit TV. Well, this time it didn't last long—the money gave out. Martha said I was paying out too much, but I had to tell her how hard it was for young fighters to get started without some kind of decent back-up money.

I tried to help out in other ways, too. When one of those government committees was investigating the Mafia involvement with boxing, I begged the California government people to pass a law making boxers put away some of their purse for the tax people. I used myself as an example.

I got to New York a lot around this time. I was either refereeing or speaking at some affair, or working out a deal with Billy. One day a real good white friend of mine and I went down to a fancy clothing showroom. We had met the owner before and he told us to come on down and that he'd give us a wholesale price. We went down and ordered a whole bunch of stuff; the owner then told us he had some "models" and he'd send them over to the hotel. I looked at my friend and he looked at me, and we said, "What the hell, why not?"

We got back to the room and the girls were there. A white one for my white friend, and the black one for me, I guess. Well, let me tell you, this girl—I'll call her Marie Harris—she was something special. Beautiful brown-skinned girl, and as wild as they make them. She came in, opened up her purse, and took out this little box and started sniffing cocaine. She told me to try it. I said no. I remembered that hell I'd been through with drugs a few years before, but some people don't learn, do they? Anyway, this girl convinced me that coke isn't habit-forming. I don't know, did I want to be convinced? Did I need something? Why did I need something? I don't know. Yeah! I snorted the coke, felt good, made love every day I was with that girl in New York.

That affair didn't stop right there. Every time I was in New York, I was with that girl and the coke and the pot. Then I found myself wanting the coke even when I wasn't in New York. It was so easy to get. Just so damned expensive for a short high.

Oh, those sixties brought a lot of heavy stuff. I remember back in '64 a good friend of mine was in trouble. Jimmy Hoffa. He was going on trial for some kind of union trouble. Something about the government having a picture of him taking a package from some other guy. Jimmy told me he was going to be indicted in Washington, D.C. That's when I told him that there were a lot of blacks in Washington and recommended Martha to him; she became one of his lawyers.

I knew Jimmy well from Detroit; he was a union man for Wonder Bread. I don't know a thing about the bribery charges; I just knew a good friend of mine was in trouble and this good friend did a lot of fine things for a lot of people.

I'd go to the court to watch the trial. Well, Attorney General Robert Kennedy thought he had Jimmy. Kennedy said, "I'll jump off the Washington Monument without a parachute if Hoffa is acquitted." Jimmy was acquitted. Funny thing, there was a Senator from, I think, from Arkansas who said, "Joe Louis is a helluva lawyer." I guess they must have thought that me just sitting there was some kind of influence.

Life moves on. I had to go to New York on business in 1965. I looked up that girl and told her to come by my hotel. When she got there she was quiet. Not like herself at all. I asked her what was wrong, and that's when she zapped me. Told me she was pregnant and I was the father. Jesus Christ! What the hell was she talking about? Yeah, I saw her often, but knowing her, I knew other people did too. When I asked her what she was going to do about it she told me she was going to have the baby.

I said to myself, "Shit, she ain't gonna trap me in this thing." I hightailed it out of New York and went to Los Angeles. Kept real quiet and didn't hear a thing. Finally, though, Marie started calling on the phone. Told me the baby boy was here and what was I going to do about it? I was in a fog. I swear before God, I didn't want to hurt Martha with this.

I played the waiting game and I lost. The baby was four months old and Marie was threatening to bring him out to L.A. and leave him on my doorstep. Well, shit, this wouldn't do. I broke down and told Martha about it. She just looked at me real hard. Then she asked me to give her all the information and a plane reservation for New York. Martha got to New York, contacted Marie, and called me, saying that the baby was the spitting image of me and she was bringing him home to Los Angeles.

When she got off the plane with the baby, I could see he was mine. Martha said, "Well, we'll adopt him and it'll be all legal." Martha didn't give me any hassles about the baby, and what could we do with a cute, helpless little baby but fall in love with him and make him part of our family? We called him Joseph. (My first son, Joe, Jr. was "Punchie.")

During the summer of 1966, I was playing golf with Bob Wilson, a friend of mine in Phoenix, Arizona. I was telling him that I'd be in Frankfurt, Germany, on September 10 to see the Muhammad Ali–Karl Mildenberger fight. He said to me: "Hey, Joe, I got a sweet idea. I'm part owner of a new club opening in London. We're calling it Pigalle. After the fight, why don't you come over and act as a temporary host?" Didn't sound like a bad idea. I'd had some good times in London, and I think I needed to get away. I was getting some real itchy feelings in America, with all the race demonstrations going on, and my personal life unsettled.

I didn't get any salary, but I did get my living expenses. And you know, I like to live high. Only problem I had was trying to understand what those English people were saying, and I guess their only problem was trying to understand what Joe Louis was saying.

They showed my fight films in a restaurant cafe they had next door and then the people would come in and ask me questions about the various fights. If the "21" table was slow, I'd use the house money to play that table until the crowds started coming around. I never used my own money in this deal. That's just as well, because a lot of my friends would come to see me. I didn't want to win their money and they didn't want to win my money.

I only lasted three weeks. That was enough. I had to get home to Martha and little Joe, Jr. I felt a little better about myself and I felt a little stronger about dealing with the problems I left. Or at least I thought I did.

Around this time, I was starting to feel nauseated, with constant pains in my stomach. I didn't know what in the hell was wrong with me. I'd be playing with Joe-Joe, Jr. (that's what his name got down to), and I'd want to stay on my knees because getting up was painful. Well, leave it to Martha. She got me to the doctor. They found out I had a gall bladder condition and they recommended immediate surgery. I don't like doctors when they're doctoring that much. I don't like them cutting into my body, but the pain was pretty severe. So there was nothing to do but go in for surgery, and I'm glad I did. Once I got out of the hospital all my big appetite returned and I felt good and strong, like a new man. I felt like I could take on anything.

While I was home trying to recuperate from the gall bladder operation and trying to get to know my new son, the reporters started coming. The Olympic Games of 1968 were being held in Mexico City. Funny how games get to be a political thing. The Russians were talking about a boycott because America was so involved in the Vietnam War, the Mexican students were upset about the games going on in Mexico City because of the war, and then South Africa was supposed to be banned because of the racial discrimination. Then they were readmitted. Then, on top of all this, the black athletes start talking about boycotting the Olympics to demonstrate how they felt about race discrimination in America.

Jesus Christ, all these people and reporters coming to me to ask me what I thought. Here I was doing my best to hold body and soul together. I gave them answers, but I don't think a lot of people were happy with what I had to say. Loud and clear, I said I didn't think blacks should boycott the Olympics. I mean, where the hell else can they prove what they can do in competition with the whole world?

Besides all that, the blacks wouldn't be able to get a real boycott going. Too many of these kids would be too scared to go against America, and that was what all those big issues were about. Hell, they had nailed Muhammad Ali because he refused to go into the Vietnam War. They took away his title and treated him like a prisoner on parole. Now, what the hell, if they treated Muhammad Ali like that, what kind of hope would these kids have if they went against America? A lot of them were counting on using their athletic skills to get them a college scholarship. A lot of them were wearing special sports equipment supplied free from big American companies. A lot of the boys were looking forward to getting on sports teams, or government work, or something related. Most kids weren't willing to take the risk, and I don't know that I blame them. What can you do, have a "Black Olympic Games" of the world? Who's going to sponsor it; who's going to come to it? There are times you have to be practical and find another way to fight.

JOE LOUIS: MY LIFE

I personally thought that the gesture made by Tommie Smith and John Carlos was beautiful. There they were, two fine black athletes on the victory stand, and they raised their fists in the black power salute while the "Star-Spangled Banner" was playing. I saw it on TV. It looked like something a movie producer would have created. Tell you the truth, it brought tears to my eyes. Those guys weren't mugging anyone, they weren't tearing up any town, they weren't drunk, they weren't on welfare—they were two American boys expressing how displeased they were about the way America was treating them, but still sticking in there.

Well, I knew what was going to happen. I wished I had a bet on, I would have made a lot of money. They threw those guys out of the Olympics and out of Mexico like they were criminals. Just like they threw Ali out of boxing.

People always kept telling me what a good influence I was on race relations in America, but when I saw what they did to Ali and Tommie Smith and John Carlos, and so many more, I couldn't find room to remember. I wondered if I ever counted for anything. I was depressed deep, deep down. I escaped the easiest way I knew how—drugs.

I was discouraged or disappointed so many times. People were still running up behind me and calling me "Champ" and I liked that. Only one thing I needed more than a handshake to make me feel like myself again. Well, I knew what I thought I needed. Cocaine was no stranger to me now. I took it whenever I could buy it. I bought it from whoever sold it to me. It made me feel like myself just after the Carnera fight, just like after the Braddock fight, when I became the Heavyweight Champion of the World, like just after I won the second Schmeling fight. I kept telling myself that nothing could be wrong with feeling that good. If Momma had been

[253]

around, she would have told me why I felt so bad and depressed between these snorts, but Momma wasn't here. And I'd already put enough on Martha.

But Martha is a nosy woman. She began to see something was wrong with me, but at first I don't think she guessed it was drugs.

I kept pushing myself through until June, 1969. Somebody sold me some bad stuff. I collapsed and they took me over to Beekman Downtown Hospital in New York and pumped my stomach. Those people at Beekman were nice. They never told anyone what was wrong with me. As soon as I came to, I called my friend Dr. Bennett in Detroit and he hopped on the first plane and got me. Oh, the news that I was sick hit the papers, but nobody knew what was wrong with me except those people at Beekman and Dr. Bennett.

My friend Doc Bennett got me together as best he could. I started feeling like my own self again. But then, you know, when you're feeling OK, some kind of nothing little thing upsets you. I started in again with the drugs after a while. I was working hard, hustling hard, and things came to a head.

1970s

UP TO THE PRESENT

AROUND THIS TIME, MARIE HAD ANOTHER BABY. I can honestly say I had nothing whatsoever to do with this one. That didn't make no difference to Martha, though. By now she and Marie were good friends. Since Marie didn't have no way of taking care of this baby, Martha decided we should adopt the boy. She argued me into it by saying that little Joe-Joe needed a brother. That it wasn't good for a child to grow up without brothers or sisters. That it would make them too selfish. Well, you know, Martha's a good lawyer, and I bought her case, so now we got little John-John. Great kid. I love him.

This time in my life is confusing and puzzling to me. I remember Martha looking upset all the time when I told her I was afraid the Mafia was after me. I still thought about the close call I had with the government when I was fooling around with Annie Mitchell. She worked for the Mafia and I really thought they would come after me. I'd pile up blankets and pillows all around me when I went to bed so they couldn't get to me in my sleep.

Martha kept telling me that if the Mafia wanted me, they'd have to have an awful lot of manpower to keep up to me. Martha was trying to joke me out of how I felt, but I told her she knew what it was all about.

Finally, she convinced me to see my old friend Dr. Bennett in Detroit. So I went out there and talked to my friend, stayed a few days, and then he turned around and told me I should go to a hospital. At first I agreed with him and said yes. Then I thought to myself, if I agree with him, I'm saying something's wrong with me. So I cut out of there and just disappeared for a while.

I stayed in touch with Billy Rowe. I'd only tell him what city I was in, but never where I was staying. Did myself a whole lot of traveling. I went to all the secret places I knew about all over the country. I didn't have any intention of rushing back home. Martha was going to Europe, so I wouldn't have to face up to her. What was wrong with me? I don't know. Only thing I knew was I wanted to keep moving and didn't want to attach myself to anything right then.

I stayed in some odd places with people who didn't want any publicity, so nothing got in papers, and I kept hidden from America for a while. Thing is, though, I got tired of running. Never been a coward in my life. Whatever had to be faced, I knew I'd have to face it eventually. So let's get the damned thing over with.

When I finally got back home to Los Angeles for a few days, I found out Martha'd been calling my son, Punchie. Punchie was enrolled in law school in Denver then, and I kept asking him why he didn't go back there. He just hung around me. Then me and Martha went to our summer home in Colorado.

Next thing I knew, the Deputy Sheriff and a handful of guys were at my house. The Sheriff apologized to me but all the same time he said he had to take me to the Colorado Psychiatric Hospital. Punchie had signed the papers on me. At first I was real mad. I was mad at Punchie, Martha, the tax people, the whole damn world. But then I thought about it and said to myself, "If Punchie and Martha are so upset about me, maybe I just better go along quiet-like."

Martha wasn't there, so I asked the Sheriff to give me a little time to get myself together. I called a press conference right away. When the reporters got to my house, they looked more embarrassed than me. I didn't know what to tell them except I'd been feeling bad and I was going to the hospital for a while. You know something, I felt foolish saying this because at that very minute I felt there was nothing wrong with me at all.

Anyway, I wound up at this hospital on May 1 on a "hold for treatment" order.

After I was in for a while, Martha came to see me. I never saw her look so shy. Right off, I told her that I thought she could of done all of this another way. She looked real sad and told me that, no, she couldn't do it any other way. She was right. Martha had tried other means to help me, but I just wouldn't follow through. Any anger or hurt I had for Martha and Punchie faded away. I realized they loved me and wanted to do what they thought was right.

Well, I figured since I was in the damn hospital I might as well make the best of it. I never wanted to be penned in anywhere. I cooperated with all the doctors and they started letting me go home on weekends. I'd play golf with Punchie and my friend Billy Eckstine and Billy Rowe.

The doctors put me on Thorazine, some sort of medicine, and I started feeling better. Not that I thought I felt bad before, but I didn't have those street drugs in my system again. Maybe that's what made me seem like I was sick.

You know, people were nice to me and I really appreciated what they did. Martha told me about all the letters I was getting from all over the world from people who were concerned about me. I know at first I just wanted to get the hell out of that hospital, but then after a while I sort of relaxed there. I was tired, tired of the running and the hustling, and I figured I might as well stay and rest some.

The thing that really had me almost crying was when I found out my friends were putting on a big "Salute the Champ—Joe Louis" party in Detroit at Cobo Hall Arena. Can you imagine, people were going to try to raise $100,000 for me—to honor me, and to help pay these hospital bills there? Martha went and represented me. Roxy was there, and Billy Conn, too.

My daughter Jackie stayed in touch with me too. By the time fall came around, I was feeling real good. Only thing is, I picked up a real bad habit. Me, Joe Louis, at the age of fifty-six, starts smoking. I sure can start some bad habits late in my life. But anyway, I'm feeling good, looking good, must have lost about forty pounds.

I was itching to get out now. My friend Ash Resnick came to visit me and said, "Hey, why don't you come to Caesar's Palace in Las Vegas and work as a greeter." Well, now, Caesar's Palace is something else again, I hear. The Palace was set up by some of the Teamsters' Union people. I liked the idea of it. Hell, I spent a lot of time in Vegas anyway.

I told my friend Ash I'd check into it. I asked Martha— she said to talk to the doctors. They dickered back and forth some and said it might be good for me to be around celebrities and people. I just kept quiet while they were talking and gave a pleasant smile now and then. I wanted to get the hell out of the place and do something new.

Oh, it was beautiful being out. Caesar's gave Martha, me, and both Joe and John a suite in the hotel; they had a great big party for me. What the hell, I wasn't in training anymore. I wasn't taking any more drugs, so I had a drink of Rémy Martin's brandy. First drink since I'd had that moonshine in Alabama. Tasted damn good to me. Tell you the truth, I don't mind a few belts of that Rémy Martin every day now.

In 1970 I started working at Caesar's Palace. Got a good boss, Murray Gennis. We get along and there are no problems. My official title is Casino Host and public relations administrator. Sounds real good, huh? It's a busy job. I really work at it, and the people I'm working for aren't doing me favors. I earn the money I make.

Say Caesar's has a party for its special people, in Detroit or Hawaii, you name it. I'm there. I greet and meet. When Caesar opened a branch in Vancouver, I was there.

Guests come to the hotel and ask if I'll play golf with them. You know, that's OK with me. Sometimes they want their picture taken with me and autographed. That's OK too. I spend a lot of the time in the "21" pit, gambling. That's part of my job, too. The bad thing about it is that I love to gamble myself. Never was afraid to take a chance, but I found out it costs money.

It feels good to walk through the casino and have people calling out, "Hey, Champ," "Hi there, Champ," "Come stand next to me for luck." Sometimes people get mixed up, though. I remember the night I was standing at the bar with my friend, Teddy Brenner of Madison Square Garden, when this tourist type came over to me just grinning away. I grinned back, of course, because that's part of my job. She looked up at me and says, "Don Newcombe. My favorite baseball player. How are you doing?" I just went along with the lady and told her I was doing fine. We talked back and forth about baseball and everything was going fine until she asked me for an autograph. I started writing "Don," and I turned to Teddy Brenner and whispered to him, "How do you spell 'Newcombe?'" He busted up laughing and messed up the whole thing.

Feeling real good these days. My body feels good, my head feels good. Got a good job and Caesar's Palace gives me a good house with a swimming pool—Johnny Carson had this house before. Murray Gennis let me know right off that I could come and go as I liked. A lot of people all over the country still want to see the champ. I go speak at meetings and dinners and to a lot of young people.

The kids are real cute. They ask me questions like, could I beat Muhammad Ali. That really puts me in a bind. Ali's carried the fight game on his shoulders for a lot of years. If he wasn't around, the heavyweight division would be nothing. He's a real idol to the kids and to black people. He's a damn fool like me—gives his money away and does a lot of unbelievable things for people. Muhammad stands real tall against the white man. He makes his people feel proud, and I love him for it.

On the other hand, though, if Ali fought in my time with me, I'd have to say he'd stay in there with me a long time, but I'd win. Guys who had Ali's style and his speed, like Billy Conn, who lasted with me for thirteen rounds, and Bob Pastor, who stayed with me for twenty-one rounds over a period of two fights—I beat them. That jabbing and running would have made it hard for me to catch a guy like Ali, but eventually I'd get him and knock him out.

Ali's a great fighter, but I think a Rocky Marciano or Jack Dempsey would rate ahead of him. So would Walcott. Ali makes too many mistakes, his hands are down a lot, and he takes too many punches to the body. That's no good. I know. While I'm talking about it, I'll tell you about the greatest fighter I ever saw. My old Army pal, Sugar Ray Robinson. He could do it all—punch, move. Nothing he couldn't do. Then I'd rate Willie Pep second to Robinson. Don't get me wrong, though, I'm not putting down my friend Ali. He'd have done real good with Max Baer, Jimmy Braddock, or Schmeling.

One thing wrong with the fight game now is that there aren't enough good heavyweights around. When Ali goes, the game'll be in bad shape. Ken Norton and Jimmy Young aren't the type to carry a championship. A heavyweight champion has to have more than his fists. There has to be something in his personality that appeals to people, or makes them mad. If you don't have that special something, you're not going to draw. You won't make money, the promoters aren't going to make it, and there you are, with all your skill and no money. I never considered that I had anything special except luck, but lots of other people did have something special. Ali's got it. I hope he keeps it long as he can.

JOE LOUIS: MY LIFE

Yeah, I'm comfortable in Vegas. Don't have to get dressed up (except on special occasions), just wear a sport shirt, of course, most times its silk, cowboy hat or baseball cap, slacks, sometimes my cowboy boots, and that's fine with me.

I see all my old friends when they come to entertain. Frank Sinatra and me go back a long time. All the way back when he was with the Harry James orchestra. I remember when I left the ring, Sinatra told me anytime I want something, just call him. I called a couple of times, and he always came through for me, and if there's any way, I'd come through for him. Sinatra does a lot of good things for people you never hear about. Then there's Sammy Davis. He's been good to me too, and Redd Foxx, and my old golf buddies, Bob Hope, and Fred Astaire. I belong to the Las Vegas Country Club, and I play there a lot too, as well as Caesar's.

Of course, the money isn't the big money I used to make, but that's thirty years ago. Then, on the other hand, I don't have that big a problem with money; its the people around me who had the problem.

Round about 1972, I went out of town to be guest host. When I got back home, Martha told me Marie had another baby. She had a baby girl. I said that's nice; I'm not worried—I'm innocent. Then Martha starts talking about how nice it would be for Joe-Joe and John-John to have a little sister. I told Martha loud and clear that I wasn't the least bit interested in the idea, but Martha kept on coming at me. She's a funny kind of a lady, she seems business-like and stern, but the good in her keeps slipping out. She wanted that baby. Martha is one of those women who really love children. Even when I met her, she was raising a pretty little baby she had adopted. Candace is now a pretty young lady, and Martha did a real fine job.

Well, then, I think to myself, I'm not your average-type

husband. I'm hard to live with. I'm a nighttime person and Martha is a day person. Her spending time with the kids seems to give her comfort and lets her give out her love. Lord knows, she has put up with me and helped me through some of the hardest times in my life. So, what the Hell, if having that baby girl will make her happy, what can I say? Now we have Joyce legally adopted, and I'm happy, too. Something special about baby girls.

The old champ is getting older now. I can tell you more about 1934 than about 1974. Busy all the time, always working or traveling, but that's the way my whole life has been. I remember so many of the real fun times I had. I remember the time Martha and me were in New York to see some fight. I found out Marva and Doc were in New York too, so I called up Marva to chew the fat. We talked back and forth and then she told me that Rose Morgan was going to give her a special free hairdo and makeup job. I told Marva, "Shoot, let me call Rose." I got Rose on the phone and said, "Hey, baby, what you doing? I can't have Marva looking better than my Martha." Rose just laughed and said of course she'd do the same job for Martha.

Well, that night, after the fight, Marva, Doc, Martha, and me went to the 21 Club and saw Earl Wilson, the gossip columnist from the *New York Post*. When he asked me how I was doing, I told him, "Must be all right. My second wife made up my first wife and my third wife. And don't they both look beautiful?" Earl cracked up. If I remember correctly, he put the story in his column the next day.

About early 1975, I got a call from Don King inviting me to New York to talk about some things. I was real interested because Don King is a very special man. In fact, he's the first black man to take on promotional boxing across the nation. I don't know if the man is extra smart or if the time is finally right for a black man to get the lion's share. I know one thing, I wanted to go and see.

In New York I talked things over with King and, let me tell you something, the man is the smartest, nicest guy you could meet. Never happened in the history of America where a black man could be allowed to do what Don King was thinking about. We talked about promoting fights, putting on tournaments, giving boxing the shot in the arm it needed and deserved. He was asking me for my help, and believe me, I jumped at the chance.

Seems like Don King was a regular hustler out of Cleveland who was always a big sports fan, especially boxing. He'd had a little trouble with the law but that was behind him now. Ali encouraged him to go into the fight promotion business, and, at the beginning, Ali became the center of his career. Now, for the first time, we had a black heavyweight champion and a black promoter. Can't miss.

Well, Martha was in New York with me, with her friend Loretta. We were in the Essex House, and one day we get a call from Marie. You guessed it, she had another baby. I don't know if it sounds odd or not, but Martha, Marie, and me are all friends. We've got a good relationship. The kids know Marie's their real mother and they call her "Marie." But Martha is their mother now, and they call her "Mother," and that's the way it's supposed to be.

I came back to Essex House after a business conference and here was Loretta with Marie's new baby girl. The baby was all dressed up. Loretta was saying how cute the baby was, and I agreed—she's got big, pretty dark eyes, fat little chubby legs—she's cute. Martha and Loretta were standing there making over the baby, and I got a funny feeling. First off, I say, "Don't bring that baby back to

JOE LOUIS: MY LIFE

Vegas. We got enough babies in the house already."
Loretta looked upset and asked me how I could think that
way. Anyway, Loretta said she had to get back to Vegas,
and was taking the baby back to Marie before she left.

Martha and I stayed in New York a few more days to
clean up some business. Well, we got back to Vegas, went
home and, sure enough, there was that baby stretched out
on the couch in the living room. What can you do? Well
now, we got Janet. Joe-Joe, John-John, and Joyce were all
excited about her, and so were Martha and Joe Louis.

The house has never been the same since the baby girls
came, and I don't suppose it ever will be. We've got a good
ranch-style house here, and I couldn't for the life of me
tell you how many rooms there are. Seems like every time
I go out of town and come back, there's a room that's been
divided or altered in some way. For sure, I know four kids
have their own rooms. And they all, except Janet who's
still in the crib, have their bed, a little couch in the room,
TV set, desk. Then there's a big master bedroom, living
room, guest rooms, den. Must be about three or four full
bathrooms. And there's Pierre, a real nice girl from
Guatemala who takes care of the kids. I think practically
every couch and chair in the house can be pulled out and
made into a bed. Of course I didn't know all this till I
came home one day and there were about thirty kids
sleeping all over the house. I don't remember what it
was—some Boy Scout or children's group meeting.

I love the kids and they love me. They make me feel
young. Those times when I'm concentrating too much on
myself, they come along with some little ache or pain
that's so important to them that I had best change my
concentration to them.

Sunday morning, bright and early, Martha's getting
them together to go to Sunday School. The boys are in the
church choir. Sometimes I even get there if I don't get
home too late from Caesar's Palace the night before. The
boys go to a Montessori school, and they're doing fine.

JOE LOUIS: MY LIFE

I don't know how Martha does it. She's got her law practice, she's got the kids, and me to take care of. You know something, that Martha does it all, and she does it right. It makes her happy, and that pleases me.

When they buried my old friend and manager, John Roxborough in Detroit, it was an especially bad time for me. It was around Christmas, 1975. He'd lived a full life. If Roxy hadn't run into me way back when, you wouldn't be reading this book now. Roxy helped a whole lot of people. I think he could leave this world feeling good about himself.

There I was, just getting used to the fact that Roxy was gone, then in March, 1976, Julian Black died. He was seventy-nine. Hell, I'm sixty-three. Makes you think back to the time when we all were young and had the world by the tail. It made me feel bad that me and Black had fallen out, and I had never reached out and tried to mend up the hole.

Everybody's being real nice to me. I went up to Ali's camp at the Concord in upstate New York, where he was training for the Ken Norton fight booked for September, 1976. He wanted me around him. Shoot! What am I going to teach Ali? But for just hanging around for ten days, he wanted to give me $30,000. I thought that was ridiculous. He's a pro fighting, the Champion. Well, anyway, for my time, he gave me $10,000, and I took it. I was trying to tell him, "Don't get in trouble like me." Then, again, what can you say? Ali feels the same way about money that I do. Is it or should it be that important?

Hell, I guess I still can influence people some. I signed a contract with Twentieth Century-Fox about doing a two-hour TV special on my two fights with Max Schmeling. Seems like those fights showed what was going on in the world in the 1930's. What with Hitler and America, they represented something people would want to see.

Everything was fine until I found out early in 1977 that

my friend, Don King, was being accused of fraud. Seems like the boxing tournaments he had set up were in question. Now, Don King wasn't in this all by himself. *Ring Magazine,* the Bible, was doing the ratings on the fighters, and they were making some mistakes, not rating a fighter proper. Now, if Don just used *Ring Magazine*'s ratings, I don't see how that could be his fault.

When all this stuff hit the papers, people came to me asking about it. A lot of black people felt it was prejudice. Like I always say, and some people don't like it, first thing black people do when something goes wrong is to say, "It's 'cause I'm black." I don't necessarily believe that. First you've got to analyze the problem, you've got to be honest with yourself and then decide if it's prejudice or not. But I'm going to tell you one thing for sure in the case of Don King; this time it was out-and-out prejudice. The people out there in big business knew Don was onto the big money, and Don is black. They tried their best to move him out of number-one position, but the committee investigating it in New York found him innocent of all charges of fraud.

Things have changed a lot. Thirty years ago that decision wouldn't have been made. He'd have been found guilty, but then thirty years ago he wouldn't have had the opportunity he's got now. You have to be tough and stick in there in spite of what the white man's heaping on you, or you wind up being nothing but a wino or a junkie.

In the Spring of '77, I remember I went to work at Caesar's, but I wasn't feeling too good. In the evening, my boss, Don Murray, asked, "What's the matter, Joe?" I'm a person who doesn't like to complain, but I was feeling a little bit scared. I told him I had slight pains in my chest and my arms, and that after tonight I thought maybe I should take a couple of days off. Well, he got all excited and told me to go home right away and see a doctor. I kept insisting that it wasn't that bad, but I went home anyway. I told Martha what happened and before I could barely get the words out of my mouth, Martha got me to the hospital.

The doctors checked me out, gave me some medicine, and told me to take it easy for a couple weeks. By the time I got home, the news was on the radio, TV, newspapers. Had to take the phone off the hook for a while. Telegrams were coming in from all over the world. I felt a real warm feeling and it made me fall in love with people again and my heart felt stronger. I get mad and bitter about the wrong things that happen to black people, then I get suckered by the concerned feelings people have. Sometimes the world is hard to live with.

Soon, though, I was back to my old self. Trying my best to follow the doctor's orders. You know, you think, or at least I do, that nothing's wrong and never will be. You know better deep down, but who doesn't cheat a little bit about that?

All kinds of good things coming up for me; I signed up to play in a TV story called "Quincy" on NBC with Jack Klugman and Moses Gunn. The story is about a boxer who dies mysteriously after a championship fight and later is found out to have been drugged.

I signed up to be on the Redd Foxx Show as a boxer. Me and Redd just going to ham it up some. Now, don't get the wrong impression—I'm not turning into an actor. I'm doing what they call cameo shots. I'll just be on the screen a few minutes.

Another thing: Joe DiMaggio and Jim Brown want me to appear on their "Hall of Fame Invitational Golf Tournament," TV event in Las Vegas. It'll be professional athletes against plain Vegas tourists. Joe asked me and Mickey Mantle, Pancho Gonzales, Eddie Arcaro, and a lot of others to participate in this. I'm looking forward to that, too.

JOE LOUIS: MY LIFE

A lot of people are still saying I was taken advantage of throughout my life. I can't feel I've been taken advantage of by anybody. When Roxie and Black died, I owed them a lot of money. Mike Jacobs also died with me owing him a lot of money. Lord help him, but if anything happens to Marshall Miles, I'll owe him a lot of money. Nobody today could prove any of those fellows took advantage of me. I almost always did exactly what I wanted to do.

I've been in a whole lot of fights inside the ring and outside the ring, too. I like to think I won most of those battles.

Well, like the man said, "If you dance you got to pay the piper." Believe me, I danced, I paid the piper, and left him a big fat tip.

RING RECORD OF JOE LOUIS (JOE LOUIS BARROW)

Born May 13, 1914, Lafayette, Alabama
Weight, 200 pounds, Height, 6 feet, 1½ inches
Managed by Julian Black and John Roxborough,
and later by Marshall Miles

* Denotes title fight

1934

July 4—Jack Kracken, Chicago .... K.O. 1
July 11—Willie Davis, Chicago .... K.O. 3
July 29—Larry Udell, Chicago .... K.O. 2
Aug. 13—Jack Kranz, Chicago .... W 6
Aug. 27—Buck Everett, Chicago .... K.O. 2
Sep. 11—Alex Borchuk, Detroit .... K.O. 4
Sep. 24—Adolph Wiater, Chicago .... W 10
Oct. 24—Art Sykes, Chicago .... K.O. 8
Oct. 30—Jack O'Dowd, Detroit .... K.O. 2
Nov. 14—Stanley Poreda, Chicago .... K.O. 1
Nov. 30—Charley Massera, Chicago .... K.O. 3
Dec. 14—Lee Ramage, Chicago .... K.O. 3

1935

Jan. 4—Patsy Perroni, Detroit .... W 10
Jan. 11—Hans Birkie, Pittsburgh .... K.O. 10
Feb. 21—Lee Ramage, Los Angeles .... K.O. 2
Mar. 8—Donald "Reds" Barry, San Francisco .... K.O. 3
Mar. 28—Natie Brown, Detroit .... W 10
Apr. 12—Roy Lazer, Chicago .... K.O. 3
Apr. 22—Biff Benton, Dayton .... K.O. 2
Apr. 27—Roscoe Toles, Flint .... K.O. 6
May 3—Willie Davis, Peoria .... K.O. 2
May 7—Gene Stanton, Kalamazoo .... K.O. 3
June 25—Primo Carnera, New York City .... K.O. 6
Aug. 7—King Levinsky, Chicago .... K.O. 1
Sep. 24—Max Baer, New York City .... K.O. 4
Dec. 13—Paolino Uzcudun, New York City .... K.O. 4

1936

Jan. 17—Charley Retzlaff, Chicago .... K.O. 1
June 19—Max Schmeling, New York City .... K.O. by 12
Aug. 17—Jack Sharkey, New York City .... K.O. 3

Sep. 22—Al Ettore, Philadelphia .... K.O. 5
Oct. 9—Jorge Brescia, New York City .... K.O. 3
Oct. 14—Willie Davis, South Bend .... Exh. K.O. 3
Oct. 14—K. O. Brown, South Bend .... Exh. K.O. 3
Nov. 20—Paul Williams, New Orleans .... Exh. K.O. 2
Nov. 20—Tom Jones, New Orleans .... Exh. K.O. 3
Dec. 14—Eddie Simms, Cleveland .... K.O. 1

1937

Jan. 11—Steve Ketchel, Buffalo .... K.O. 2
Jan. 27—Bob Pastor, New York City .... W 10
Feb. 17—Natie Brown, Kansas City .... K.O. 4
June 22—James J. Braddock, Chicago .... K.O. 8
    (Won the Heavyweight Championship of the World)
*Aug. 30—Tommy Farr, New York City .... W 15

1938

*Feb. 22—Nathan Mann, New York City .... K.O. 3
*Apr. 1—Harry Thomas, Chicago .... K.O. 5
*June 22—Max Schmeling, New York City .... K.O. 1

1939

*Jan. 25—John Henry Lewis, New York City .... K.O. 1
*Apr. 17—Jack Roper, Los Angeles .... K.O. 1
*June 28—Tony Galento, New York City .... K.O. 4
*Sep. 20—Bob Pastor, Detroit .... K.O. 11

1940

*Feb. 9—Arturo Godoy, New York City .... W 15
*Mar. 29—Johnny Paycheck, New York City .... K.O. 2
*June 20—Arturo Godoy, New York City .... K.O. 8
*Dec. 16—Al McCoy, Boston .... K.O. 6

1941

*Jan. 31—Red Burman, New York City .... K.O. 5
*Feb. 17—Gus Dorazio, Philadelphia .... K.O. 2
*Mar. 21—Abe Simon, Detroit .... K.O. 13
*Apr. 8—Tony Musto, St. Louis .... K.O. 9
*May 23—Buddy Baer, Washington, D.C. .... W disq. 7
*June 18—Billy Conn, New York City .... K.O. 13
July 11—Jim Robinson, Minneapolis .... Exh. K.O. 1
*Sep. 29—Lou Nova, New York City .... K.O. 6
Nov. 25—George Giambastiani, Los Angeles .... Exh. 4

1942

*Jan. 9—Buddy Baer, New York City .... K.O. 1
        (Donated purse to Naval Relief Fund)
*Mar. 27—Abe Simon, New York City .... K.O. 6
        (Donated purse to Army Relief Fund)
June 5—George Nicholson, Fort Hamilton .... Exh. 3

1944
(Exhibitions)

Nov. 3—Johnny Demson, Detroit .... K.O. 2
Nov. 6—Charley Crump, Baltimore .... W 3
Nov. 9—Dee Amos, Hartford .... W 3
Nov. 13—Jimmy Bell, Washington, D.C. .... W 3
Nov. 14— Johnny Davis, Buffalo .... K.O. 1
Nov. 15—Dee Amos, Elizabeth .... W 3
Nov. 17—Dee Amos, Camden .... W 3
Nov. 24—Dan Merritt, Chicago .... W 3

1945

Nov. 15—Sugar Lip Anderson, San Francisco .... Exh. 2
Nov. 15—Big Boy Brown, San Francisco .... Exh. 2
Nov. 29—Big Boy Brown, Sacramento .... Exh. 2

Nov. 29—Bobby Lee, Sacramento .... Exh. 2
Dec. 10—Bob Frazier, Victoria .... Exh. 3
Dec. 11—Big Boy Brown, Portland .... Exh. 2
Dec. 11—Dave Johnson, Portland .... Exh. 2
Dec. 12—Big Boy Brown, Eugene, Ore. .... Exh. 3
Dec. 13—Big Boy Brown, Vancouver .... Exh. 3

1946

*June 19—Billy Conn, New York City .... K.O. 8
*Sep. 18—Tami Mauriello, New York City .... K.O. 1
Nov. 11—Cleo Everett, Honolulu .... Exh. 4
Nov. 11—Wayne Powell, Honolulu .... Exh. 2
Nov. 25—Perk Daniels, Mexicali, Mexico .... Exh. 4

1947

Feb. 7—Arturo Godoy, Mexico City .... Exh. 10
Feb. 10—Art Ramsey, San Salvador .... Exh. 3
Feb. 10—Walter Haefer, San Salvador .... Exh. 3
Feb. 12—Art Ramsey, Panama City .... Exh. 3
Feb. 12—Walter Haefer, Panama City .... Exh. 3
Feb. 19—Arturo Godoy, Santiago, Chile .... Exh. 6
Feb. 27—Art Ramsey, Medellin, Colombia .... Exh. 2
Feb. 27—Walter Haefer, Medellin, Colombia .... Exh. 2
Mar. 10—Walter Haefer, Havana .... Exh. 2
Mar. 10—Art Ramsey, Havana .... Exh. 2
June 6—Rusty Payne, San Diego .... Exh. 2
June 6—Dick Underwood, San Diego .... Exh. 2
June 13—Tiger Jack Fox, Spokane .... Exh. 4
June 23—Harry Wills, Los Angeles .... Exh. 4
*Dec. 5—Jersey Joe Walcott, New York City .... W 15

1948

Jan. 29—Bob Foxworth, Chicago .... Exh. 4
*June 25—Jersey Joe Walcott, New York City .... K.O. 11

Sep. 30—Pat Comiskey, Washington, D.C. .... Exh. 6
Oct. 28—Bob Garner, Atlanta .... Exh. 3
Oct. 28—Merritt Wynn, Atlanta .... Exh. 3
Oct. 29—Bob Garner, Norfolk .... Exh. 4
Oct. 31—Bob Garner, New Orleans .... Exh. 4
Nov. 1—Bob Garner, New Orleans .... Exh. 3
Nov. 3—Bob Garner, Nashville .... Exh. 4
Nov. 8—Johnny Shkor, Boston .... Exh. 4
Nov. 9—Bernie Reynolds, New Haven .... Exh. 4
Nov. 17—Jimmy Bivins, Cleveland .... Exh. 6
Nov. 19—Vern Mitchell, Detroit .... Exh. 6
Nov. 23—Kid Riviera, St. Louis .... Exh. 6
Nov. 24—Ray Augustus, Oklahoma City .... Exh. K.O. 2
Nov. 25—Curt Kennedy, Kansas City .... Exh. 4
Nov. 29—Billy Smith, Cincinnati .... Exh. 4
Dec. 10—Billy Conn, Chicago .... Exh. 6
Dec. 14—Arturo Godoy, Philadelphia .... Exh. 6
Dec. 16—Pat Comiskey, Paterson .... Exh. 6
Dec. 20—Willie James, Lewiston .... Exh. 4

1949

Jan. 10—Sterling Ingram, Omaha .... Exh. 4
Jan. 11—Orlando Ott, Topeka .... Exh. 4
Jan. 12—Hubert Hood, Wichita .... Exh. 4
Jan. 17—Art Swiden, Toledo .... Exh. 4
Jan. 18—Dick Hagen, Moline, Ill. .... Exh. 4
Jan. 19—Orlando Ott, Rochester, Minn. .... Exh. 4
Jan. 25—Elmer Ray, Miami .... Exh. 6
Jan. 27—George Fitch, Palm Beach .... Exh. 4
Jan. 28—Nino Valdez, Tampa .... Exh. 4
Jan. 31—Dixie Lee Oliver, Orlando .... Exh. K.O. 4
Feb. 1—Elmer Ray, Jacksonville .... Exh. 4
Feb. 3—Bill Graves, Daytona Beach .... Exh. K.O. 3
Feb. 4—George Fitch, Savannah .... Exh. 4
Feb. 23—Edgar Edward, Kingston, Jamaica .... Exh. 3

Mar. 1
(Louis announced his retirement as undefeated
World Heavyweight Champion.)

Mar. 1—Ed Crawley, Nassau .... Exh. 4
Mar. 4—Omelio Agramonte, Havana .... Exh. 4
Mar. 5—Omelio Agramonte, Oriente, Cuba .... Exh. 4
Mar. 16—Elmer Ray, Houston .... Exh. K.O. 4
Mar. 18—Tex Boddie, Dallas .... Exh. 4
Mar. 22—Hubert Hood, St. Paul .... Exh. 6
Mar. 22—Abel Cestac, Washington, D.C. ....Exh. 4
Oct. 10—Curtiss Sheppard, Baltimore .... Exh. 4
Oct. 24—Bill Weinberg, Providence .... Exh. 4
Oct. 25—Joe Domonic, Hartford .... Exh. 4
Oct. 31—Bill Gilliam, Atlantic City .... Exh. 4
Nov. 14—Johnny Shkor, Boston .... Exh. N.D. 10
Nov. 22—Joe Chesul, Newark .... Exh. N.D. 10
Nov. 28—Johnny Flynn, Kansas City .... Exh. N.D. 10
Dec. 7—Pat Valentino, Chicago .... Exh. K.O. 8
Dec. 14—Roscoe Toles, Detroit .... Exh. 5
Dec. 14—Johnny Flynn, Detroit .... Exh. 5
Dec. 19—Al Hoosman, Oakland .... Exh. K.O. 5
Dec. 21—Jay Lambert, Salt Lake City .... Exh. 5
Dec. 21—Rex Layne, Salt Lake City .... Exh. 5

1950

Jan. 6—Willie Bean, Hollywood .... Exh. 6
Jan. 10—Jack Flood, Seattle .... Exh. 6
Jan. 12—Clarence Henry, Wilmington .... Exh. 4
Jan. 13—Al Spaulding, San Diego .... Exh. 4
Jan. 20—Andy Walker, Stockton .... Exh. 4
Jan. 24—Rex Layne, Salt Lake City .... Exh. 4
Feb. 1—Gene Jones, Miami .... Exh. 8
Feb. 7—Nino Valdez, St. Petersburg .... Exh. 4
Feb. 8—Candy McDaniels, Orlando .... Exh. 5
Feb. 14—Johnny Haynes, Tampa .... Exh. 4

Feb. 21—Sid Peaks, Jacksonville .... Exh. 6
Feb. 23—Dan Bolston, Macon .... Exh. 1
Feb. 23—Leo Jackson, Macon .... Exh. 3
Feb. 27—Willie Johnson, Albany, Georgia .... Exh. 4
Feb. 28—Dan Bolston, Columbus, Georgia .... Exh. 4
Mar. 3—Leo Johnson, Waycross, Georgia .... Exh. 4
Mar. 18—Kid Carr, Lubbock .... Exh. 4
Mar. 20—Sterling Ingram, Odessa .... Exh. 4
Mar. 22—Joe Santell, El Paso .... Exh. 4
Mar. 22—John McFalls, El Paso .... Exh. 4
Mar. 24—Henry Hall, Austin .... Exh. 4
Mar. 25—J. K. Homer, Waco .... Exh. 4
Apr. 22—Walter Haefer, Rio de Janeiro .... Exh. K.O. 2
*Sep. 27—Ezzard Charles, New York City .... L 15
Nov. 29—Cesar Brion, New York .... W 10

1951

Jan. 3—Freddie Beshore, Detroit .... K.O. 4
Feb. 7—Omelio Agramonte, Miami .... W 10
Feb. 23—Andy Walker, San Francisco .... K.O. 10
May 2—Omelio Agramonte, Detroit .... W 10
June 15—Lee Savold, New York City .... K.O. 6
Aug. 1—Cesar Brion, San Francisco .... W 10
Aug. 15—Jimmy Bivins, Baltimore .... W 10
Oct. 26—Rocky Marciano, New York City .... K.O. by 8
Nov. 18—U.S. Serviceman, Tokyo .... K.O. 4
Nov. 18—U.S. Serviceman, Tokyo .... K.O. 4
Nov. 18—U.S. Serviceman, Tokyo .... Exh. 3
Nov. 18—Cpl. Buford J. DeCordova, Tokyo .... Exh. 4
Nov. 18—Cpl. Buford J. DeCordova, Tokyo .... Exh. 4
Nov. 18—Cpl. Buford J. DeCordova, Tokyo .... Exh. 5
Dec. 14—Sgt. Lindy Brooks, Sanda, Japan .... Exh. 3
Dec. 14—Chang Pulu, Taipei, Formosa .... K.O. 1
Dec. 14—Sgt. Seth E. Woodbury, Taipei,

Formosa .... Exh. 2

Dec. 14—D. H. Cantrell (U.S. Navy), Taipei,
Formosa .... Exh.   2
Dec. 14—Cpl. Buford J. DeCordova, Taipei,
Formosa .... Exh.   3
Dec. 16—Cpl. Buford J. DeCordova, Taipei,
Formosa .... Exh.   3

Row 1

40

20th CENTURY SPOR
Presents

JOE
LOUIS
CHAMPION

V
S

W

FOR THE HEAVYWEIGHT CHAMPIONSHIP OF THE

MADISON SQUARE
GARDEN

DEC

TWENTIE

WORKING PRESS

427

ENTER AT
GATE

6

YANKE
161 ST STREET

TWENTIETH CENTUR

WORLD'S
CHAM

JOE LO

MAX SCH

Challenger

Wednesd $ 3 v

Mezza Stand
EST. PRICE $3.0305
Federal Tax .31
State Tax .1595